M¹⁰⁰

The

fine

art of

MURDER

HERBERT ASBURY

STEWART H. HOLBROOK

A. J. LIEBLING

CARL CARMER

ARCHIE MCFEDRIES

CLEVELAND MOFFETT

EDMUND PEARSON

WALTER B. GIBSON

AVERY HALE

S. N. PHILLIPS

ALAN HYND

The fine art of

MURDER

Edited by
WALTER B. GIBSON

Illustrated by
CAL SACKS

GROSSET & DUNLAP
Publishers   New York

ACKNOWLEDGMENTS

Grateful appreciation is expressed to the following persons for their courtesy in permitting the inclusion in this book of the stories listed below:

THE MONSTER OF SIXTY-THIRD STREET. Copyright, 1940 by Alfred A. Knopf, Inc. Reprinted from "Gem of the Prairie" by Herbert Asbury by permission of the publisher.

Mrs. Sibyl Holbrook, BELLE OF INDIANA. From "Murder Out Yonder" by Stewart H. Holbrook. Copyright 1941 by Stewart H. Holbrook.

THE CASE OF THE SCATTERED DUTCHMAN by A. J. Liebling. Reprinted by permission. Copyright © 1955, *The New Yorker Magazine, Inc.*

Carl Carmer, THE TALE OF THE MURDEROUS PHILOLOGIST WITH BUT ONE BIG TOE. From "Listen for a Lonesome Drum" by Carl Carmer. Copyright 1936, 1950. By permission of Carl Carmer and David McKay.

Alan Hynd, THE CASE OF THE LITTLE EXTERMINATOR, by Archie McFedries. Copyright 1945 Alan Hynd.

THE END OF THE BORDEN CASE. Copyright 1928 by Forum Publishing Company, from the book "Five Murders" by Edmund Pearson. Reprinted by permission of Doubleday & Company, Inc.

Walter B. Gibson, THE GHOST FROM THE GRAVE. Copyright © 1952 Whitestone Publications. Reprinted from *Daring Detective Magazine,* November, 1952.

Alan Hynd, THE SHE-DEVIL OF NAGYREV by Avery Hale. Copyright 1942 Alan Hynd.

Alan Hynd, THE MONSTER OF AURORA by Alan Hynd. Copyright 1947 Alan Hynd.

Introduction

MURDER is the ultimate crime.

Of all the arts, murder is perhaps the most neglected. Which is fortunate. It needs no encouragement.

Happily, no one has yet endowed a Center for the Destructive Arts, with murder as its major course. It is true that people have been trained as cool, calculating killers by the military services and police schools. But their approach has been scientific rather than artistic, and therefore beyond our interest. There have also been cliques that have plied their trade in wholesale slaughter all the way from the days of the Persian assassins through the eras of the Thugs in India, the Borgias in Italy, the head-hunters in Borneo, up to the time of that highly modern and thoroughly American institution, Murder, Incorporated.

But such "co-op" projects in mayhem and massacre lack the spontaneity and subtle touch of the lone hand.

It was Cain, you remember, who set the basic pattern for murder, when he slew his brother Abel. He had a motive—hatred; he committed the deed in cold blood; he faced the full consequences imposed by society of that period. It is possible that he didn't greatly care about that final point. Society then consisted solely of Adam and Eve. Since they had already been ejected from the Garden of Eden because of their own misconduct, they were hardly in a position to

v

voice an unbiased opinion. (There was another inexplicable Land of Nod, you remember.) We don't know about opinion there, but the Lord seems to have been sufficiently concerned to equip the first murderer with the sign of Cain—not to brand him as a murderer (as most people think) but to protect him from retribution.

So we must believe that murder is ancient. If you are willing to concede that Eve, in her search for knowledge, was merely experimenting with a strange mixture of serpent and apple (and women are irresistibly attracted to new recipes) —then I think that you must call murder not only the ultimate crime, but also the first. Cain slew Abel—the third person in the world killed the fourth. You can't do much better than that and still populate a planet.

Since then, murder has gone on, moving from the simple to the complex. Motives are now more varied; methods of inflicting death have become numerous and ingenious; consequences range from the dreadful to the trivial. Moral dissuasion and physical punishments have been devised as deterrents, but to little avail. The pattern of murder has remained the same. Statistically it has kept pace with other crimes.

Indeed, added threats have sometimes become challenges to would-be murderers, rather than obstacles. This applies particularly to those who see murder as a fine art, for as such, the art consists chiefly in circumventing the established hazards. The more numerous the pitfalls, the greater the thought applied to the problem. The artistic murderer has three main aims: to conceal the motive, disguise the deed, and avoid the consequences.

In theory, the perfect murder should have no apparent motive, the crime itself should appear to be a normal or accidental death, and there should be no resultant problems or inconveniences to the perpetrator. According to some authorities, the undetected murder may well happen more often than is generally supposed. The conjectures of the experts are alarming. And based on solid reasoning. But

I must tell you that I think there are far fewer perfect crimes than you think. There are some, I suppose. But they are few and they usually depend on unpredictable conditions that seldom apply. Don't try your luck.

Let's be practical. The instances where a person with many potential enemies suddenly disappears. The case of Judge Joseph Crater, of New York, is a classic example. He vanished in 1930, and has never been seen since. Many criminals hold grudges against judges, and Crater's legal and political connections brought up names of other persons who might have been imbued with lethal notions. But none of the motives was strong enough to sustain indictment until the crime itself could be established. And it never was.

Nor is the Crater case unique. The "missing person files" in many cities could supply dozens of names that might easily topple into the lap of the homicide squad with the slightest provocation. This applies also to those happy-go-lucky characters known as "skips" who disappear into parts unknown, presumably to get rid of wives and children, debts, and other responsibilities. Sometimes, however, instead of *taking off*, they are *taken off*. But until they show up dead, there is no way of marking them as murdered.

Artistry in the disposal of murder victims as missing persons is nullified unless the job is permanent. Otherwise the slayer must be prepared to meet eventualities. The old adage, "Out of sight, out of mind," is too simple an opiate in murder. Corpses rise to destroy their destroyers.

One woman's husband had been missing for six months. A body, possibly his, was washed up from a river so badly decomposed that even the fingerprints seemed indistinguishable. On the corpse was a vestige of a corduroy shirt resembling one the man had worn. But his wife said, no, it couldn't be his. She had given that shirt away a few months before he disappeared.

That should have ended it. But word came from Washington that the decomposed fingerprints had been put through a new and special process that had rendered them distinguishable. They were identified as the missing husband's. And the woman was suddenly confronted with a murder charge, since her statement regarding the shirt was obviously false.

Evasions and alibis are only one way to face murder charges. Persons who have met every charge head on have frequently come out ahead. Lizzie Borden was a capable exponent of that technique. She had a motive, in that she despised the people she allegedly murdered; she stood to profit from their deaths. But was that strong enough to counteract her natural scruples against murder? She was on the premises when the victims were viciously slain. But was she strong enough physically to have indulged in such brutality? She was a bit of a girl, and when she underwent trial, there was a question whether she was mentally strong enough to stand the two-week ordeal.

She stood it. With *three* strikes against her, Lizzie Borden still wasn't out. She stood her ground, and today, if there is anything more baffling than the Borden case, it is Lizzie herself.

In contrast to such artistry, we find grossly overrated murders like the Snyder-Gray affair of 1927, where Ruth Snyder and her lover, Judd Gray, murdered Ruth's husband, Albert, in a project combining profit with a love pact.

Beforehand, Ruth took out a life insurance policy on her husband, with a double indemnity clause of nearly $100,000 in case of accidental death. This not only supplied the motive, but set the conditions of the crime, a simple and transparent slaying that the killer would attribute to an imaginary burglar. So clumsily handled was this attempt that detectives cracked the case practically on sight.

Nevertheless, the Snyder-Gray trial made nationwide headlines, with all the gruesome details, including the executions of both Ruth and Judd in the electric chair at Sing Sing. Their bungling, however, may have inspired some people to do better, for not long after the Snyder-Gray debacle, a woman in another city arranged her husband's death in a far more sensible manner.

All three flaws were carefully avoided: there was no great amount of insurance involved. The woman had no man. She simply shot her husband. Then rushed out to tell the police. She got rid of the gun through an accomplice, a youthful relative who thought the woman's husband had been mistreating her.

She, too, blamed it on a burglar. Very plausibly. The script called for the "burglar" to remove the screen from a downstairs window, come upstairs, shoot the husband, and jump from a high window to the ground below. After "witnessing" that, the horrified woman ran downstairs, unlocked the front door and dashed to the nearest corner to summon the police.

It all worked perfectly—even the disposal of the gun—until the police tried to figure the burglar's route. Then, they couldn't find how he had gotten into the house to start. Between them, the woman and her accomplice had been so eager to conclude the act that they neglected the preliminary detail. Each thought the other had removed the screen, but neither had. That lack of artistry sent them both to prison.

The weakness in clever murder devices is that they arouse suspicion because they are so ironclad. Thereby they lay themselves open to the most trivial and unexpected details. In Florida, a would-be murderer established the exact time that he and a companion left a beach in their car. They drove inland, hell-for-leather, along little-used secondary highways and stopped on a sand road outside a bungalow. There the slayer aimed a shotgun point-blank through the window and killed his victim. He hopped back into the car with his companion. They made a record run back to the beach and again they fixed the exact time, immediately on their arrival.

Since the slayer was an obvious suspect, he was arrested, quizzed, and came up with his ironclad alibi. It was supported by reliable witnesses. The time interval was so incredibly short that no jury would have believed that the murderer could have made the trip inland and back, unless there was supporting evidence. So a keen detective looked for it. And he found it.

He studied the edge of the sand road that the killer and his companion had purposely scuffed so as not to leave incriminating footprints. He noted some white flecks in the grayish sand and dipped up a sample. Under a microscope they proved to be grains of beach sand that had trickled from a rip between the upper and lower sole of a man's shoe. That cracked a murder. It was just a trifle too good to be perfect.

In contrast to such fiascos, the Hall-Mills case, which occurred in New Jersey in 1922, ranks favorably with the Borden murders of thirty years before. A philandering parson, the Reverend Edward Hall, and a choir singer, Mrs. Eleanor Mills, were shot to death near a lonely lane. It was their last tryst. The minister's wife, Mrs. Frances Hall, and a few of her close relations, were charged with the murders and eventually brought to trial.

Public sympathy switched from the victims to the accused. If Mrs. Hall and her relations had been unjustly convicted, the law would be doubly at fault, for they had borne the brunt of scandal before being charged with murder. They met the ordeal with a forthright simplicity that resulted in a "not guilty" verdict that put the Hall-Mills case in the limbo of the great unsolved.

The murderer, of course, must not think too far ahead and outwit himself. That can prove fatal. The classic example was the calculating killer who met his victim in New Hampshire, drove him across a bridge into Maine, and murdered him there. Clever, indeed, for New Hampshire law provided capital punishment for murder, whereas Maine had abolished it.

They caught the culprit on his way to Canada and brought him back to New Hampshire, where he confessed his crime so they would send him to Maine and let him stand trial there. But a hard-headed New Hampshire grand jury decided that the murder might have been committed before he reached the bridge, and that all he took into Maine was a dead body. So they tried him in New Hampshire and convicted him. He was sentenced to be hanged, but on the eve of the execution, he died from a heart attack. There are ways to cheat the gallows.

This case of the horse-and-buggy era raises the perennial question: how much does capital punishment discourage murder, if at all? I have come to believe that it probably discourages it greatly, though there are cogent reasons to think otherwise. The New York State law of 1965 is perhaps the most disturbing one on the books for the peaceable citizen, since it eliminates the death sentence *except* when the victim is a police officer. Then, of course, the killer gets the chair, because no cop is willing to be a sitting duck even if the State declares an open season on murder where the general public is concerned.

The law does have some unpublicized aspects that could be exploited. Instead of increasing sales taxes, the State might do well by selling honorary deputy sheriff badges which would bestow on the holder the status of a lawman. At $50 each, the treasury would probably be swelled by $50,000,000 by granting extra immunity to murder. It would be cheap insurance.

Now that we are really deep in the subject, let's study the fine points of the murderer's art through the case histories of some of the more notorious practitioners. The ones you will find here have been chosen because they show the knack of killing—or lack of it—from the most practiced hand to that of the outright bungler.

Two things, I think, can be said about these cases. They are well told. They have an indisputable finality.

Which makes it excusable to read about anything—even murder.

Contents

Contents

The Monster of Sixty-third Street

C AN hex and hate be linked in homicide? Does the art of murder include the delivery of death from afar? Is witchcraft still with us? Do ancient curses still work?

Very possibly, according to data compiled by Charles Fort, whose off-trail philosophies won him a host of followers during the 1920's.

Fort delved into the famous case of Lizzie Borden, who was accused of two axe murders that involved both extreme hate and remarkable force. While she was languishing in jail, a Boston reporter named Henry Trickey faked a story, building up the case against her. When Trickey was indicted for libel, he lived up to his name by skipping to Canada.

"There may," remarks Fort, "have been something more deadly than an indictment, from which there was no escape for Trickey. While boarding a train at Hamilton, Ontario, he fell and was killed."

Fort cites the equally famous Hall-Mills case of thirty years later. "In the fall of 1922," he relates, "Mrs. Jane Gibson was a sturdy woman farmer. It was her accusation that upon the night of the murder of Dr. Edward Hall and Elinor Mills, she had seen Mrs. Hall bending over the bodies. So she testified. At the retrial, in November, 1926, she repeated the accusation, though she had to be carried on a cot into the courtroom."

1

By Fortean logic, the whammy could also have been applied in that instance. The press, too, was hit by a hoodoo
during the Hall-Mills case, though Fort apparently overlooked it. The case was reopened by Philip A. Payne, sen-
sation-seeking editor of the *New York Mirror*.

After Mrs. Hall and the other defendants were acquitted,
they sued the *Mirror* for libel, and Payne, like Trickey, decided to leave the country. He took off from Maine in a
plane called Old Glory, which was scheduled to land in
Rome—a follow-up of Lindbergh's New York-to-Paris flight
of a few months before. But Old Glory never made it. The
wreckage was found off Newfoundland with no trace of
Payne or his companions.

Charles Fort may have found something when he delved
into the hex stuff. Perhaps he was ahead of his time, for
when he died in 1932, parapsychology and ESP were just
coming into vogue. Today, many respected students of those
subjects would agree with most of Fort's findings.

They should revel in the case of Henry H. Holmes. On
the gallows, he hurled imprecations upon all who had
brought him to his unhappy end, and his words seem to
have carried a sinister weight. The judge who had sentenced
Holmes died soon after the trial. Within six months, the
warden of the prison committed suicide. That horrible example so shook the man who had served as Holmes's jailer
that he, too, took his own life.

The foreman of the jury laughed at the superstitious
warnings of friends until, of all things, he was struck by
lightning. That was too much for the undertaker who had
buried Holmes. Feeling that he might be next on the list, he
prudently went insane. By a strange coincidence, he died on
the twentieth anniversary of the day when he had lowered
the murderer into the grave.

Quite a score for a killer to run up after death. But in life,
as you will see, he was even more active, though perhaps not
quite so vindictive.

The Monster of
Sixty-third Street

HERBERT ASBURY

IN the middle 1890's Chicago temporarily forgot the disturbing revelations of William T. Stead and the Civic Federation to marvel at the extraordinary career of a young doctor named Herman W. Mudgett, but better known as Henry H. Holmes. Gentle and almost effeminate in appearance and manner, with mild blue eyes and a soft and musical voice, and possessing an almost irresistible attraction for women, Mudgett was nevertheless a forger, a bigamist, a swindler, a horse thief, and a murderer who maintained a fantastic "castle" equipped with trapdoors, secret stairways, soundproof rooms, torture chambers lined with sheet iron and asbestos, a crematory, vats of corrosive acids and quicklime, and apparatus with which he articulated the skeletons of several of his victims and prepared them for sale to medical schools. This thrifty butcher was finally hanged for the

3

murder of one of his accomplices in a bizarre insurance fraud, and enough evidence was available to have hanged him for a dozen other killings. But the actual number or persons who met death at his hands was never known, although police and newspaper estimates ranged from thirty to several hundred. He once described himself as "an honest dealer in human remains," but the New York *World* called him "the first criminal of the century," and the Chicago *Journal* said of him:

"The nerve, the calculation and the audacity of the man were unparalleled. Murder was his natural bent. Sometimes he killed from sheer greed of gain; oftener, as he has himself confessed, to gratify an inhuman thirst for blood. Not one of his crimes was the outcome of a sudden burst of fury—'hot blood'—as the codes say. All were deliberate; planned and concluded with consummate skill. To him murder was indeed a fine art; and he reveled in the lurid glamor cast upon him by his abnormal genius. Even with the shadow of the noose dangling over his head, he evolved a so-called confession, detailing with horrible calmness how he had exterminated twenty-seven fellow creatures, and coldly setting forth the varied and bloody tortures he employed. One could almost see the fiendish grin on his thin and bloodless lips as, in the gloom of his cell, he set down the terrible tale. But the man was an atrocious liar, and several of those with whose murder he charged himself have since denied his story with their own lips. The statement was prompted by a perverted ambition to be regarded as the 'greatest' monster who ever walked in the form of man, and an incongruous desire to win for the education of his little son the $5,000 offered for the 'confession' by a newspaper."

Mudgett, or Holmes, was born in 1860 at Gilmanton, New Hampshire, where his father, a respected and prosperous citizen, had been postmaster for almost a quarter of a century. He was notoriously a bad boy, frequently in trouble, and in later years was principally remembered for his cruelty to animals and smaller children. His only redeeming trait appears to have been a fondness for study; he was the brightest pupil in the local schools. In 1878, when he was eighteen years old, young Mudgett eloped with the seventeen-year-old daughter of a well-to-do farmer of Loudon, New Hampshire, and that same year he began to study medicine at a small college in Burlington, Vermont, paying his tuition with a small legacy which had been inherited by his wife. In 1879 he transferred to the medical school of the University of Michigan, at Ann Arbor, and while studying there committed his first serious crime with the aid of another student who is said to have become, in later years, a prominent physician in New York. The accomplice insured his life for $12,500 and soon thereafter disappeared, while Mudgett stole a corpse from the dissecting-room of the medical school, identified it as that of the missing student, and collected the insurance. A few months after this coup Mudgett completed his medical studies and left Ann Arbor, abandoning his wife and infant son. Mrs. Mudgett returned to Gilmanton and is said never to have seen her husband again.

Not even Pinkerton detectives, who procured most of the evidence which sent Mudgett to the gallows, were able to learn very much about his activities during the half-dozen years that followed his departure from Michigan, although they came across his trail in several cities and states. For a year or so he was engaged in legitimate business in St. Paul, and so gained the respect and goodwill of his neighbors that he was appointed receiver for a bankrupt store. He immediately stocked the place with goods bought on credit, sold them quickly at low prices, and vanished with the proceeds. From St. Paul he went into New York State as agent for a New England nursery, and for a while taught a district school in Clinton County, boarding at the home of a farmer near the village of Moore's Forks. He seduced the farmer's wife, and disappeared one night leaving an unpaid board bill and a pregnant landlady. In 1885 he opened an office in the village of Wilmette, a North Shore suburb of Chicago, posing as an inventor and using the name of Holmes. Without troubling to divorce his wife in New Hampshire, he married Myrtle Z. Belknap, daughter of a wealthy resident of Wilmette, but she left him after he had twice tried to poison her father and had attempted to obtain possession of his property by means of forged deeds. When Belknap threatened to have him arrested, Homes hastily left Wilmette and went to St. Louis, where he served three months in jail as the result of an attempted land swindle. It was in St. Louis that Holmes met the two men who were destined to bring about his destruction—Marion Hedgspeth, a famous train robber who was awaiting sentence to the penitentiary; and Benjamin F. Pietzel, a small-time swindler who was finding it extremely difficult to earn a dishonest living for his wife and five children.

Early in 1889 Holmes appeared in downtown Chicago with the A.B.C. Copier, a machine for copying documents, and about the only honest device with which he was ever connected. He operated from an office in the Monon Block on South Dearborn Street, but the copier was a failure, and Holmes again vanished, leaving his creditors with worthless notes aggregating nine thousand dollars. A few months later he turned up in the Englewood section on the south side, as a clerk in a drugstore owned by a widow named Holden, at Wallace and Sixty-third Streets, a neighborhood which served as a base for his operations during the next several years. About the first of 1890 Mrs. Holden disappeared, and Holmes told the neighbors that she had sold him the business and "moved away." Apparently no one was sufficiently interested to find out what actually had happened to her, and she could not be found when the police finally began to investigate Holmes's activities.

In 1892 Holmes built on the southwest corner of Wallace and Sixty-third Streets, directly opposite the drugstore which he had "bought" from Mrs. Holden, the building which was popularly known as Holmes's Castle—an imposing structure of three stories and a basement, with false battlements and wooden bay windows covered by sheet iron. It occupied an area of fifty by one hundred and sixty-two feet, and contained between eighty and ninety rooms. Holmes himself drew the plans and closely supervised every detail of construction, and, as far as the police could learn, never paid anyone a cent for the materials which went into the building. He also changed workmen frequently, often discharging them in a great fury and refusing to pay their wages, so that no one else knew the terrible secrets of the Castle until he was arrested in the summer of 1895.

The detectives who devoted several weeks to searching and making a floor plan of the Castle found nothing out of the ordinary on the first and third floors; the latter was cut up into small apartments which were apparently never occupied, and the former into larger rooms which were rented for business purposes. Three or four were used by Holmes himself for a drugstore, restaurant, and jewelry store. But the second floor of the building proved to be a veritable labyrinth, with narrow, winding passages leading to hidden stairways, cleverly concealed doors and rooms, blind hallways and trapdoors, all so arranged as to facilitate escape and confuse pursuit. Holmes's private apartment, consisting of bedroom and bath and two small chambers which he used as offices, was on the second floor front, facing Sixty-third Street. In the floor of his bathroom, concealed under a heavy rug and carefully fitted, the police found a trapdoor, from which a stairway descended to a small room about eight feet square. There were two doors to this chamber, one opening on a stairway which led downward to the street, and the other giving access to a chute which extended to the basement.

Besides Holmes's quarters, the second floor contained thirty-five rooms. Half a dozen were fitted up as ordinary sleeping chambers, and there were indications that they had been occupied by the various women who had worked for the monster, or to whom he had made love while awaiting an opportunity to kill them. Several of the other rooms were without windows, and could be made airtight by closing the doors. One was completely filled by a huge safe, almost large enough for a bank vault, into which a gas pipe had been introduced. Another was lined with sheet iron covered by asbestos, and showed traces of fire. Some had been soundproofed, while others had extremely low ceilings, and trapdoors in the floors from which ladders led to smaller rooms beneath. In all of the rooms on the second floor, as well as in the great safe, were gas pipes with cut-off valves in plain sight. But these valves were fakes; the flow of gas was actually controlled by a series of cut-offs concealed in the closet of Holmes's bedroom. Apparently one of his favorite methods of murder was to lock a victim in one of the rooms and then turn on the gas; and the police believed that in the asbestos-lined chamber he had devised a means of introducing fire, so that the gas pipe became a terrible blowtorch from which there was no escape. Also in Holmes's closet was an electric bell which rang whenever a door was opened anywhere on the second floor.

The basement of the Castle, which was seven feet deep under the entire building and extended under the sidewalk on Sixty-third Street, was Holmes's disposal plant, where he burned or otherwise destroyed the bodies of his victims, or removed the flesh from their bones and prepared the skeletons for articulation. In a corner of the huge underground room, beneath the chute which ran from the second floor, was a dissecting table and a case of gleaming surgical knives, with sufficient evidence to indicate that they had frequently been used. Under the table was a box containing several skeletons, all of females. Built into one of the walls was a crematory, with a heavy iron grate to hold the fire, and another grate, fitted with rollers, by means of which a body could be slid into the flames. "A curious thing about this retort," said the *New York World,* "was that there was an iron flue leading from it into a tank. There was no other entrance to this tank. . . . A white fluid was discovered in the bottom of the tank which gave forth an overpowering odor." Buried in the floor of the basement the police found a huge vat of corrosive acid and two of quicklime, in any of which a body would have been devoured within a few hours. A pile of loose quicklime was also found in a small room built into a corner, and in it was the naked footprint of a woman. Scattered about the basement were several mysterious machines, the purpose of which was never learned, although it was believed that one, in shape somewhat similar to the rack of the medieval torturer, was the "elasticity determinator" with which Holmes once said he had been conducting experiments. He had a theory that the human body, by proper manipulation, could be stretched to twice its normal length, and held that universal application of the process would produce a race of giants. Another unexplained mystery was encountered by workmen who were digging a tunnel through the cellar wall toward Sixty-third Street. Said the *New York World:*

". . . They encountered a wall that gave forth a hollow sound. As soon as this wall was broken through a horrible smell was encountered and fumes like those of a charnel house rushed forth. A plumber was sent for, and the workmen gathered about while he proceeded to investigate. The first thing the plumber did was to light a match. Then there was a terrific explosion that shook the building, while flames poured forth into the cellar. The plumber was the only man who escaped uninjured, and an ambulance took the other workmen to the hospital. Then a thorough search of this mysterious chamber was made by the police. They found that the brick wall had concealed a tank curiously constructed. This tank had contained an oil whose fumes, the chemists say, would destroy human life within less than a minute. There were evidences about the cellar of this mysterious and deadly

oil having been used. . . . A small box was found in the
center of the tank. When this was opened by Fire Mar-
shal James Kenyon an evil-smelling vapor rushed out. All
ran except Kenyon, who was overpowered by the stench.
He was dragged out and carried upstairs, and for two
hours acted like one demented."

Half a dozen human bones, and several pieces of jewelry
which were identified as having belonged to one of Holmes's
mistresses, were found by detectives in a large wood-
burning stove in the center of the basement, and scraps of
blood-stained linen were discovered in a nearby ash heap.
"In a hole in the middle of the floor," said the *World,* "more
bones were found. These have been examined by physicians, who declare that they include, among others, the
bones of a child between six and eight years of age. There
were seventeen ribs in all, part of a spinal column, a collar-
bone, and a hip bone. In spite of the retort, the deadly oil
tank, and two vaults of quicklime, all working at the same
time, is it possible, it was asked, that Holmes was murdering
people so fast that he had to bury some of them?"

When Holmes built the Castle he told his neighbors that
he intended to operate the second and third floors as a
boardinghouse during the World's Fair, which opened in the
spring of 1893, a few months after the completion of the
building. The *New York World* declared that there were
many reasons to believe that the monster contemplated
gathering in victims among the visitors to Chicago. "There
are hundreds of people," said the *World,* "who went to Chicago to see the Fair and were never heard of again. The list
of the 'missing' when the Fair closed was a long one, and in
the greater number foul play was suspected. Did these visitors to the Fair, strangers to Chicago, find their way to
Holmes's Castle in answer to delusive advertisements sent
out by him, never to return again? Did he erect his Castle
close to the Fair grounds so as to gather in these victims by
the wholesale, and, after robbing them, did he dispose of

their bodies in his quicklime vats, in his mysterious oil tank with its death-dealing liquids, or did he burn them in the elaborate retort with which the basement was provided?"

These questions were never satisfactorily answered, although detectives did learn that Holmes had advertised the Castle as a boardinghouse. No fewer than fifty persons, reported to the police as missing, were traced to the place, but there the trail ended, and the detectives were unable to find sufficient evidence to justify the popular belief that Holmes had killed any or all of them.

The police believed that the first persons murdered in the Castle were Mrs. Julia Conner, the wife of I. L. Conner, of Davenport, Iowa, and her eight-year-old daughter, Pearl. The Conner family came to Chicago in 1890, soon after the disappearance of Mrs. Holden, and Holmes employed both Conner and his wife in the drugstore, the former as a clerk and the latter, a strikingly handsome woman, as bookkeeper. Mrs. Conner soon became the monster's mistress and Conner quit his job and left Chicago when Holmes told him that his wife had been unfaithful. Mrs. Conner and the little girl remained with Holmes for almost two years, the longest period that any woman except his first wife ever lived with him. During some six months of that time she ran the drugstore alone while Holmes went to Texas, where he was a member, and probably the leader, of a gang of swindlers, murderers, and horse thieves which operated in that state and in Arizona. The gang was finally dispersed by Texas Rangers, but Holmes escaped and returned to Chicago before a warrant which had been issued for his arrest could be served.

While he was in Texas Holmes became acquainted with a young girl named Minnie Williams, who with her sister, Nannie, owned property in Fort Worth valued at about fifty thousand dollars. In the late summer of 1892 Minnie Williams came to Chicago and moved into the Castle, and Holmes introduced her about the neighborhood as his private secretary. Actually she was his mistress, and her mad infatuation with the monster was obvious to everyone who saw them together. Within two hours after her arrival she had quarreled with Mrs. Conner over Holmes, and within ten days Mrs. Conner and her daughter had disappeared. After his arrest Holmes told detectives that Mrs. Conner had died while he was performing a criminal operation and that the little girl had "wandered away." Eventually, however, he admitted that he had murdered both the woman and her child because of Minnie Williams' jealousy. "But I would have got rid of her anyway," he said. "I was tired of her."

Minnie Williams lived at the Castle for more than a year and probably knew more about Holmes's affairs than any other person. The police said that it would have been impossible for her not to have had guilty knowledge of many murders. Besides being responsible for the killing of Mrs. Conner and her daughter, Minnie Williams was believed to have instigated the murder of Emily Van Tassell, a Chicago girl who worked for Holmes early in 1893 and vanished within a month; and of Emeline Cigrand, a nineteen-year-old blonde who is said to have been the prettiest of the monster's victims. Miss Cigrand, a girl of good family and excellent character, was a stenographer in the Keeley Institute at Dwight, Illinois, when Holmes's friend Ben Pietzel went there in the fall of 1892 to take the gold cure for drunkenness. Upon his return to Chicago Pietzel told Holmes of the girl's beauty, and Holmes offered her a large salary to work for him in Chicago. She accepted the job, came to the Castle, and never left it. Holmes said afterward that he had locked her in his soundproofed room and forced her to have illicit relations with him, and that he had killed her because Minnie Williams objected to sharing him with another woman. Miss Cigrand was engaged to Robert E. Phelps, a wealthy man many years her senior, who was never seen again after he had called at the Castle. Holmes told the police that Phelps had died during the course of an "experiment."

In the early summer of 1893 Nannie Williams came to the Castle from Texas to visit her sister. Holmes made violent love to her and apparently had no trouble in persuading her to sign over to him her share of the Fort Worth property. Nannie Williams disappeared in July, 1893, and it was understood by those who had met her in Chicago that she had gone back to Texas. In the fall of 1893 Ben Pietzel took charge of the Castle, and Holmes and Minnie Williams went to Denver, where the monster, under the name of Howard, married Miss Georgianna Yoke of Richmond, Indiana, whom he had met in Indianapolis several years before. After living in Denver for several weeks with the two women, neither of whom knew of the existence of the other, Holmes sent Miss Yoke back to her home in Indiana, telling her that he would soon join her, and returned to Chicago with Minnie Williams. He made several trips with Miss Yoke during the next two years, but was never with her more than a few weeks at a time. Apparently, however, he really loved her. At any rate, as she testified at his trial, he was always kind to her and made no attempt to take her life.

About the first of December, 1893 Minnie Williams transferred her Texas property to Holmes, and soon afterward she disappeared; she was last seen alive on December 15. When he was questioned by detectives after his arrest Holmes at first insisted that Minnie Williams had killed her sister in a fit of jealous fury and had fled to Europe with a young man; but he finally admitted that he had killed both the Williams sisters, and that their skeletons, as well as those of Emily Van Tassel and Emeline Cigrand, were in the box found in the basement of the Castle.

The facilities of the Castle were also utilized by Holmes in innumerable swindling operations, in some of which he was assisted by Mrs. Conner and Minnie Williams. He served good food in his restaurant, but virtually every article offered for sale in the jewelry and drugstores was a fake; the gold jewelry was brass, the diamonds were glass, and no matter what sort of pills were ordered, the customer received powdered chalk, occasionally colored and perfumed. For more than a year Holmes sold water from Lake Michigan over the counter of his drugstore at five cents a small glass, assuring the people of Englewood that it was the finest mineral water in the world and had come from an artesian well in his basement. Perhaps the most elaborate of his swindles was the celebrated gas generator, which deceived many people and was hailed as an important invention by which gas could be manufactured from water. In the basement of the Castle Holmes built a queer-looking contraption of pipes and tanks, with a furnace underneath, and when everything was ready he notified the gas company, which sent an expert to make an examination. "What the expert saw," said the *Chicago Tribune,* "was a contrivance such as he had never seen before, with a stream of water running in at one end and a strong flow of gas at the other. Holmes assured him that the cost of manufacture was next to nothing, and the result was that the gas company gave the invention such a strong recommendation that Holmes was enabled to sell it to a Canadian for $2,000. When the machine was taken out it was discovered that Holmes had tapped the gas company's mains and thus generated his great illuminator."

While in jail in St. Louis, Holmes told Marion Hedgspeth, the train robber, that he had evolved a foolproof scheme to defraud an insurance company, but that he required a shrewd lawyer to help work out the details. Hedgspeth referred Holmes to his own attorney, Jeptha D. Howe, of St. Louis, and Holmes promised to send the bandit five hundred dollars if the plan was successful. Apparently Holmes did nothing about this particular idea for several years, though in the meantime he attempted an insurance swindle without assistance. He took a cadaver to a seaside resort in Rhode Island, registered as H. H. Holmes, and then burned and otherwise disfigured the head of the body and left it on the beach. Shaving his beard and making other alterations in his appearance, he returned to the hotel, registered under another name, and inquired for his friend Holmes. When the body was found on the beach he identified it as that of Holmes, and presented an insurance policy for twenty thousand dollars. But the insurance company suspected fraud and refused to pay, and Holmes returned to Chicago without attempting to press his claim.

In the early summer of 1894 Holmes held a conference with Ben Pietzel and Jeptha D. Howe, and the three compounded a plot whereby Pietzel was to take out life insurance and then disappear, while Holmes was to procure a body, identify it as that of Pietzel, and collect the insurance. As soon as the plan had been completed, Pietzel insured his life for ten thousand dollars at the Chicago office of the Fidelity Mutual Life Association, and in August went to Philadelphia, where he opened an office at No. 1316 Callowhill Street under the name of B. F. Perry, posing as a patent attorney. On September 3, 1894, Pietzel's body, with the face blackened and blistered as if from burns, was found on the floor of his office. Near by was a broken bottle which had contained benzine, and the first theory evolved by the police was that Pietzel, who of course they thought was Perry, had been killed in an accidental explosion. But an autopsy showed that his death had been caused by chloroform. Meanwhile the police had learned that "Perry" had come to Philadelphia from St. Louis, and the police of that city were asked to find his relatives. About three weeks after the finding of the body Jeptha D. Howe appeared in Philadelphia and said that the dead man was in reality Ben Pietzel, and that he was empowered by Mrs. Pietzel to collect the insurance. Later Holmes arrived in Philadelphia with Pietzel's daughter, Alice, and he also identified the body as that of Pietzel. The insurance was paid without question. Of the ten thousand dollars, Howe took twenty-five hundred and Holmes the remainder. Holmes afterward gave Mrs. Pietzel five hundred dollars, but took the money back within a few days on the pretense that he would invest it.

The ironic feature of the business was that actually no fraud had been perpetrated on the insurance company. Pietzel's life had been insured, and Pietzel was certainly dead; Holmes had murdered him three days before his body was found. But neither Howe nor Mrs. Pietzel knew this; they thought that Pietzel was alive and that Holmes had substituted a body in order to collect the insurance, and that Pietzel would return to his family in a few months. Howe regarded the whole matter as a closed incident, and when he returned to St. Louis he told Marion Hedgspeth about the scheme and how well it had worked. But when Hedgspeth failed to receive the five hundred dollars which had been promised him by Holmes, he told the warden of the prison about the conversation he had held with Holmes while the latter was in jail. The warden notified the insurance company, and the Pinkerton Detective Agency was employed to investigate. Detective Frank P. Geyer of Pinkerton's Philadelphia office was assigned to the case, and he was soon convinced that the body found in Callowhill Street was really that of Pietzel, and that Pietzel had been murdered. Geyer suspected Holmes, partly because of Holmes's unsavory record as a swindler, and partly because he had identified the body and was known to have called upon Pietzel several times while the latter was masquerading as B. F. Perry. Police departments throughout the United States were asked to arrest Holmes, and the Texas authorities were requested to revive their warrant charging him with horse-stealing, so that he could be held if caught.

But Holmes proved to be very elusive. After he had collected and divided the insurance with Jeptha Howe, he returned to St. Louis, where he found Mrs. Pietzel ill and frightened. He persuaded her to take her eldest and youngest children and go to her parents' home in Galva, Illinois, and promised to meet her in Detroit in two weeks with Alice, Nellie, and Howard. Her husband also, he said, would be in Detroit. Holmes arrived in Detroit several days before the appointed time and put the three children in a

boardinghouse. Then he went to Richmond, Indiana, returned to Detroit with Georgianna Yoke, and installed her
in a second boardinghouse. When Mrs. Pietzel arrived she
was lodged in still another house. Then he began to move
about the country, apparently having learned that Pinkerton's were on his trail. "During these travels," said the *Chicago Journal,* "Holmes carried with him three separate de-
tachments—Mrs. Pietzel, Miss Yoke, and the children—all
within four blocks of each other in all the different cities,
almost traveling together, under Holmes's leading strings,
and yet each detachment ignorant of the presence of the
other two." This fantastic journeying continued for nearly
two months, but on November 17, 1894, Holmes appeared
in Boston, alone, and was arrested and sent to Philadelphia.

A week after Holmes's arrest Miss Yoke was located at
her parents' home in Indiana, and Mrs. Pietzel was found in
Burlington, Vermont, where Holmes had established her in
a rented house to await the arrival of her family. Holmes
had lived at the house for several days, but left in great an-
noyance when she found him digging a hole in the back
yard. The police believed that he was digging her grave, but
for some unknown reason decided not to kill her. Mrs. Pietzel was arrested and taken to Philadelphia, but was soon
released, and no charge was ever made against her.

Holmes flatly refused to tell what had become of the three
Pietzel children, Nellie, Howard, and Alice, and Detective
Geyer set out to find them and so complete his case against
the monster. In Chicago he learned that Holmes's mail had
been forwarded every day to Gilmanton, New Hampshire;
from Gilmanton it had been sent to Detroit, from Detroit to
Toronto, from Toronto to Cincinnati, from Cincinnati to
Indianapolis, and so on. For more than eight months Geyer
followed Holmes's trail throughout the Middle West and
Canada, stopping at every city to investigate every house
that had been for rent at the time Holmes was supposed to
have been there—literally hundreds of them. In Detroit the
house that Holmes had occupied with the children was still

vacant, and there was a big hole in the cellar floor. But nothing was found in the hole. In Toronto Geyer searched for eight days before he found a house at No. 16 Vincent Street which had been rented to a man with two little girls. Holmes had borrowed a spade from a neighbor with which to dig a hole for storing potatoes, and Geyer borrowed the same spade and dug in the same place. Several feet under ground he found the bodies of Nellie and Alice Pietzel. In an upstairs bedroom was a large trunk, with a piece of rubber tubing leading into it from a gas pipe. It was clear that Holmes had induced the girls to enter the trunk, probably during a game of hide-and-seek, and had asphyxiated them.

During the few days in which they lived in Toronto the Pietzel girls had told neighbors that they had a little brother in Indianapolis, and with this clue in mind Geyer went to the Indiana city and painstakingly searched nine hundred houses. Finally, in the suburb of Irvington, he found the place that Holmes had rented and in which he had lived for nearly a week. Fortunately for Geyer's investigation, the house had been vacant since the departure of the monster, and the stove used by Holmes was still in the kitchen. And in the stove the detective discovered the charred body of Howard Pietzel. Holmes told a great many different stories when confronted with the evidence which had been unearthed by Detective Geyer; he insisted that Pietzel had committed suicide, and declared that the three children had been murdered by a mythical young man who had made the mythical trip to Europe with Minnie Williams. But in his famous "confession," which he wrote while awaiting execution, Holmes said that he suffered greatly when he was informed that Geyer had found the bodies of Alice and Nellie Pietzel in Toronto. "I saw again," he said, "the two little faces as they had looked when I had hurriedly left them—felt the innocent child's kiss so timidly given—heard again their earnest words of farewell."

The indictment returned by the Grand Jury charged Holmes with the murder of Ben Pietzel. His trial, which began on October 28, 1895, was one of the most sensational of the century, and the newspapers reported it in a manner which would have done credit to the modern tabloid. And they had first-rate material with which to work. Besides the mysteries of the Castle, which were recounted at length in the testimony of various witnesses, Holmes created several exciting scenes in the courtroom, broke down and wept when Georgianna Yoke appeared as a witness for the state, and at length discharged his lawyers and attempted to conduct his own defense. But the skill and shrewdness he displayed in questioning witnesses and arguing points of law were of no avail; the trial ended in six days with a verdict of guilty of murder in the first degree. Afterward the jurors said that they had agreed in one minute, but had remained out for two hours and a half "for the sake of appearances."

Holmes's case was appealed to the Pennsylvania Supreme Court, which affirmed the verdict, and on April 30, 1896, the Governor refused to intervene. On May 7, 1896, nine days before his thirty-sixth birthday, Holmes was hanged in Moyamensing Prison.

"It is safe to assume," said the *Chicago Journal* on the afternoon of the execution, "that a sigh of relief will go up from the whole country with the knowledge that Herman Mudgett or Henry H. Holmes, man or monster, has been exterminated—much the same as a plague to humanity would be stamped out."

Belle of Indiana

ALONG in the early 1950's, the following ad appeared in various popular magazines:

> LONELY? Let us help you find that certain someone. Join Old Reliable Club. 50 years of dependable, confidential service. Correspondents most everywhere seeking congenial mates, proven results. Interesting photos, descriptions FREE.

The real pay-line in that come-on was the statement, "50 years of dependable, confidential service," for it showed that this outfit was actually in operation at the time of Belle Gunness, who flourished half a century before. After what Belle accomplished in the way of proven results all other lonely hearts organizations should have closed up shop.

Belle didn't need a staff of experts to help her. She was a one-woman club all on her own, and what a club she wielded! Whoever felt it knew it, but never lived to tell.

Companionship clubs continued to flourish, but Belle's technique was unique. The lonely-hearted are usually faint-hearted as well, which is why they rely on go-betweens.

Belle was far ahead of her time. She advertised direct, thus
saving commissions and keeping facts strictly to herself.

Her pleas for companionship encouraged replies from reticent gentlemen who might ordinarily have shied from the
standard lonely heart pitch. Moreover, Belle had money and
could prove it, which softened the suspicions of miserly cor-
respondents who feared that tugs at their heartstrings might
eventually reach their purse strings.

All in all, Belle not only wrought well, but wrote well. So
well, in fact, that for many years, a well-faked ad purporting to come from a sincere but wealthy widow was termed
"a Belle Gunness" in the lonely hearts trade.

> DIVORCED? WIDOWED? SINGLE?
> Why be lonely and blue? Are you seeking
> friendship-companionship-marriage with a
> sincere, refined, and worthwhile person?
> Introductions arranged. Meet your "ideal"
> among our members.

> ROAD TO ROMANCE
> America's Finest Social Register for person-
> alized, selective introductions, invites YOU
> to meet its thousands of refined lady and
> gentlemen members. Write for beautiful photo
> album with actual pictures of members. En-
> close coin (10¢) and mention your age.

It sounds like fun, so what's wrong with it—other than a
few murders cropping up now and then?

One thing that the ads *don't* mention is that there's no
sure way of balancing up the lonely hearts candidates. That
lopsided situation didn't exist in the time of Belle Gunness.
Perhaps it was the other way about. It could very well have
been, considering the influx of male moths that hovered
about the gleaming candlelight that shone so bright through
the sycamores surrounding Belle's Indiana home.

Belle of Indiana

STEWART H. HOLBROOK

Had it not been for an unfortunate hired man and a fire, Belle Brynhilde Poulsatter Sorenson Gunness might have been in business indefinitely; and a very profitable and interesting line it must have been. She was an extremely retiring and uncommunicative person and until fire destroyed her home near La Porte, Indiana, on April 28, 1908, she was practically unknown except to a circle of what one shudders to call her intimates.

Belle first appeared in La Porte in 1901. She was then the Widow Sorenson, relict of Mads Sorenson, who died in 1900 leaving her with two children and eight thousand dollars in life insurance. From sale of the Sorenson home in Illinois the widow received another five thousand dollars. Thus she was financially well fixed when she bought a forty-eight-acre farm about a mile out of La Porte and moved there with two children of her own and another youngster, Jennie Olson, daughter of one Antone Olson.

The Widow Sorenson was forty-two years old in 1901.[1] Neighbors describe her as "rugged," which would seem wholly inadequate. She was five feet seven inches tall and weighed two hundred pounds, most of which was pure brawn. When her household effects arrived at the farm, the truckers were amazed at the ease with which she juggled heavy trunks, boxes, and crates. One of them, who may have been drinking that day, swore that he saw the woman pick the big upright piano clean off the floor of the porch, lug it unaided into the front room, and set it down as gently as she would have handled a basket of eggs. "Ay like music in home," Belle had beamed.

"Weigh three hunnert pound, easy," the awed trucker said later, referring to the piano.

In spite of her retiring disposition, neighbors soon learned that the Widow Sorenson was an accomplished farmer who could pitch hay and milk cows and who did her own butchering of hogs and calves, the meat of which she sold in La Porte. She wasn't a widow long. How they first met isn't clear; but in April of 1902 she married Peter Gunness, a Norwegian who seemed to be a jolly, honest person and became well liked by neighboring farmers. But Peter wasn't long for the world. In December, after only seven months of wedded bliss, he was killed when, as Mrs. Gunness explained the matter, he was struck on the head by a sausage grinder that fell from a shelf.

It is of course idle to speculate on whether or not the shelf had been jiggled. The La Porte coroner was called and, although later he admitted that the sausage-grinder affair "looked a little queer," he found officially that Peter Gunness, God rest his soul, had been the victim of an accident.

The Widow Gunness, who henceforth was known as Belle Gunness, was no doubt glad of the four-thousand-dollar life-insurance policy which the oddly animated sausage

[1] She was born Brynhilde Poulsatter at Selbe, Norway, in 1859, and came to the United States in 1868. Her first marriage was in 1883.

machine had liquidated. But she continued to live modestly, even frugally, and it soon became apparent that in spite of her forty-three years Belle was in an interesting condition. A son whom she named Philip was born in 1903. In addition, her brood included daughters Lucy and Myrtle by her previous marriage and the Jennie Olson she was caring for.[2]

Although it was not known until later—tragically later—Belle Gunness was addicted to the use of matrimonial journals.[3] That is, she advertised in them—listing, as was the custom, her desire for a good husband and being not too coy regarding her own personality and qualifications. What Belle wanted, it seemed, was a man of Scandinavian birth, preferably Norwegian, who was kind and honest and who would help a lovable and hard-working widow to lift the mortgage on her little farm. The "kind and honest" part of the desired man's qualifications might be winked at, one gathers; but the mortgage-lifting end of the deal was nothing short of imperative. "Triflers," Belle's advertisement said coldly, "need not apply."

A photograph of Belle Gunness at this period shows a squat, powerfully built woman in a long plain dress with puff sleeves, a Gibson Girl hair-do, and an exceeding dull and heavy face. Looking at the photograph, one is hard put to explain the undoubted attraction the woman exercised on a large number of men. To term the woman in this photograph "plain" is mere flattery. But either this picture is a gross libel on Belle or her personal charm was such that no photograph could catch and hold it.

[2] I dislike to use the term "caring for" in connection with *anything* in which Mrs. Gunness was concerned, but it must suffice for the present.

[3] Matrimonial journals are still flourishing in the United States, but today they usually operate under euphemisms such as "correspondence clubs" and "acquaintance societies." In former times they came right out with it and used *Wedding Bells* and other direct-action names. Any male could get a copy free and there read all about the wondrous charms of the ladies as described by themselves. But to get the names and addresses of these jewels the boys had to pay—six for a dollar. I once knew a lumberjack who got a very good wife by mail order. I also knew a farmhand who got a frightful witch in the same manner and was forced to strangle her to regain his peace of mind.

Shortly after the death of Mr. Gunness, Belle engaged a hired man to work around her place; but she herself was still active in butchering pigs, of which she had many, and in caring for the garden. The hired men changed from time to time, some of them very suddenly indeed; but none of them entered Belle's life very deeply until the next to last one, of which more later.

In 1906 a Mr. John Moo arrived at Belle's farm from Elbow Lake, Minnesota. He was a husky, good-looking man of about fifty years of age, well dressed by country-town standards, and a native of Norway. His object was matrimony, and he had been fetched by one of Belle's advertisements in the wedding-bells periodicals. With him John Moo brought one thousand dollars to "pay off the mortgage" on his intended's farm.

John was introduced to callers and neighbors as Cousin John, and for almost a week he was seen about the house every day. Then, one day, he wasn't there. That was fifty-odd years ago. John Moo hasn't been seen since.

Hard on the heels of the disappearing Moo came George Anderson of Tarkio, a village in the northwestern corner of Missouri. George, like both Peter Gunness and John Moo, was a native of Norway. Living in Missouri must have given him some of the skepticism for which that state is famous: George Anderson did not bring very much money with him to Belle's place.

He was mighty glad he hadn't. Long afterward he related why.

Attracted by Belle's description of herself in one of the marriage papers, Anderson had made the long trip to La Porte with the intention of matrimony. After the usual amenities—and by now Belle must have been getting pretty good at amenities—the woman brought up the little matter of raising the mortgage. Really charmed by the husky Belle, George was seriously considering returning home to get what might be termed the entrance fee and then marrying the woman.

Early on his visit at the farm, however, he suddenly

awoke in the middle of the night. "All in a cold sweat," he recalled. Bending over him and peering intently into his face was Belle herself, a lighted candle in her hand. What she intended to do, if anything, George Anderson never found out. He was so startled at the odd expression in the eyes and on the usually phlegmatic face of his intended bride that he let go a yell. Belle ran out of the room. So did George. He put on his clothes and got the hell out of there as fast as he could go, and kept going until he reached the La Porte railroad station, on foot, where he got a train for Tarkio, Missouri.

After Anderson's departure they *may* have been a lull, a sort of brief hiatus, between the arrivals of men with matrimonial intentions. Again, there may have been no break at all. It is difficult to say. In any case, Belle was not idle. She changed her advertising copy in the wedding-bells journals, and she also engaged a new hired man—a rather dim-witted young French-Canadian by name of Ray l'Amphere, who presently anglicized his name into plain Lamphere. What his relations with Belle were, other than as hired man, are not positively known; but probably they were rather interesting, as events were soon to indicate.

Either just before or just after Lamphere came to live and work at the farm, young Jennie Olson, the sixteen-year-old girl who had been put in Belle's care by the child's father, Antone Olson, disappeared. Possibly "disappeared" is too strong a word to use at this point, for Belle explained everything to neighbors. Jennie had "gone to California," she said, and was in school there. It certainly is a fact that Jennie went somewhere in midsummer of 1906. That was fifty-odd years ago. She hasn't been seen since.

During the lull in the mortgage-raising Belle began to be something of a mystery woman in the neighborhood. Hack drivers of La Porte told of delivering trunks to the Gunness farm at night. One of the drivers was Clyde Sturgis. One night he drove out there with a big, heavy trunk which was well bound with rope. Sturgis, always a helpful man, unloaded the trunk and started to cut the rope with his jack-knife. Belle was at him in a fury. "What are you trying to do!" she fairly screamed. "I'll take care of this trunk." And with that she picked it up off the porch like a box of marshmallows and lugged it inside.

Added to the business of the mysterious trunks, which doubtless became more mysterious every time it was retold, was that neighbors noted Belle kept the shutters on her house tightly drawn, both day and night, for a long period. And farmers going by late at night often saw Belle herself on the prowl, around her barn or in a small yard some fifty by seventy-five feet which Belle had recently enclosed with an *eight-foot* fence of stout and fine wire mesh. Entrance to this yard was by a rugged gate of tough oak which rumor said was always locked and to which Belle alone had the key.

The cellar of the house, too, was always kept locked except at hog-butchering season. At these times a stray neighbor or two had happened to call when Belle was in the cellar, her sleeves rolled up, wielding knife and cleaver like the best man Mr. Swift or Mr. Armour ever had. The cellar was admirably rigged for such work. It contained a long, heavy table of hardwood, twelve inches thick, and a large tub for scalding purposes. In the ceiling over the tub was a hook and pulley. Leather strips along the wall held a professional assortment of fine butcher's implements.

The lull in the stream of callers—if lull there was—came to an end in April of 1907. In that merry spring month Mr. Ole Budsberg, a native of Norway but long a citizen of Iola in Waupaca County, Wisconsin, packed his extension suitcase and took a train of steamcars for La Porte. Belle met him at the station in her own buggy. The loving couple had long since exchanged photographs, as is the happy custom in mail-order matrimonial circles, and they had no trouble recognizing each other.[4]

Mr. Ole Budsberg was a middle-aged man, the father of

---

[4] You can say what you want to about Belle, but not that she ever attempted to seduce men by retouched pictures; the ones she sent out to prospective mates looked cruelly like her.

several grown sons. He had done very well with certain log-
ging jobs in the white pine of Wisconsin and had saved his
money. With him to La Porte he brought two thousand dollars in cash. This was, as one might guess, for the purpose of
raising that apparently immutable mortgage on the forty-
eight acres of the Widow Gunness.

Mr. Budsberg arrived on the farm late in April of 1907.
That was fifty-odd years ago and he hasn't been seen since.

Nineteen hundred and seven had been a rather slow year
at the farm, but 1908 opened very auspiciously indeed when
Mr. Andrew K. Helgelein arrived at the place in January
and was made welcome by the charming chatelaine of what
soon was to be known as Abattoir Acres. Mr. Helgelein was
a native of Norway, but for years past he had been living
near Aberdeen, South Dakota, where he successfully raised
wheat.

Mr. Helgelein came with the most honorable intentions
of matrimony. In his big wallet he carried no less than three
thousand dollars in cash, with which to—but never mind.
What had fetched him was obviously a series of letters, the
last one of which happily has survived to give a good sample
of Belle's literary style and general technique. It was written
in Belle's own clear hand on January 13, 1908, and was in-
advertently but fortunately left at his South Dakota home by
Mr. Helgelein when he started for La Porte. Wrote the Belle
of Indiana:

> To the Dearest Friend in the World: No woman in the
> world is happier than I am. I know that you are now to
> come to me and be my own. I can tell from your letters
> that you are the man I want. It does not take one long to
> tell when to like a person, and you I like better than any-
> one in the world, I know.
>
> Think how we will enjoy each other's company. You,
> the sweetest man in the whole world. We will be all alone
> with each other. Can you conceive of anything nicer? I
> think of you constantly. When I hear your name men-
> tioned, and this is when one of the dear children speaks

of you or I hear myself humming it with the words of an
old love song, it is beautiful music to my ears.

My heart beats in wild rapture for you. My Andrew, I
love you. Come prepared to stay forever.

And, by God, he did. That was thirty-three years ago and
he hasn't been seen since.

Now affairs at the farm departed from their usual hum-
drum quiet. Ray Lamphere, the hired man, had a frightful
quarrel with Belle. He, like many another poor man, had
fallen in love with her and he was jealous of the latest star
boarder, Helgelein. In a terrible temper he packed up his
belongings and left. In La Porte he told friends that Belle
owed him back wages. He said he knew enough about Belle
to make her pay him not only his wages but to keep his
mouth shut, too.

Lamphere must have done a deal of talking, for it got to
Belle's ears. She promptly had him arrested on complaint
that he was insane and a menace to the public. He was given
what passed in those days for a sanity hearing and was
found sane. He made a call on Belle at the farm. They
argued heatedly about something. She had him arrested
again, for trespass.

Lamphere was a man who could take it. He paid a fine
for trespass and he remained in the neighborhood. It is even
thought that he called on Belle again. He also continued to
make various veiled threats about her, and once mentioned
to farmer William Slater that "Helgelein won't bother me
no more. We fixed him for keeps."

Trouble also assailed Belle from another quarter. She got
a letter from Mr. Asle Helgelein, a substantial citizen of
Mansfield, South Dakota, who wanted to know what had
become of his brother Andrew. Belle wrote in reply that
Andrew had gone away, doubtless on a visit to his native
Norway. To this whimsey Asle Helgelein answered that he
was positive his brother had done no such thing.

Now we get a real sample of how Belle met a challenge of
this sort. She sat right down and wrote Asle that she wished

he would come to La Porte to aid her in a search for Andrew. She intimated, too, that searches of this kind cost money. If Asle replied to this invitation it is not of record.

For once in her life Belle Gunness was worried. Or so she seemed to M. E. Leliter, prominent attorney of La Porte, to whom the woman came on April 27, 1908. She told him she was mortally in fear of Ray Lamphere, the ex-hired man. He had threatened to kill her, she said. He had promised to burn her house around her ears. In view of these things hanging over her she wanted to make her will. It is significant, perhaps, that she did not ask for police protection from Lamphere.

Attorney Leliter drew up a will and she signed it. It left her estate to her two children by the late Mr. Sorenson and her one child by the late Mr. Gunness. In case the children did not survive her, the estate was to go to a Norwegian children's home, a sort of orphanage, in Chicago.

Leaving Mr. Leliter's office, Belle proceeded to the La Porte bank—where she paid off a five-hundred-dollar note. Then she returned to the farm.

Early next morning farmers on the McClung road saw the Gunness home in flames. It burned to the ground. Only the hired man, one Joe Maxon, escaped, and he said he barely made it. Noise of the flames licking at his room had awakened him, he said, and he jumped out his second-story window in his underwear. He vowed that just before jumping he had shouted loudly to wake Mrs. Gunness and the children but had received no reply. They had been in the house when he went to bed.

When the embers had cooled slightly, searchers found four bodies. Three were readily identified as those of Lucy and Myrtle Sorenson, Belle's daughters, and of Philip Gunness, her son. The other corpse was the headless body of a woman. All four were found on a mattress in the cellar. On top of them were the charred remains of the pride of Belle's parlor, the fine upright piano.

Sheriff Albert H. Smutzer was called. He viewed the scene and arrested Ray Lamphere, the farmhand who had been doing so much talking about Mrs. Gunness. Immediately upon his arrest and without so much as one question asked him, Lamphere asked one of his own. "Did Widow Gunness and the kids get out?" he inquired.

But Lamphere denied any knowledge of how the fire started, even when he was confronted by John Solyam, a neighbor's boy, who identified Lamphere as the man he had seen running from the Gunness place just before the flames were noticed. "You wouldn't look me in the eye and say that," Lamphere asserted.

"Yes, I will," the lad said, and continued, "You found me hiding behind the bushes and you told me you'd kill me if I didn't get out of there."

Lamphere was indicted for murder; and a charge of arson was left, as you might say, hanging over him, just in case the other charge wasn't sufficient. The victim named in the murder charge was of course Mrs. Gunness. But, and the doubts began piling up one on top of the other, *was* the headless body that of Mrs. Gunness?

Swan Nicholson, neighboring farmer who had known Mrs. Gunness over a period of six years, viewed the headless corpse and said, without qualification, no, it wasn't that of the hefty widow. It wasn't tall enough, it wasn't big enough, and, well, it just didn't look like her at all. C. Christofferson, another farmer who had often called at the mystery place to do plowing and other work, was as positive as Nicholson had been. No, he said, that body had never been Belle. And so said Mrs. Austin Cutler, an old acquaintance.

From Chicago came Mrs. Nellie Olander and Mr. Sigurd Olson, sister and brother of the Jennie Olson who had lived with Belle and had "gone to California" not long before. Mrs. Olander and Mr. Olson told authorities they had known Belle ever since they could remember and that the headless body was of someone else, not Belle.

A tragic visitor at this time was Antone Olson, father of the missing girl. He came from Chicago to view the charred bodies. Jennie's was not among them. Mr. Olson told police he had planned to visit the Gunness home on the following Sunday to see if Jennie was all right. He said he had dreamed a few nights before that the Gunness home had been burned to the ground and Jennie was in the fire. It had worried him.

Physicians measured the charred remains of the headless woman. Making proper allowances for the missing head and neck, they concluded that the corpse was that of a woman five feet three inches tall and weighing about one hundred and fifty pounds. Belle, as those who knew her agreed, had not been a hair under five feet seven and weighed at least one hundred and eighty-five pounds, possibly more. Swan Nicholson was quite definite. The Widow Gunness, he said with sober assurance, weighed two hundred pounds if she weighed an ounce.

Clerks in La Porte stores who had sold Mrs. Gunness various articles of wearing apparel were interviewed for their knowledge of clothing sizes. These figures were compared with estimates of acquaintances. Physicians had meanwhile made careful measurements of the corpse. The two sets of measurements, one real, the other estimated, indicated that the body found in the cellar must be that of someone other than Belle. This is how they compared:

	Victim (inches)	Mrs. Gunness (inches)
Biceps	9	17
Bust	36	46
Waist	26	37
Thigh	25	30
Hips	40	54
Calf	12½	14
Wrist	6	9

Despite these discrepancies and admitting they would like to have more definite proof, police authorities said the headless corpse was that of Belle Gunness. Three rings on the left

hand were considered additional proof. One was set with
diamonds and had no markings. A plain gold band was en-
graved "M.S. to J.S. Aug. 22 '94"; another gold band was
marked "P.G. to J.S. 3-5-'95." It was reasonable to believe
that these rings had to do with Belle's first marriage, to
Mads Sorenson, and her second, to Peter Gunness. Because
of the condition of the flesh it was impossible to say if these
rings had been on these fingers for a long time.

Presently, as in all such cases of doubt, there came forward those witnesses who are apparently present, in swarm-
ing numbers, when any skulduggery has come to light. Half
a dozen persons volunteered the information that they had
seen Mrs. Gunness driving a woman to the farm on the
night of the fire. Descriptions of this mysterious party varied
from "slim" to "fairly stout." All agreed she had been "a
dark woman."

What the harassed authorities needed was a head for the
corpse, or at least a skull. Search of the barns and outbuild-
ings and of the near-by swamp revealed nothing in the form
of a head. The sheriff was prepared to call it a day—to let
the whole confusing matter rest as it was and to go ahead
with prosecution of the farmhand, Lamphere, for murder of
Mrs. Gunness. Doubtless that is exactly what would have
happened had it not been for the appearance on the scene of
Asle Helgelein of Mansfield, South Dakota. This was the
brother of Andrew, the man Belle had reported to Asle as
on his happy way to Norway. Asle had not known of the
Gunness fire until his arrival at La Porte. He had come simply to find his brother.

Asle went to Sheriff Smutzer with his suspicions that Andrew had somehow been done in by this woman he had
come to marry. The sheriff didn't seem very interested, but
Asle was persistent and the sheriff finally agreed to make
another inspection of the premises. In the high-fenced yard,
the gate to which had to be broken by police, were noted
several soft depressions in the ground. Joe Maxon, Belle's
last hired man, the one who barely had escaped from the
burning house, told officers that Belle once had him wheel

dirt into the yard to level the partly filled holes. Contained rubbish, Belle had said. At the urging of Asle Helgelein deputies took shovels and started digging.

The first layers under the soft earth were indeed rubbish —old cans, bottles, and so forth—but suddenly a digger let out an exclamation. He came up with a good fat gunny sack. In it was a body well hacked but still in fair condition, everything considered. Helgelein looked closely at the remains. "That's Andy," he said.

The deputies now dug with a right good will. Before sundown that day, which was May 3, 1908, they had uncovered the remains of at least four more bodies. One of these was identified as that of Jennie Olson, the girl who had "gone to California." One of the others was of a tall man with a dark mustache. The two others were of children.

Next day the yard yielded four more bodies. On the third day only one body was found. That made a total of ten in the yard. If the four in the cellar were added, the grand total was fourteen—an impressive number for so small a farm.

When he was informed of the bodies found in the yard, Lamphere, the ex-hired man, screamed in his cell. "Bodies, murder, Helgelein!" was his curious cry. "My God, that woman! Now I know what was going on!"

Not all of the bodies could be identified, but positive identifications were made of those of Jennie Olson, Andrew Helgelein, John Moo, and Ole Budsberg. For reasons that need not be gone into here, three other bodies were presently presumed to be those of one Olaf Lindblom and one Eric Gerhalt, both Norwegians who had come, separately, to visit Belle, and that of a hired man whose name was never known.

The remains of several *other* bodies were mere fragments —fingers and other small bones for which comparative skulls and trunks were missing. As physicians attempted to sort the hundreds of spare parts, the heavy table and the vat in the Gunness cellar took on a possible new meaning that made strong men shudder. Had that vat been used for purposes other than the scalding of hogs? One couldn't know, but police and physicians now looked at the several cleavers found in the ashes with new interest.

With Belle's private boneyard apparently exhausted, police felt that the investigation was completed—finished. They hadn't reckoned with the growing public rumor about that headless corpse and its possible connection with the mystery woman seen with Belle in her buggy on the night of the fire. New witnesses came forward. They had seen this same dark woman get off the evening train from Chicago. Belle had met her at the La Porte depot. They had driven out the McClung road together, toward the farm.

Maybe so; but Joe Maxon, Belle's final hired man, had seen no strange woman that night, although he admitted it was possible one could have been in the house without his knowledge. "It sure was a queer place," he allowed in what was a fair attempt at an understatement.

No matter what Joe Maxon said, local opinion had it settled that the headless corpse was that of a woman the crafty Belle had imported to the farm for just such a purpose. Belle herself was safe elsewhere, somewhere. So the story grew and solidified.

Dr. Ira P. Norton, La Porte dentist, had been very busy at the time of the Gunness fire and had not then connected the fire with a former patient. With the Gunness farm and its odd harvest now on the front pages of the nation's press, Dr. Norton recalled that he had done some dental work for the late Mrs. Gunness. He told police he could easily identify his own work, which was a bridge of gold and porcelain.

Police doubted Dr. Norton would have anything to work on. They said that fire hot enough to consume a head would also consume, or at least melt, both gold and porcelain. Not so, said Dr. Norton. The gold caps would not fuse under 1800 degrees Fahrenheit. The porcelain would not disintegrate at less than 2000 degrees. "That would call for a blowpipe flame," the dentist said.

The next problem was how to sift the ashes and debris of a large house and find a few small teeth—even if they existed, which the police seemed to doubt. Louis Schultz, a

public-spirited citizen of La Porte, heard of the quandary
and went to the officers with a suggestion. He was an old
sourdough, he said, not long since returned from the Yukon, and if he had a little lumber and some encouragement
he would build a regular gold-mine sluice box right there on
Belle's place. With plenty of running water handy he would
sluice every measly bit of stuff in the ruins of the house,
and if there was any gold to be found in the claim he
damned well would find it.

This Louis Schultz was plainly God-given. The sluice was
built in Belle's front yard; water was piped from the barn;
and old Klondike Louis, the ninety-eighter, went to work on
the strangest mining job of his career, while thousands
cheered.

The thousands who cheered Louis at his work came not
only from La Porte and surrounding towns but from Chicago, where the daily papers were whooping up the biggest
story of the year and one of the best horror stories of all
time. Klondike Louis, indeed, was a sensation. With his
sluice box roped off and scores of extra deputies needed to
handle the huge crowds, he shoveled tons of debris and
washed it down over the riffles before the largest audience a
sourdough ever had. At that time newsreels were in infancy
and seem not to have caught the epic event; but newspaper
photographers were all over the place, catching Louis in
pose after pose.

Bets were made on the outcome. Chicago bookies formed
pools on the day and hour Louis would strike pay dirt in
the Belle Gunness Mine. Vendors of popcorn and tonic cir-
culated in the crowd, which on its peak day was estimated to
be six thousand persons. On May 19, after four days of hard
work, Klondike Louis struck the vein. Washed out from the
muck and debris of the house was a piece of dental bridge-
work containing two lower bicuspids capped with gold, and
four porcelain teeth between them.

Dr. Norton looked closely. "My work, positively," he
said. "Those are Mrs. Gunness' teeth."

In November, Ray Lamphere, the ex-farmhand, went on

trial in La Porte for the murder of Mrs. Gunness. He was ably defended by Wirt Worden and was acquitted. Tried for arson, he was convicted. Obviously the jury did not believe Mrs. Gunness was dead. Lamphere was sent to prison at Michigan City, where he died in 1909.

Before his death Lamphere told a long and sometimes disconnected story of his affairs with Mrs. Gunness to a trusty at the prison by name of Harry Myers, and after Lamphere's death Myers retold it to prison officials. Highlights of this account were that Belle did *not* die in the fire. Despite the evidence of the dental work, the body was that of a woman Belle had lured from Illinois on the promise of housework, then killed and beheaded to preclude identification. The head had been destroyed by use of quicklime, "in a hole dug in the swamp."

Lamphere painted a horrible picture of the female monster on the prowl. With the stand-in woman butchered, Belle went methodically to work on her own three children, killing them one after the other with practiced hand, then piled the four bodies onto the mattress after dressing the woman's in some old clothes that would readily be recognized as Belle's clothing.

In all, Lamphere said, Belle had lured forty-two men to her house.[5] Only one had escaped, presumably the alert George Anderson of Tarkio, Missouri, who had awaked to find Belle standing over his bed peering into his face so intently.

From her dupes Belle had got amounts of cash varying from one thousand dollars to thirty-two thousand dollars each, Lamphere said. Usually she first drugged their coffee, then bashed in their heads while they were in a stupor. She then dissected the bodies on the big table in the cellar, tied

[5] I was immensely relieved to come across this figure "forty-two" in the record. There is something magic about forty-two in connection with apocryphal accounts of murders in series. Folklore has it, for instance, that Harry Orchard killed forty-two men; that Billy Gohl of Grays Harbor, Washington, killed forty-two; that Lydia Sherman of Connecticut accounted for a similar number.

the parts into neat bundles, and buried them in the locked yard. On occasion she varied the monotony by putting the bodies into the hog-scalding vat and adding generous amounts of quicklime.

Lamphere admitted to Myers that he had helped Belle bury "several bodies" but denied he ever had a part in the killing. Jennie Olson had been killed because "she knew too much." It was the same with Belle's own children. The other unidentified children had been put in Belle's care by mothers or fathers of broken homes.

As for the late Peter Gunness, alleged victim of the bounding sausage grinder, Belle had killed him with an axe.[6]

Not all of the dying Lamphere's story made sense. No doubt it was also grossly exaggerated. Some of it was sheer fantasy. And he was oddly silent regarding his own relations with Mrs. Gunness. But on the subject of the headless corpse he was positive; it was not Belle. She was safely away.

And that is the opinion today of many oldsters around La Porte, who believe that Belle, who left only a small amount in her bank account, had killed the unknown woman, fired the house, and left for other parts.

On a somewhat different plane Belle lives on just as Ambrose Bierce, the old journalist, did for many years in spite of his probable death in Mexico in 1916. As recently as 1931 Belle was "seen" in a Mississippi town. In the same year the body of a woman found in Los Angeles was thought to be hers. It wasn't. For more than twenty years the sheriff's office at La Porte received an average of two queries a month about Belle—Belle the Hoosier Monster, the Queen of the Abattoir, the Female Bluebeard. During the past decade the queries have been fewer, but they continue.

Belle Gunness, in fact, seems assured of an enduring

[6] This part of Lamphere's story was given weight when a youngster of La Porte recalled having heard little Myrtle Sorenson, Belle's daughter, remark that "Mama brained Papa with an axe. Don't tell a soul."

place in the folklore of the region. I base this guess on the
fact that she is the subject of at least one ballad, and when a
person or an event gets into song it is not likely to be forgotten as soon as one not in a ballad. The literary or musical
merit of the ballad has nothing at all to do with its lasting
qualities, as witness the doggerel about Jesse James, Jim
Fisk, Floyd Collins, and other folk heroes.

The ballad about Belle I heard sung to the air of "Love,
O Careless Love," and the verses I have been able to un-
earth are as follows:

> Belle Gunness lived in In-di-an;
> She always, always had a man;
> Ten at least went in her door—
> And were never, never seen no more.

> Now, all these men were Norska folk
> Who came to Belle from Minn-e-sote;
> They liked their coffee, and their gin:
> They got it—plus a mickey finn.

> And now with cleaver poised so sure
> Belle neatly cut their jug-u-lur [sic];
> She put them in a bath of lime,
> And left them there for quite some time.

> There's red upon the Hoosier moon
> For Belle was strong and full of doom;
> And think of all them Norska men
> Who'll never see St. Paul again.

One of the last direct links between Belle Gunness and
the present day is an old, old woman confined in the Long-
cliff Hospital for the Insane at Logansport, Indiana. She has
been a patient there for a good many years and is one of the
characters of the institution. She worked at Belle's place for
several months and is not adverse to talking about it. The

favorite question asked this old woman is "What did Belle Gunness do with all those men?" And the invariable reply, accompanied by a truly horrible leer, is "She fed 'em to the hawgs."

On the subject of Belle being alive or dead the old crone is noncommittal. "Who knows?" she says.

If Belle still lives, as many believe, she is eighty-two years old in 1941. That's getting on, as they say; but should I happen on a farmhouse in some back-country place and the proprietor is a husky old woman who kills her own hogs, I'll be on my way—no matter the road or the weather.

The Case of the
Scattered Dutchman

COMPETITION was keen when "penny journalism" flourished in the Gay Nineties. There were three times as many newspapers then, but only one-fourth the number of readers. Even less, probably, considering the eager repeat buyers who snatched every new edition from the newsboy's hands whenever he voiced the cry, "Uxtry! Uxtry! Read all about it!"

Though newspaper publishers complained that they were steadily losing money, all seemed eager to buy other papers and all were reluctant to sell. It is said that William Randolph Hearst, owner of the *Evening Journal,* once heard that James Gordon Bennett, Jr., then living in Paris, was eager to sell the *New York Herald.* So Hearst sent a cablegram, "State price of *Herald.*" Back came Bennett's prompt reply, "One cent weekdays, five cents Sundays."

Pennies spelled profits in those days, and the amazing thing about the daily sheets was that they contained very little except news. Features such as daily "comic" strips were totally unknown, the comic pages being strictly for the Sunday trade. Happy Hooligan and the Yellow Kid were real laugh-getters in those days.

Occasionally, the Sunday "funnies" introduced a character like "Hairbreadth Harry," or "Hawkshaw the Detective" as a take-off on the fictional Sherlock Holmes. But a daily comic strip in the form of a crime sequence would have shocked the readers of that period.

The crime buffs got their kicks from the real stuff whenever it cropped up, which could be frequently. When murder hit the headlines, avid readers gorged the grisly details during breakfast, digested further developments during the noontime dinner hour, and—if further findings were anticipated, as usually they were—gained those from a night extra on the way home to supper. There were usually enough obscure points to make it worthwhile going to the corner in the cool of the evening to pick up a final.

Actually, the regular readers of the Nineties were more than half a century ahead of their time, for they were getting the benefit of a two-weeks' continuity of Dick Tracy, all in a single day with half a dozen different slants. Fact, it seems, was more grotesque then than fiction is today. That was the era when killers like Jack the Ripper specialized in repeat jobs and murderers returned regularly to the scene of the crime—presumably because they had nowhere else to go. So newspaper readers shuddered over homicides and gazed at other horse-car passengers secretly hoping that one might turn out to be the culprit.

All the while, they kept reading the newspaper accounts, episode by episode, much to the profit of the penny journalists. They, in turn, devoutly wished that someday a body would be discovered bit by bit, so as to start the pennies dropping even before the crime was fully established.

And one day, like an answer to a pious publisher's prayer, a body did appear just that way—bit by bit.

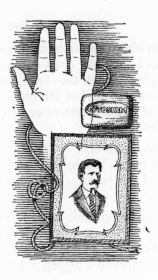

The Case of the
Scattered Dutchman

A. J. LIEBLING

THE afternoon of Saturday, June 26, 1897, was warm and
moist in New York City, and it is probable that boys
were swimming off every idle dock in the North and East
Rivers. James McKenna, thirteen years old, of 29 Avenue
C, and John McGuire, fourteen years old, of 722 East
Twelfth Street—both addresses within a few steps of the
East River—were among those who at three o'clock were
swimming in the slip on the south side of what was then a
disused dock at the foot of East Eleventh Street.

I will lift the next five paragraphs bodily from a story at
the top of the first page of the Sporting Edition of the *Evening Telegram* of that date, because I cannot think of any
sound way to amend them:

They saw an object slip into the line of vision past the edge of the dock, and the cross current gave it the appearance of trying to enter the slip. It looked much like a package of merchandise, but the article in which it was wrapped looked like a bright piece of bunting or a flag, with the sun striking it.

The two boys swam eagerly toward what they thought would prove a prize. The bright covering they found to be oilcloth, and the package was carefully tied up with good strong string.

McKenna got on one side and McGuire on the other and between them the package was brought inside the slip and one of the boys pulled one end of the string from around the oilcloth and dropped it over the edge of the stringpiece.

There was a general rush on the part of the dock hangers-on to furnish a knife, and McGuire slipped back over the edge of the dock and dug the knife in the oilcloth covering.

The knife stuck and refused to come out, and the boy gave it a wrench. Then he tried again, and succeeded in working a small hole in the cloth. He saw something white, and the sticky feeling of the knife blade sickened him.

The *Telegram*, which specialized in sporting news, had a later final edition than the city's other afternoon papers, since its readers counted on it to report the winner of the last race at Sheepshead Bay. (The race that day was a steeplechase, won by Mars Chan, at 2-1.) On Saturdays, the *Telegram*'s Sporting Edition was even later than on other days, because there were seven races instead of six. The story of the discovery in the East River was the only important nonsporting item on the first page, and over it were these headlines:

MAN'S TRUNK
FLOATS IN RIVER

HEADLESS AND LEGLESS BODY WRAPPED
IN OILCLOTH GETS INTO EAST
ELEVENTH STREET SLIP

FOUND BY SWIMMING BOYS

THEY THINK THEY HAVE A FIND, BUT
MAKE A GHASTLY DISCOVERY

IS THE WORK OF AN EXPERT

CUTS LOOK LIKE THOSE OF DISSECTING
TABLE—MAN WAS IN PRIME

The other top headlines on the page dealt with a bicycle
race at Manhattan Beach, the victory of the New York
Giants over the Washington Senators (both in the National
League then), and the triumph of a two-year-old named
Blueaway in the Zephyr Stakes, twenty-five hundred dollars
added. (A well-played second choice, he also paid 2-1).

After telling of the sickened boy, the unknown *Telegram*
writer continued:

It was not until a half hour later that someone reported
the matter to the Union Market police station [this was
on First Avenue, near Tenth Street], saying merely that
something securely wrapped in cloth was knocking
against the end of the dock.

Policeman Winter was detailed to take care of the matter. With the assistance of some laborers, he got the package upon the boards.

The policeman cut the cords and rolled back the oilcloth, disclosing to view the trunk of a man, in an almost perfect state of preservation.

The neck had been severed cleanly from the body, almost on a line with the shoulders, and the work was done in such a manner as to lead to the conclusion that it was that of someone accustomed to handling amputating instruments.

The work of amputating the legs had not been done so cleanly. They had been severed from the trunk just below the abdomen, in a rather slovenly fashion, not at all like the work of a dissecting table.

The chest had been marked and scarred in a peculiar manner. The flesh had been lifted from the bones just below the left breast and cut off cleanly all the way across the chest to a point almost on a line with the shoulder. The cut was even and laid open to view several of the ribs.

This, in connection with the clean amputation at the neck, inclines the police to the theory that the trunk was fresh from the dissecting table when found.

The only drawback to this is the unprofessional work on the lower half of the trunk.

The possibility that the dissection had been performed by two persons working in great haste—the more professional member of the team on the neck, the other on the torso—had not occurred to the *Telegram* man.

A district reporter for the *Telegram* may have been in the police station when the tip came in, and accompanied policeman Winter to the dock, or he may have learned of the find from the station blotter and hurried to the dock while the parcel was being dragged from the water. In either event, he —or a police surgeon he may have talked to—was clearly an excellent observer, and the further development of the case was to confirm not only the details he phoned in to the rewrite man but many of the rewrite man's immediate deductions from them. It may be, of course, that my own deductions about how the *Telegram* story was put together are in error, and that the city editor, apprised by telephone of the interesting nature of the find (he could hardly have been informed of it before four o'clock), dispatched a star reporter straight to the scene in a hack. Even with the prevailing speed limit of twelve miles an hour, the reporter could have got from the *Telegram* office, in Herald Square, to the foot of East Eleventh Street in twenty minutes, made his notes from his own observation, and returned to his desk by five, after which he could have written his story between the fifth and seventh races. This would have been drawing it fine, however, even for the newspaper titans of 1897, when, according to an old journalistic friend of mine named Ned Brown, "what they call a porterhouse now wouldn't have counted as a chuck steak."

The rewrite job, as I therefore judge it to be, continues:

The trunk is that of a man who was evidently in the prime of life. He must have weighed fully 180 pounds, and the arms are big and powerful. The chest is that of a man accustomed to unusual exertion and regular calls for increased lung power.

The flesh is clear and white, and indicates that the man was in perfect health, and the muscles of the body show plainly that their possessor was a giant in strength.

The hands are small when figured in proportion to the evident weight and height of the man. The fingers are small and well shaped and do not resemble in any way the fingers of a man accustomed to manual labor.

On the inside of the left palm is a small blue mark, evidently extending deep into the cuticle. It looks as though it might have been burned in with powder. There are no needle pricks to indicate it is a tattoo mark, nor is there any regular formation to it.

The oilcloth in which the body was enclosed was brand

new. It had never been placed on a floor as a covering, the underside bearing no mark. It was of good quality. The pattern was red squares with small gilt stars.

The string was white, very heavy, and after the knots were tied had been cut cleanly with a sharp instrument. Scissors or a small pocket knife would not have been able to cut it so cleanly.

A curious crowd surrounded the object as it lay on the Eleventh Street dock. A messenger was sent to the coroner's office.

The police are taking an extraordinary amount of interest in the case, owing to a great extent to the signs of refinement and the fact that the body had been but such a short time in the water.

Between the oilcloth and the spine of the trunk was found a sheet of new cheesecloth, a little heavier than the ordinary kind, more like that used in hospitals, but in no way resembling absorbent cloth.

This discovery has served to strengthen the theory of the police that the work is that of a band of medical students from the dissecting table of a hospital.

In substantiation of the rumor of foul play, its adherents point to the peculiar wound on the breast, claiming that the strip of flesh may have been taken off to destroy tattoo marks or other marks that would help toward an identification.

They also claim that the legs may have been marked in some way, and they too were taken off and disposed of in some way.

None of the other afternoon papers—the *Evening World,* the *Evening Journal,* and the *Evening Sun*—had so complete and incisive a story. Their city desks had been put off by the first reports from the police of the precinct, who, the *Evening World*'s brief story said, "incline to the belief that the body may be that of a medical subject." The police claimed later that they had taken this position in an effort to keep the newspaper sleuths out of their way while they got started on the serious business of investigation, but the *Journal,* having been caught flat-footed, continued for weeks to charge that the police had tried to squelch the story just to save themselves trouble. The *Journal's* implication was that Lord knew how many other crimes had been shrugged off in this fashion; only the enterprise of newspaper reporters—the *Journal's,* of course—had forced the police to revise their attitude in the torso case.

The next morning's *Sun,* on behalf of its teammate, the *Evening Sun,* attributed the medical-subject theory to pure stupidity on the part of the police, and the *World* of that Sunday morning took the same position. The paper was on to the possibilities of the story and gave it two columns on the first page, under the headline "BOYS' GHASTLY FIND." In the course of its account, the *World* observed, "It does not appear that the police made any attempt at investigation, but jumped at and accepted the theory that the portion of the human being had been cast into the river by the students of some medical college who had been studying anatomy." According to the *World,* the discovery that it was probably a case of murder had been made by doctors at the morgue, after the torso was removed there.

None of the Sunday papers had anything substantial to add to the *Telegram* account, although they padded it out with direct quotations from the coroner, a Dr. Tuthill; the medical examiner, a Dr. Dow; and the Superintendent of Bellevue, a Mr. Murphy. (First names of such well-known civic characters were evidently considered superfluous in news stories of that golden age.) Both the *World* and the *Herald* were skeptical about the likelihood of a solution. "The finding of the upper portion of the headless trunk of a man in the East River yesterday furnishes a mystery that will not easily be solved." the *World* reported, and went on, "All indications point to an atrocious murder. There is, however, no apparent clue by which the identity of the victim may be discovered, or his slayer brought to justice." The

Herald stated, "There is nothing to tell when or where the crime was committed, whether on land or on sea, and there is not one chance in a million that the identity of the victim will be discovered." The suggestion that the man had been murdered and dismembered aboard a ship evoked the romantic possibility that he had been a Spaniard spying on Cuban gunrunners. The police said he could not have been a sailor, because there were no calluses on his hands.

The morning *World* and the *Evening World* had different staffs but shared the eleventh floor of the proud new Pulitzer Building, on Park Row, and dovetailed their coverage of running stories. The Pulitzer Building, with its sixteen floors, was the tallest building in New York, and from their city rooms the men of both *Worlds* could look over to and beyond the North River or out to sea, as well as at Brooklyn, across the only bridge there was over the East River at that time. All Manhattan lay visible at their feet, and it accentuated their cockiness. The *World* had a circulation of 370,000, which was almost as much as the four other morning papers had among them. These were the *Herald* and the *Sun, ex acquo* with 120,000; the *Times,* with 75,000; and the *Tribune,* with 76,000. The *World*'s predominance had been achieved within a few years after Joseph Pulitzer came to New York from St. Louis and bought the paper from Jay Gould, in 1883. The *Evening World,* founded by Pulitzer four years later, had overshadowed its afternoon contemporaries just as decisively until it was challenged by a newer newcomer—young William Randolph Hearst's *Journal,* which made its appearance in 1895. Hearst was trying to take over Pulitzer's afternoon field by imitating all Pulitzer's circus tricks and then adding an extra elephant for the clowns to jump over. By 1897, despite brilliant retaliatory strokes on the part of Pulitzer, Hearst was beginning to show results. The *Evening World* still led the afternoons, with a circulation of 360,000, but the *Journal* claimed 309,000, and was gaining. The *Evening Sun* and the *Evening Telegram,* with 100,000 each, were out of the hunt; Edwin

Godkin's *Evening Post,* with 25,000, had become a symbol of the unpopularity of virtue.

The Hearst-Pulitzer feud made for virulent competition, and in its course reporters became direct rivals of the police. A *World* or a *Journal* man finding a useful clue at the scene of a crime would bring it back to his newspaper, in which it would appear as a chalk-plate illustration over the vainglorious line "Made from a photograph taken in the *World* [or *Journal*] office." Had reporters reached the East Eleventh Street dock before the police on the day the torso was found, the officers would have attached no significance to the chunk missing from the victim's brisket. They would have been sure that a *World* or a *Journal* man carried it away.

Reporters developed their own leads in solving crimes, outbidding the police for stool pigeons and at times outbidding the detective branch for details observed by uniformed men. Then they would follow through in person "arresting" suspects, if the latter didn't appear dangerous, and extorting confessions from them. These they would publish as scoops. The practice sometimes proved momentarily awkward when it developed that a reporter had abducted an innocent party, but there were few such mistakes a ten-dollar bill couldn't square. Neither the *World* nor the *Journal* begrudged outlays occasioned by excessive zeal. In making "arrests," the reporters, who had shiny badges and pistol permits, usually represented themselves as detectives, but when printing the story their papers invariably said they had "made the arrest as citizens." Some of the reporters, as one might expect, became better detectives than most city detectives, and when a big case broke, the Police Department would put tails on the leading newspapermen, while the newspapers would put tails on the more resourceful detectives. This was a form of recognition the latter enjoyed to the point of sticking to familiar disguises in order not to throw the journalists off their track. Naturally, there were exchanges of information between friends in the two professions, by which cops helped

reporters to discredit rival reporters and reporters helped
cops to discredit rival cops.

The *World* and the *Journal* assumed airs of independent
sovereignty. In headlines as well as editorials, the rival
sheets gave themselves credit for defeating candidates they
had opposed, rectifying conditions they had deplored, stopping outbreaks of leprosy they said they had detected, setting fashions, making slang, and, above all, solving crimes.
Even the sportswriters conveyed the impression that they
were not merely reporting games but coaching both teams
and refereeing. "Being a newspaperman gave you stature
then," says Ned Brown. "Everywhere except in society. It
didn't cut any ice there. But elsewhere a first-string reporter
on any recognized paper—especially one of the *Worlds*—
had a lot of prestige. *Civis Romanus erat.* He was a citizen of
no mean state."

Today, Ned Brown, a small man, is as spare and brisk as
a whippet, with a sharp, inquisitive profile and lively blue
eyes. He prides himself on his penetrating *coup d'oeil,* which
makes him a master at rapid chess and crossword puzzles,
and at sizing up situations. Mr. Brown has worked for only
one newspaper in his life—the *World.* The job lasted thirty-
four years, until the paper ceased publication in 1931. During most of his service with the *World,* he was a boxing
writer, but he didn't begin as one. When the mysterious
torso was fished from the river, Ned was a very junior member of the *World* staff; he was working there during the summer vacation following his first year at Bellevue Hospital
Medical School, which was then situated at Twenty-sixth
Street and First Avenue, across the street from the hospital,
with its wards and morgue. He did small assignments,
mostly legwork, at space rates—five dollars a column if he
telephoned the stuff to a rewrite man and seven dollars and a
half if he wrote it himself. The bits he wrote personally were
for the most part humorous items he picked up at night in
the Tenderloin—the bright-light district that, by his definition, ran from Thirtieth Street to Forty-second, between

Sixth and Eighth Avenues. He liked the Tenderloin beat because it permitted him to spend his nights in saloons—
looking at people, listening, and fancying himself a young
man about town—without having to disguise the fact from
his father, who was Frederick Sherwood Brown, the telegraph editor of the *World*. The elder Brown had established
his family in Flatbush, a remote *faubourg* of the independent City of Brooklyn.

Ned found Flatbush slow. His official hours were from
two in the afternoon until midnight, but often when he was
covering the Tenderloin he worked an extra hour or two,
business merging with pleasure. On such occasions, the long
journey home to Flatbush—by steam elevated train to
Brooklyn Bridge and then by trolley car into the dark in-
terior of Long Island—frequently seemed too dismal to en-
dure, and then he would spend the rest of the night in the
Murray Hill Baths, on Forty-second Street. The Murray Hill
Baths were not on Murray Hill but between Broadway and
Sixth Avenue, and, like all the other Turkish bath establishments of the region, they stayed open all night. Turkish
baths were infinitely more popular and numerous then than
they are now; men on the town for the evening regularly
wound up in one or another of them. An individual cubicle
cost a dollar, a bed in the dormitory fifty cents; the ticket
for either one included a scrubbing and use of the steam
room and the plunge, universally esteemed specifics for over-
indulgence; an alcohol rub cost an extra two bits. There was
always a tip for the rubber, who would not scorn a dime. The
baths all favored a fanciful Oriental décor, like the tiled in-
terior of a mosque. The Murray Hill was one of the largest
and most ornate.

In those days, Mr. Brown says, few medical students went
to a liberal arts college; he himself entered medical college
straight from Erasmus Hall High School, in Brooklyn, and
in 1897 he was still in his teens. He was a hard-liquor
drinker, but not when he was working; on those nights, he
would buy a beer or two in each establishment he visited,

"just to hold the franchise." When he retired to the baths, therefore, his mind would still be clear and his curiosity active; he would engage the rubbers in conversation and sometimes land a boulevardesque anecdote worth a dollar and a half at space rates, or a bit of information that might come in handy someday as background. He was keenly interested in anatomy, which was then, as it is now, the principal subject of the medical first year. At the baths, he had before his eyes a living exhibit of anatomical and dermatological peculiarities, and he was accustomed to discuss these with the rubbers; at heart every masseur is a doctor *manqué*.

Ned doesn't recall being in the *World* city room when the torso was first reported, and he is sure he wasn't sent uptown to the dock. But when he read the Sunday papers the next morning he was fascinated—both as a medical student and as a newspaperman. Coroner Tuthill, he noted, had told reporters at the morgue that the disaggregated man could not have been dead more than twenty-four hours when his chest was taken out of the river; Dr. Dow had said "ten hours at the most." Even if one accepted the longer estimate, and added a few hours for possible error, the man could not have been killed earlier than Friday. The conclusions different doctors reached as to his height and heft varied a bit— one doctor explained that his estimate of five feet ten inches depended on the premise that a man's height is equal to the reach of his outstretched arms—but all agreed that he had been taller than average. Every newspaper account mentioned the solid but unworkmanlike hands. He had been a man who kept himself in good physical trim, but not by hard labor. A wealthy sportsman? A college athlete? An army officer? Any one of them would make a corking good victim from a newspaper point of view. Ned had a special family interest in this kind of murder, because his father, while a reporter on the *Cincinnati Enquirer,* had cleared up the murder of a girl named Pearl Bryan, whose severed head had been thrown from the suspension bridge over the

Ohio River between Cincinnati and Covington, Kentucky. The guilty wretch may have hoped thus to create a conflict of jurisdiction; the elder Brown, however, proved that the actual crime had been committed on the Ohio side of the river. It is a spiritless son who would not like to outdo his father, but Ned, as he rode the trolley over the bridge to work that Sunday afternoon (like all young and single men on seven-day newspapers at that time, he worked Sundays and had a weekday off), had small hope that he would be assigned to the Ghastly Find story. The Ghastly Find would be in the competent hands of Gus Roeder, the *World*'s homicide specialist, and of Bill Reitmeier, who covered Police Headquarters, on Mulberry Street. They would need no help in keeping the story fresh for a day or two, after which, if it was as hopeless as the morning-paper stories indicated, it would lapse and be forgotten.

When Ned stepped off the elevator on the eleventh floor of the Pulitzer Building, he had no need of his peculiar gift to recognize that something extraordinary had happened. The day staff on Sunday was always light, but on that particular afternoon the city room was perfectly empty except for one early copyreader and the man on the desk—a Sunday substitute for Edward J. Casey, the *World*'s assistant city editor. The man on the desk was telephoning, and as he saw Ned come in he put his hand over the mouthpiece and beckoned him with a sweep of his arm. When other reserves are exhausted, even the summer soldier is welcome. The man on the desk took less than a minute to tell Ned that a second parcel wrapped in oilcloth with a pattern of red squares and small gilt stars had been found, this one on the Bronx side of the Harlem River, at about the latitude of 176th Street, or ten miles from where the torso had turned up. Two boys out berrying with their father had come upon it in a sylvan setting, into which it had apparently been tossed from Undercliff Avenue, a winding carriage drive on the side of a hill. When the parcel was opened at the High Bridge police station, in the Bronx, it had yielded another section of the cadaver. The captain there had dispatched it to the morgue to be matched up with the East River bit. "If the pieces fit, it's the same stiff," the man on the desk said. "If it's part of a different stiff, then the guy with the red oilcloth has murdered them both," He spoke, Ned remembers, with the pleasure of a man who cannot lose. From the moment the first tip about the second bundle came in from Reitmeier, the Sunday city editor had been calling every member of the staff he could reach by telephone—directing those who lived uptown to the region of the find and ordering the downtown fellows to converge on the morgue or Police Headquarters. He had also been sending out the regular Sunday men as they reported for duty. He told Ned to hustle up to the morgue and report to Gus Roeder, who was running the Pulitzer operation there. "Do whatever Gus tells you," he said, unnecessarily. "The *Journal's* probably got forty guys there already." Mr. Brown recalls his emotion on being assigned to his first big story, even though he anticipated only a legman's role (for which he was well fitted, being a tireless runner and weighing precisely a hundred and nineteen pounds). The field of his début could not have been better chosen, for, owing to his year at medical school, he was familiar with the morgue, and if there was one subject on which he would back his own opinion, it was a cadaver. The steam elevated bore him to the vicinity of the morgue in quick time, and he ran the rest of the way at a quarter-miler's pace.

Gus Roeder, the homicide man, was a red-faced German-American, already in his forties and therefore, to Ned, a hoary veteran. He could express himself well in English but spoke the language with a perceptible accent. (He worked from pencilled notes, which he surrounded with rhetoric as he dictated his stories to an office boy who, unlike him, knew how to run a typewriter.) He wore conservative dark clothes and a hard hat, and was not enough of a bohemian to be popular with his fellow reporters. He was on good terms with a powerful faction of the detective force, however, and exchanged information with his police friends, to their advantage and his. He was also a friend of Frederick Sherwood Brown's, and knew that Ned was a medical student. The Bronx portion of torso had by this time been brought downtown, and the two fragments, put together, matched as neatly as pieces of a jigsaw puzzle; so did the cut edges of the two sheets of oilcloth. The second piece of victim included everything from the adbomen to a point above the knees, where the saw or knife had been employed again to detach the legs. These hadn't turned up yet. Ned found the juxtaposed segments of great interest. "The gaping ends of the blood vessels at the neck, where the head had been severed, and the thighs, where the legs had been cut off, indicated that the man had lost a considerable amount of blood before expiring," he says now, relapsing into his freshman patter. "In other words, the guy had been alive while they were cutting him up. That knocked out the medical school idea." Ned also had a long look at the highly publicized hands. When he finished, he told Roeder what he suspected, and Roeder instructed him to follow his hunch. Roeder already had a score of men out working on even longer shots.

Some indication of the number of paths Roeder's men explored was to be found in the *World* of Monday, June 28th. A five-column top head on the first page thundered:

THE FRAGMENTS OF A
BODY MAKES A MYSTERY

Under it, in lines three columns wide was:

A PIECE OF A MANGLED TRUNK FOUND
YESTERDAY IN HARLEM FITS AN-
OTHER PIECE FOUND SATURDAY
IN THE EAST RIVER

BOTH WRAPPED IN RED
AND GOLD OILCLOTH

Then, in single column:

A MAN OF THE MIDDLE OR BETTER
CLASS HAS EVIDENTLY BEEN
BRUTALLY KILLED

MANY STABS WOUNDS AND BRUISES

PORTIONS OF THE BODY, WHICH MAY
HAVE CONTAINED MARKS OF IDEN-
TIFICATION, CUT AWAY

THE POLICE ARE AS
YET ENTIRELY AT SEA

CARL WEINECKE, WHO DISAPPEARED
MAY 17, HAD MARKS WHICH
WOULD FIT PLACES CUT
AWAY ON THE DEAD
TRUNK

CORONER TUTHILL HAS
A THEORY OF HIS OWN

THINKS THE VICTIM WAS ATTACKED
AND KILLED IN A FIGHT AFTER A
HARD STRUGGLE

The text of the lead, set in bold type, was exclamatory and consecrated to the obvious. "Somewhere in Greater New York or near it since late Friday afternoon an awful crime has been committed" is a fair sample.

The layout of pictures on the front page illustrated the peculiar attraction of the great Pulitzer's journalism. Nestling under three columns of the top headline was a chalk-plate reproduction of the "Hand of the Headless Murdered

Man—Exact Size (from a flashlight photograph made in the morgue last night by a *World* photographer)." The hands of the victim had been described in various accounts as large, small, and medium-sized. When I first saw the "exact-size" illustration in a bound volume of *Worlds,* I could not resist an impulse to put my hand over it and compare the two, and I suspect that three of every four readers of the paper in 1897 did the same thing. (From my comparison, I judge that the victim, like me, wore a size-8½ glove with a wide palm and short fingers.) The stubby thumb in the *World*'s photograph was superimposed on a map showing "Route headless shoulders would take in floating from spot where other part of body was found." This had been drawn in accordance with a theory, enunciated in an interview granted by a former Chief of the United States Secret Service named Andrew L. Drummond, that the murder had been committed in the Bronx and part of the body thrown from High Bridge into the Harlem, which leads into the East River. "It would be foolish for a man to carry the body from the Battery, say, to High Bridge in order to throw it into the water," Mr. Drummond had told a *World* reporter. Next to the upper, or Bronx, end of the map was a sketch of "where the trunk of the body was found," and, next to the Eleventh Street end, a sketch of "where boys found the headless shoulders." The layout was completed by illustrations of the oilcloth ("reproduced from sample brought to the *World* office") and of the "clumsy knot with which each bundle was tied" (also "photographed in the *World* office").

Inside the paper were a dozen stories on assorted angles of the case. The wife of a Dane named Weinecke—an unemployed lumber inspector, of 82 East 15th Street, who had disappeared on May 7th—thought the installments might be of him. The *World* had to take some account of her views, although it did so with patent unenthusiasm; he would have made an anticlimactic victim, despite a half-hearted effort on the part of the editors to supply him with a mysterious past before his arrival in this country. There was a long story on efforts that were being made to trace the red-and-gold oilcloth pattern through jobbers to retailers, in order to question everyone who might remember selling any recently. Police authorities had wisely refused to theorize about the murder, and in revenge the *World* and the other morning papers said they were incompetent and "all at sea." The medical men had allowed themselves to be drawn more easily, and the reporters had induced Dr. Philip F. O'Hanlon, the coroner's physician who performed the autopsy, to venture a surmise as to how the man had been killed. "From what I can learn from the condition of the body, I should say that this is what occurred," the *World* quoted Dr. O'Hanlon as extrapolating. (It was the decade of Sherlock Holmes, and every physician felt that Dr. Watson had been unfairly dealt with.) "The man, who was a big, powerful fellow, was attacked. He made a strong resistance, but I should say he was overpowered by numbers. That he was knocked down I think is proved by the imprints of the toe and boot-heel on his arm. Some of the other bruises on his body may have come from kicks. I should say that he struggled to his feet and was standing erect when someone, who must have been very muscular, stabbed him in the collar-bone with a big knife. This was followed immediately afterward by another wound—that which cut the heart. That caused death immediately. The blood under the thumbnail shows that he struggled hard or else that he clasped his hand to his bosom after he had been stabbed."

A *World* story on the autopsy itself reported:

> A close inspection was made of the hands with a view to determining the man's position in life. They were long and broad, the fingers were well formed, and while the palms were not callous, yet they indicated that the man had done some work, not recently, perhaps. The nails were cut down almost to the quick, evenly rounded, as though their owner had taken some care of them.
>
> The fingertips of the left hand were smooth and even;

on the forefinger was a scar extending from the nail back to the second joint. It was an old one, and in the opinion of the examining physician, might have been caused by an operation. . . . There was little hair on the body, the arms or the hands, and the latter showed little of the effect of the sun.

Not a man who could live without work, was the judgment of those who examined the trunk, nor yet a man whose livelihood was earned by hard manual labor; he might have been a policeman, a carpenter, a bartender.

The most romantic reconstruction of the crime was furnished by Drummond:

> Andrew L. Drummond, for twenty-two years Chief of the Secret Service of the United States Government, and now head of a great detective agency in this city, with offices at No. 1 Park Row; is greatly interested in the developments in the murder case [the *World* reported].
>
> "I read the account in Sunday's *World*," said Mr. Drummond last night, "and from what you tell me now of the finding of another part of the body near High Bridge and of the result of the autopsy, I believe that this most atrocious murder was committed by a foreigner.
>
> "In the whole history of crime in this country murders which were done with like ferocity as this have always been committed by foreigners, usually those of a warmer climate than ours.
>
> "I should judge, from what I have heard of this case, that the murderer is a Sicilian, or possibly a Spaniard or Cuban. Maybe a Spanish spy has been put out of the way by Cubans.
>
> "But the theory of the murder which strikes me as the most likely one is that it is the result of a family feud among Sicilians. I know the ways of the Mafia so well that this strikes me as the most plausible theory. The red oilcloth points to Sicilians, who love bright colors. . . .

"Probably the murdered man was invited to a friendly game of cards at the home of the murderer, who had sworn a vendetta against him for some wrong to his wife or sweetheart. Then, in an unguarded moment, the man was killed and his body cut up for disposal by one or several men."

The Drummond story was the last on the murder in the *World* (it brought the total space the paper devoted to the case to eight and a quarter columns, not counting pictures), and was followed by this plug, in boldface type: "Further developments in New York's great murder mystery will appear in the editions of the *Evening World.*"

Ned Brown, reading the story about the hands in the Monday morning *World,* may have feared that a couple of the details would set somebody else to thinking along the line he was already following. But if so, there was nothing he could do about it, and he had a full program for the day. Ned was searching for a kind of soap called Cotaspam, or Kotaspam—he is no longer sure of the exact spelling. Not that he looked as though he needed soap; that morning Ned was probably the cleanest man in Greater New York. His naturally pink skin was now positively translucent. He had in a pocket ten dollars that he had drawn from the *World* treasurer, on the authorization of Gus Roeder, to use as expenses. Cotaspam was expensive soap—twenty-five cents a cake. Ned had to walk over to Broadway to find a druggist who stocked it, and when he did, he bought two boxes containing a dozen bars each, for a total of six dollars.

The reason Ned wanted Cotaspam specifically, he says, was that once, before having dinner at the home of a wealthy boy he was tutoring in Brooklyn, he had washed his hands in the bathroom there and had been so impressed with the fragrance of the soap that he asked the name of the brand. "It smelled Elysian to me," Mr. Brown says now. "Sandalwood, verbena, geranium, Sen-Sen, and Ed Pinaud's Eau de Quinine all in one." With the two boxes under his arm, Ned took a Broadway car as far as Herald

Square, where he transferred to a westbound Thirty-fourth Street crosstown and rode to Ninth Avenue. Then he walked half a block north and entered a tenement at 441 Ninth Avenue. It was a family neighborhood of working people, mostly respectable and chiefly German or Irish. During the years after the end of the Civil War, brick tenements had replaced frame houses as the city marched north. They were mostly small buildings, three or four stories high, with two families on a floor, and sometimes a store on the street level. A parking lot occupies the west, or odd-numbered, side of the block now, but some even-numbered houses still standing on the east side of the avenue in the next block north give at least an idea of what the neighborhood must have looked like. Ned climbed the stairs to the top floor of No. 441 and worked his way down, knocking at each door in turn. There was a woman in practically every flat, and to each Ned presented a cake of soap and delivered a little spiel. The company he represented was trying to find a larger market for its soap, he said, and so was making a special introductory offer. Each recipient was to use the soap for a day, just to experience how good it was. If she liked it, she could give him a nickel for it when he returned in the evening; if not, she was privileged to return the soap without any obligation. "One smell and they fell for it," Mr. Brown says. "They could tell it was expensive soap. Some of them wanted to give me a nickel right then, but I said no dice. 'The company wants to get your opinion of its product after you have used it,' I would say. 'I will be back at six o'clock.'" Such door-to-door canvassing was more common then than it is now; Ned had heard the routine scores of times in his own home. His appearance was plausible; he was young and thin, and wore a cap and a shiny second-best suit. He got rid of half a box of soap in No. 441 and then went through the same performance in Nos. 439 and 437, omitting only one apartment. This was on the second floor, above a drugstore, in No. 439, and a nameplate on its door bore the legend, "Mrs. Augusta Nack, Licensed Midwife." When Ned had finished with No. 437, he had only a couple of cakes left, and he stuck them in his pockets. It was nearly noon, and he walked out of the neighborhood to a café near Herald Square to eat lunch and look over the afternoon papers as they came out. Talk about the elegant soap would spread through the three tenements, he knew; the women visited across the halls or from their fire escapes in warm weather, and in the afternoon there would be knots of them on the sidewalk getting a breath of cool air.

"There is nothing like a sweet smell to catch a woman," Mr. Brown says. "I know it from experience now, but at the time I had to figure it out for myself. I was what you might call precocious." Ned read the afternoon papers with apprehension, which turned to smugness as he found more and more signs that they were off what he felt was the right track. Monday morning's papers had had a big new development to report—the discovery of the second segment. All the afternooners could do was ramify speculation.

RIVER'S MURDER MYSTERY
GROWS STRANGER AND DEEPER

the three-o'clock edition of the *Evening World* proclaimed, listing Clues (no new ones) and Theories (same) in its lead. It had on its front page a portrait of the missing Weinecke (which it spelled Weincke), three columns wide, with question marks at either side of his head, but he bore an unexciting resemblance to a testimonial writer in a patent-medicine ad. "Is he the murdered man?" the caption writer asked, and most readers' reaction to Mr. Weinecke's photograph must have been "Who cares?" The *Evening World* had balanced its front page with an equal display of a story headed "JOHN L. SPARS WITH WORLD MAN," written and illustrated by the *World* man, W. O. Inglis; his account of this terrifying experience took the form of a letter addressed to Bob Fitzsimmons, the heavyweight champion, to fight whom the thirty-eight-year-old John L. Sullivan had announced his emergence from retirement. (Sullivan's advertised comeback had a patriotic motive. On losing his championship to James J. Corbett, in 1892, he had said, "I am glad I was beaten by an American." On March 17, 1897, Corbett had lost the title to Fitzsimmons, a New Zealander born in Cornwall.) "Friends tied on our four-ounce gloves," Inglis wrote. "I could not have tied a knot in a two-inch hawser, much less in the laces of a boxing glove. You will feel that way, Mr. Fitzsimmons, when you are getting ready to go into the ring with Sullivan." It was the true *World* tone, and it amused Ned, who correctly suspected that the comeback would go no further than the first time Sullivan raised a thirst.

In the *Evening World,* the exact-size picture of the victim's hand had been moved back to page 2 and reinforced with a diagram of the body, in which the recovered portions were printed in black and missing areas in gray. "The inhuman, fiendish manner in which the butcher cut up the remains of his victim seems to suggest that it was the work of a maniac," a hard-pressed rewrite man had ventured, and there were a couple of sidelight stories on the Jack-the-Ripper murders in London and other unsolved mysteries. "The superb handling of this interesting case in the *World* this morning, both as regards writing and illustration, made all other morning papers look like second-rate provincial sheets," a house plug at the bottom of the page announced. "If there is anything left to tell about the mystery when today's *Evening World* is done with it the *World* tomorrow morning will again show the little imitation morning papers how to handle a big local story. From the *Evening World*'s last night extra the thread of the strange crime will be taken up and carried on by the morning edition. The *World* is a continuous performance of newsgiving—morning, noon, and night. It never stops. It has no rival. Remember that." Despite this advertised unity, there was hot rivalry between the staffs of the *World* and the *Evening World*.

The *Evening Sun,* which had lost the dash of its Dana days, took a thoroughly dim view of the case and assailed the police. "Indications in Mulberry Street this morning pointed to the conclusion that the police had not yet waked up to the serious import of the case," it grumbled. "Chief Conlin wasn't there. . . . Chief Conlin is a man who has no taste for murder mysteries. . . . Capt. O'Brien [the chief of detectives] has even less than Conlin. Like every other policeman not possessed of distinct detective genius, his one wish is to get rid of a case of that kind, and, consciously or unconsciously, the wish will take the form of pooh-poohing it at first and letting it slip out of sight and out of mind as soon as the excitement about it dies out."

The *Telegram,* its field forces outnumbered by the hordes of *World* and *Journal* reporters, tried to sell papers with the headline:

DR. WESTON
SAYS BODY
WAS BOILED

"Coroner's Physician Weston has advanced a most important theory in regard to the great murder mystery," a *Telegram* reporter had written. "He was at the morgue this afternoon on another case, and while he was there he examined the mutilated, headless, and legless trunk. He said to me afterward: 'It appears to me that an attempt has been made to dispose of this body by boiling it. The flesh of the stump of the legs appears to have been dipped in boiling water. It is probable that the murderers thrust the legs into a kettle, hoping to boil the flesh off, but found they could not do it quickly or easily enough, and that they then cut up the remains.' " The doctors made decidedly better copy than the detectives.

Ned moved along to other bars as the afternoon wore on, avoiding those most frequented by newspapermen. Had he been one of the *World*'s stars, he would have had to take precautions against being trailed, but he knew he was too inconspicuous for that. All he had to avoid was a chance encounter. The dark interiors, cooled by electric fans, offered escape from the afternoon sun, and each time he changed saloons he bought a later batch of papers to read over his next nickel beer. The Late Edition of the *Evening World,* which went to press at four o'clock in the afternoon, headlined a typical Pulitzer stroke—a five-hundred-dollar reward. *"The World* will pay $500 in gold for the correct solution of the mystery concerning the fragments of a man's body discovered Saturday and Sunday in the East River and in Harlem," an announcement read. "All theories and suggestions must be sent to the City Editor of the *World,* in envelopes marked 'Murder Mystery,' and must be exclusively for the *World.* Appearance of the solution in any other paper will cancel this offer of reward." There followed a "suggestion" of what the solution should include: motive, identity of the criminal or criminals, time, place, and method of crime, actions of the criminal or criminals after commission of the crime, and, last but not least, identification of the murdered man.

This was the final regular edition of the *Evening World,* and it ordinarily coincided with the *Journal's* final, but within minutes of its appearance the latter paper hit the street with an extra run of its Night Edition, in which a three-column head on the right-hand side of the first page read:

$1,000 REWARD
THE NEW YORK JOURNAL WILL PAY
$1,000 FOR INFORMATION OR
CLEWS, THEORIES OR SUG-
GESTIONS WHICH WILL
SOLVE THE UNIQUE
MURDER MYSTERY
OF THE EAST
RIVER

IF NONE OF THE THEORIES OR
SUGGESTIONS IS PERFECTLY EX-
ACT THE $1,000 WILL BE DIVIDED
AMONG THE TEN THAT COME
NEAREST TO SOLVING
THE MYSTERY

It was the familiar Hearst technique, infuriating to *World* men, of waiting for Pulitzer to think of something and then raising his bid.

The *Journal*, Ned noted with distaste, had followed the *World*'s example in its play of the striking hand picture. The first page of the *Journal* bore detailed illustrations of the unknown's right hand, his left hand, his injured finger, and his broken fingernail. "The *Evening Journal* has the Most News, Latest News, Best News," the left ear of the paper's masthead boasted, and the right ear stated, "The *Evening Journal* Prints the Best Local, Telegraph, Cable News." It was enough to raise the hair of Ned's blond, James J. Corbett pompadour haircut.

The *Journal* was also playing up its own favorite candidate of the moment for corpus delicti, with a slashing first-page head:

LOUIS A. LUTZ THE VICTIM?
NEPHEW ALMOST SURE HE RECOGNIZES THE REMAINS AT THE MORGUE

The missing Mr. Lutz, a carpenter in a piano factory, had not been home for five days, the *Journal* said, and while he had no known enemies, and no money on his person when he left his house, his nephew was sure he had been killed, because he didn't think he would have committed suicide. (No other possible explanations of his absence were considered.) The *Journal* presented a boxed, signed, and undoubtedly paid-for statement by the nephew, who was named Louis E. Lutz, in which, as a clincher, he remembered that his uncle had once hit himself on the left hand with a hammer, injuring a finger. Stephen O'Brien, the Chief of Detectives, had furnished a signed statement to the editor of the *Journal* to the effect that until they found the missing sections of the body, his detectives had little to work on. "LITTLE TO WORK ON" was the headline. Dr. Nelson A. Conroy, of Bellevue, still another medico out to vindicate

Dr. Watson, had given the *Journal* a personal statement, in which he declared irrefutably: "It is hard to say just what the man's face looked like." Apparently something of a palmist, Dr. Conroy added, "The conical hand of the man indicates a practical temperament. This man must have been engaged in some useful art—an artist of some sort— for it is evident he had not done any hard work for some time." All references to the dead man's hands had a special interest for Ned, and he was relieved to see that Dr. Conroy was as far off the track as the rest.

If the *Journal* ventured gingerly into palmistry via Dr. Conroy, the *Evening World,* in a Night Extra that shortly followed the *Journal*'s, went all the way.

$500 REWARD TO ANYBODY WHO UNRAVELS THE MURDER MYSTERY

a headline across the first six columns bellowed, and then:

THEORY OF WOMAN
AND A PALMIST

A four-column cut under the reward line showed the "Hands of the Murdered Man," and under this was a two-column cut of "The Broken Nail."

"An analysis of the hand of the dead man of the river mystery was made this morning for the *Evening World* by Queen Stella Gonzales," the first-page story began. (The paper's editors brushed off the *Journal*'s Mr. Lutz with a one-paragraph sneer under the lower-case line "Alleged Identification." "The morgue people take no stock in the identification," the item ended.) "Queen Stella and Cheiro are the two most famous palmists of America, Queen Stella's drawing-room reputation excelling that of Cheiro." Queen Stella, the story went on, admitted that she was handicapped by having only a photograph of the back of the hand to work from. "She said it impressed her at once as a tragic hand," the *Evening World* reported. " '. . . Having square nails, that denotes ruling power. His little finger, pointed and reaching above the third phalange, denotes business capacity in a higher degree. . . . Through his domineering disposition and rashness in speech he must have made one or more deadly enemies.' "

Queen Stella's analysis was the beginning of a complete coverage by the *World* of the occult aspects of the case, which included appeals to another palmist (a man, who was smuggled into the morgue), a phrenologist (slightly handicapped by the absence of the head), a clairvoyant, a physiognomist (working from a photograph of the supposed victim after his identity became fairly certain), a handwriting expert, and, finally, a spirit medium.

The woman's-angle theory mentioned in the *Evening World's* head got equal play with Stella's. It was written by a Mrs. McGuirk, not otherwise identified and possibly invented. It wasn't a woman's work, Mrs. McGuirk ruled, and continued, "There is just one thing in the whole business that might suggest a woman's hand. The knots with which the parcels were fastened are the clumsy, uneven ones which women are prone to make." Mrs. McGuirk thought the victim might have been a peddler and the oilcloth part of his stock in trade. "Women poison," she concluded. "It is easier. They seldom use knives, unless very hot blood runs in their veins." The *Evening World's* Night Extra had a total of thirteen masterly columns on the case, which make good reading even after fifty-eight years. They included a remarkable collection of mystery-solution letters, which the editors claimed had been written by readers and delivered by hand between four o'clock, when its reward offer appeared, and about five, when the Night Extra went to press. A biting bit next to the reiterated reward offer contrasted honest and dishonest journalism and accused the *Journal* of snitching the letter-contest idea.

By the time Ned had finished with the evening papers, it was nearly six o'clock, and he accordingly made his way back to the west side of Ninth Avenue between Thirty-fourth and Thirty-fifth Streets. One reason Ned chose the time he did to return was that in such a neighborhood it was an hour when the man of the house was almost sure to be at home, except on Saturday night or unless something had happened to him. The women with whom Ned had left soap that morning and who had their nickels ready to clinch their bargain must have been doubly delighted, because he never came back to collect. Instead, he went directly to No. 439, climbed to the floor above the drugstore, and rang the bell at the door—slightly more pretentious than the others—of Mrs. Augusta Nack, Licensed Midwife, which he had skipped a few hours earlier. He waited in hot-and-cold anxiety. It was possible, of course, that Mrs. Nack wasn't at home, or that if she was, she wouldn't come to the door. These were the longest days of the year; it was full daylight, and he hadn't been able to tell by a lighted or unlighted window whether anyone was in. The greatest blow to his hopes would have been the heavy tread of a man coming to answer the doorbell, but, instead, he heard the slupping sound of the advance of a woman in house slippers. Then the door was ajar and Mrs. Nack stood in the aperture. She was just about Ned's height—five feet six—but she must have weighed at least two hundred pounds. Her face was wide and flat and lardy white, with small eyes, not much of a nose, and what Mr. Brown still remembers as an extremely sullen mouth. She was wearing an apron over her house dress, and there was a smell of cooking sauerkraut that has left Mr. Brown with a permanent distaste for the stuff. Ned would have given anything to see into the room behind her, but she was a hard woman to see around.

Before Mrs. Nack could ask what he wanted, Ned began, "Good evening, Madam. Have you enjoyed your trial bar of Cotaspam soap? Hasn't its fragrant lather left your hands feeling as if freshly kissed?"

"You didn't giff me any!" Mrs. Nack replied angrily, and Ned understood immediately why she had looked sore from the moment she laid eyes on him. The other women had described him while telling her about the wonderful soap, and Mrs. Nack felt she had been slighted, as usual. (Feeling slighted is a characteristic of especially high incidence among Germans and unattractive women, and Mrs. Nack was both.)

"I would have sworn I'd been to every flat in the house," Ned said. "But I guess I wasn't, or I would have remembered you sure."

It was coquetry lost on Mrs. Nack, who said merely, "Giff me the soap now."

"I'm sorry, madam, but I'm afraid I can't," Ned said. "You see, I have to get a report for my company on what each lady thought of the soap. That was the purpose of our special offer."

"Leaf it and come back tomorrow," Mrs. Nack commanded.

"I'm sorry, ma'am, but I can't do that, either," Ned said. "Tomorrow I'll be working up in Yonkers." Then he tried to look as if he had just had a bright thought, and went on, "But I happen to have a couple of bars left over. If you could give the soap a trial now, while I wait, I'd be glad to let you have one."

After thinking this over for a minute, Mrs. Nack said, "All right. Giff me the soap." Ned moved toward her, fumbling in a pocket and being careful not to give her the soap until he was inside the apartment. He knew she wouldn't shut the door in his face before he came through with the special introductory sample. As she pulled back from the door, he went through it as if in the suction set up by her big body.

"Here it is, ma'am," he said after he was safely inside. Mrs. Nack took the soap in her pale, shovel-like paws, raised it to her nose, and sniffed it. She looked mollified. "As a matter of fact," Ned continued, "I've got just two left, and since I'm putting you to all this trouble, I'm going to let you have both of them, if you like the first one. But I get awfully thirsty, climbing stairs all day in this heat, and I wonder if I might ask you for a glass of water before you start washing your hands."

"I guess so," Mrs. Nack said. "Sit down on the chair there while I get you the water."

Ned sat down in a black leather upholstered chair and looked around him while the woman went to the kitchen, in the rear of the flat, to get his drink. Within a few days, the newspapers were to describe the contents of Mrs. Nack's apartment in much more detail than Ned was in a position to take in, but his eyes fell on one item that subsequent newspapermen were destined never to see. "Leaning against a lamp, on a kind of a knicknack stand, there was a studio photograph of a big blond guy with little turned-up mustaches under his nose—a kind of Dutch version of a sport," Mr. Brown recalls. "The minute I saw it, I was sure I had seen him around, without ever knowing his name." The floor was bare, and Ned noticed that the rug was rolled up and tied, as if Mrs. Nack were getting ready to move. When Mrs. Nack brought the water, he downed it thirstily, just as if he hadn't been drinking beer all afternoon.

"Now, madam," Ned said after thanking her, "you will have the rare pleasure of making the acquaintance of the world's most luxurious hand soap. Do not hurry it, but run a basin of warm water and then work up a creamy lather. Let your hands soak in it! You will feel each finger separately caressed. When you withdraw your hands, hold them to your nose! The fragrance is a secret formula, copyrighted by the makers of Cotaspam. You have beautiful hands, Madam. They deserve Cotaspam!" The midwife slupped away again, and as soon as Ned heard water running in the rear of the apartment, he grabbed the photograph and slipped it under his jacket. He now passionately desired to leave at once, but he knew that to do so, if his suspicions were correct, would be likely to frighten Mrs. Nack into immediate flight. He also had a hunch that the longer he waited, the more he would learn. All Mrs. Nack's actions indicated that she was alone in the apartment, but the apparently substan-

tial nature of the meal she was preparing hinted that she
expected company for dinner. If it was the man in the photograph, all Ned's theories would come tumbling down and
he would probably feel obliged to invite the fellow out to the
nearest saloon and buy him a sidel of beer. But if it wasn't
the man in the photograph, it might be Mrs. Nack's accomplice in his murder. Ned had formed a most unfavorable
impression of Mrs. Nack; she looked capable of murdering
an infant—and probably had, for midwives often doubled
as abortionists. But he was not physically afraid of her, despite her lardy bulk. He was an athletic young fellow, who,
with his brother, had rigged a trapeze and flying rings in the
attic at home in Flatbush; Ned could chin himself innumerable times with one arm, and fancied himself as an amateur
boxer. The dinner guest, however, would almost certainly
prove to be a large adult male, armed and with a nasty taste
for fragmentation. While Ned was pondering this prospect,
Mrs. Nack returned, a smile for once suffusing her desk
blotter of a face. "It is nice soap as possible," she said.
"Very elegant."

Ned whipped out his reporter's notebook and started
writing in it. "May I quote you, madam?" he asked. "We
intend to publish testimonials in the newspapers, and a testimonial from a midwife would have double value. It would
do a good ad for you, too."

"I don't need ads," Mrs. Nack replied. "I am going soon
anyway back to Germany." For a moment, she seemed
sorry she had said so much, but Ned's look of bland innocence evidently reassured her. "Now you give me the other
soap also," she said. "Here is a dime." Ned felt sure she had
been told by other women that the soap regularly sold for
twenty-five cents—that they knew it did because they had
priced it in the drugstore downstairs. "It is wonderful how
with any woman the idea of a bargain will obscure larger
issues entirely," Mr. Brown says. "She was looking at me
and talking about the soap, and it never occurred to her to
look around the room and notice that the picture was missing."

Ned gave Mrs. Nack the second bar of soap, took her dime, said goodbye, and walked through the doorway. Then he stopped, because a man was coming up the narrow stairs. "He was a husky man—no giant, but a full-sized middle-weight," Mr. Brown says. "About thirty years old, I should guess. He was wearing a derby hat, although it was summer —only the dudes wore straw kellies—and he had long black mustaches. I remember them as black, although the papers said afterward they were light brown. Maybe he had dyed them. Still later, he shaved them off. What I particularly remember about him, though, was his eyes. They were deep-set and glaring, and they shone like a cat's. At his trial, the artists had a field day drawing those eyes. He was furious at seeing me there—the door to the apartment was still open— and he grabbed me by the shoulder. '*Wer ist's?*' he yelled in German—'Who is it?'—and then he started giving the woman hell. I could see she was frightened—he had her buffaloed. I had learned enough German at Erasmus to understand that he was bawling her out for not keeping the door closed. He said he had told her not to let anybody in. She started explaining who I was, and telling him if he made so much noise the neighbors would come to see what was the matter. Finally, he took his hand off my shoulder—I certainly didn't look dangerous—and went inside. 'Donkey-head!' I heard him call the woman, in German, and then the door slammed, and I heard a slap you could hear right through it. I ran down the stairs and kept going. From the way those two had acted, I was sure that I had the right man's picture and that they were the ones who had killed him."

The reason Ned's skin had appeared translucent that Monday morning was that during the previous evening it had been buffed to gauzy thinness by successive pairs of large, powerful, clean, untanned, uncallused, well-kept hands with nails trimmed extremely short in order not to scratch customers. He had spent a good part of that night, after leaving the morgue, in a series of Turkish baths, making discreet inquiries about rubbers who might be missing from work.

"The minute I saw the hands on the mystery stiff at the morgue, I noticed that the skin on the tips of the fingers was crinkled, like a baby's sometimes after a hot bath," Mr. Brown says. "I remembered I'd seen the same thing recently on an adult's fingers, and then I remembered where it was —on a fellow named Bill McPhee, who was giving me an alcohol rub at the Murray Hill Baths. And I'd asked Mc-Phee, 'Do your hands get that way permanently from the hot water and soap, or do the crinkles go away when you go home?'

" 'Oh, they stay that way for a couple of days, maybe a week, it you aren't working,' he said. 'But then they go away and the skin looks just like anybody else's.'

"I sized the stiff up. Good muscular development— massaging twenty or thirty customers a day is hard work, and some of those fellows used to pride themselves on how hard they could grip. Clean, white skin—where could you keep cleaner than working in a bath, and where would you get less sun on you? Carefully trimmed fingernails, but too short for a dude or a society fellow. The big fuss about the 'extraordinary refinement' of the hands was cleared up in a minute. I told Gus Roeder that Sunday afternoon in the morgue, 'This guy was a rubber in a Turkish bath,' I said, 'and he must have worked not long before he was killed, or the crinkles on his hands would have smoothed out.' Then I explained what McPhee had told me about the crinkles lasting only a few days. 'If we check the Turkish baths in the city and find one that has had a rubber missing for less than a week and more than a day, we've got our man,' I said. Gus was a hard fellow to get excited. He pointed out that there were hundreds of baths in the city; they were popular on the East Side and in Harlem as well as in the Tenderloin, and you'd have to check those in Brooklyn, too, and anyway the man might have been lured or shanghaied from out of town. The *World* didn't have enough men to spare for that kind of quick check. Gus said. We had a dozen hot crime men—

real sleuths—but they all wanted to try out theories of their own. If we passed my idea on to the police and they thought much of it, some detective would be sure to spill it to the *Journal* and we would get no credit for it. 'But if you want to work your hunch yourself, kiddo, go ahead,' Gus said. 'I assign you to it. All the baths you take you can put on the swindle sheet, but more than a quarter tip the auditor won't believe, so don't try to get away with it.' "

Thus admonished, Ned hit out straight for his favorite district, the Tenderloin—first, because the biggest establishments were there, and, second, because he thought the rubbers in that area were more worldly types, and so more likely to get in trouble, than their confreres elsewhere. He did not begin with the Murray Hill, his habitual retreat—probably because we never expect the strange and mysterious in surroundings that are familiar to us. He began, instead, at the Everard, on West Twenty-eight Street, and tried three more before he arrived at the Murray Hill, at about nine Sunday evening. By that time, he had been scrubbed until all his surfaces felt like Jimmy Valentine's sandpapered fingertips. In each place, he had asked the attendants to put him through fast because he had a heavy date and wanted to get rid of a hangover before he picked her up. He began his quest at each bath by asking where the big fellow was who didn't seem to be on the floor that night. In each, he was told that the staff was at full strength, and upon hearing this he mumbled that he must have been thinking of some other Turkish bath. At the Murray Hill, since he was known there, he varied the approach slightly by remarking to the rubber, McPhee, that the place looked kind of shorthanded, and asking him if anyone was missing. McPhee, an irascible type, said there damn sure was. Bill, the big Dutchman, who always had Sundays off, had taken Friday that week, trading days off with a man who normally would have been working Sunday. The other man had worked Friday and Saturday and then stayed home, but the big Dutchman had failed to show, leaving them one man

short. Naturally, there had been more of a rush than they
expected. The previous night had produced an unusually
heavy crop of bad heads; it always happened that way when
you were short a man. "He took Friday off because he was
going to look at a house in the country with his girl—or so
he said," McPhee snarled. "Saturday, some Dutchman
called up to say Guldensuppe wouldn't be in to work Sunday because he was sick. Guldensuppe is his name," Mc-
Phee added in a tone of distaste. "Drunk someplace, of
course. Today, when he didn't show, the boss said he was
fired." Ned submitted to his fifth scrubbing in five hours
without feeling any discomfort. He was anesthetized by pre-
occupation. "About how big is this big Dutchman?" he
asked. "I must have seen him around here, but I can't place
him in my mind."

"Oh, probably around five eleven," McPhee replied.
(That was taller for a man in those days than it is now.)
"And he's built big—big shoulders and a fine big chest on
him. He's just built like a big Dutchman. You must have
noticed him. He has the upper half of a woman tattooed all
over his chest—used to be a sailor on one of them Heinie
windjammers when he was a kid. He has one of those trick
mustaches like two half-moons on his lip. Not a bad Dutchman," McPhee conceded, "but skirt-crazy."

When McPhee mentioned the tattoo, Ned's heart jumped.
"I remembered the torso I had looked at that afternoon,
with a slab of integument—of whole skin—removed from
the chest, apparently to get rid of some distinguishing
mark," Mr. Brown says.

Stopping at the cashier's desk on the way out to pay for
his massage, Ned asked the cashier where Bill Guldensuppe
lived. "I borrowed a dollar from him last time I was in here,
and now I hear he's not coming in any more, so I want to
send it to him," he explained. The cashier looked at a list
and said that he didn't know where Guldensuppe lived but
that he got his mail at a saloon on Ninth Avenue, near
Thirty-sixth Street—not an unusual arrangement. "And if

you're going to write to him, you might add that he's fired,"
he said. "That'll save us a stamp." When Ned got out of the
Murray Hill Baths, he didn't write. He grabbed a hack and
told the driver to get down to Thirty-sixth and Ninth and
not to spare the horse on the way. He felt like Richard Har-
ding Davis, who at that moment was covering a war between
Greece and Turkey, after attending the coronation of Czar
Nicholas II in St. Petersburg.

The saloon on Ninth Avenue was quiet that summer evening. It was a Raines Law hotel, with the ten bedrooms upstairs and the petrified sandwich on every table that entitled
it to remain open on Sundays, under the statute passed not
long before to appease the Sabbatarians upstate. (The bedrooms established its status as a hotel; the sandwiches represented the food that was legally required to be served with
every drink.) The Irish bartender had the cowlick center
part in his hair and the handlebar mustaches that were
tonsorial caste marks. The sandwich man, on hand in case
anybody wanted one that could really be eaten, was an old
German. Ned sized the saloon up as a neighborhood
headquarters—the most pretentious place for a hundred
yards in any direction. He ordered a schooner of beer and
knocked it off with unaffected enthusiasm; the baths had de-
hydrated him until his shoes felt large. He ordered another
and bought one for the bartender, at the same time ordering
a ham-and-cheese on rye, for he had not eaten since noon.
Having established relations, he asked the bartender if he
knew big Bill Guldensuppe, the Dutchman who worked at
the Murray Hill Baths. Acquaintance with a masseur in a
flashy Turkish bath was a social reference over on Ninth
Avenue. The bartender said he knew the big Dutchman who
worked in the baths, but the last name didn't sound right. He
thought it was Nack. The sandwich man, arriving with the
ham-and-cheese, said the name was Guldensuppe, all right;
he and the rubber belonged to the same Low German death-
benefit society. "He even gets mail here under the name
Guldensuppe," he said. "He goes by Nack in the neighbor-

hood because he lives with his sweetheart—Mrs. Augusta Nack, the midwife, right over Werner's drugstore." The sandwich man winked. "She got plenty of cash," he said. "She treats him good."

Ned, trying to seem casual, said that he'd happened to be in the neighborhood, so he'd stopped by, hoping to meet Guldensuppe and have a beer with him, since he knew Sunday was the rubber's night off. "He always talks about this place," he said. "He's a hot sketch!"

The bartender said he hadn't seen the big Dutchman for a couple of nights. "Maybe they've went to Coney for the day —him and his lady friend," he suggested. Come to think of it, he added, he hadn't seen him around since late Thursday night. "He usually be in for a few beers after he gets through at the baths," he said. "The work takes the moisture out of them. I hope he isn't deserting us, because he's a good customer." Ned felt like a poker player who, peeking at the second card dealt him, sees it is another ace. If Guldensuppe had been on a protracted drunk, as McPhee had supposed, it was inconceivable that he wouldn't have once poked his nose into his favorite barroom in seventy-two hours.

"He's a hot sketch!" Ned said again, to dissemble the depth of his interest in Guldensuppe's absence. "Always after dames."

"You bet!" the sandwich man said. "You should see some of the letters he gets here. Pink envelopes! No wonder he don't want Mrs. Nack should know."

Ned said, "He's got a hell of a build. If he had been born in this country, he might be fighting Fitzsimmons."

The bartender said he had heard the big Dutchman could handle himself pretty good, at that. "There was a fellow trying to beat his time with some dame, I heard, and the Dutchman give him a good going over," he said. "The fellow pulled a gun and the Dutchman took it away and kept it."

Walking down Ninth Avenue, after a valedictory beer, Ned had a good look at the building that housed Werner's drugstore—No. 439. There were no lights in the windows on the second floor. Back in the *World* office, he found Roeder just finishing off his lead story on the mystery—the one declaring that an awful crime had been committed. After Roeder had dictated and sent away the last take of his two-and-a-half-column story, which would earn him $18.75, he consented to listen to Ned. Roeder was still not overly impressed by Ned's theory. "The fifth place you visit, you find a man missing," he said. "Maybe if you went to all of them you would find two dozen. The tattoo sounds good, all right, and the jealous dame and the fellow with the gun he took away from him. What you got to do tomorrow is have a talk with this Mrs. Nack and get a good look inside the flat. Maybe there are signs of a struggle—bloodstains. Maybe the head is still in the apartment. And get a picture of Guldensuppe."

Ned thought up the soap scheme on his long journey home to Flatbush.

With Guldensuppe's picture under his jacket and the other man's glare still vivid in his memory, Ned made his way down to the *World* again on Monday evening. He was now dead certain he had the solution of the mystery. The sequel was inglorious. Colleagues of greater prestige had turned up what the city desk thought was a better bet. When the Early Edition of the next day's *World* came off the presses Monday night, the front-page headline on the murder read, promisingly enough:

WORLD MEN
FIND A CLUE

But the story under it was a letdown for Ned.

The most interesting discovery of the day was made by reporters for the *World* [it read]. It was that a wagon, in which were two men and which contained two packages, crossed to New York on the ferry from Greenpoint, L. I., on Saturday afternoon, a short time before the finding of the headless shoulders in the East River at Eleventh Street.

The Greenpoint ferry landing on the New York side is at Tenth Street, and a bundle thrown from an incoming boat would have been carried towards the Eleventh Street pier, with the tide running as it was that afternoon. . . .

That a saloonkeeper from that very section was reported missing last night, having left home on June 2 with a considerable amount of money, makes this phase of the case especially interesting.

All day Monday, while Ned was making the rounds with his soap, the *World*'s torso campaign was being run by Casey, the assistant city editor, under constant inspirational prodding from the front office. Roeder, Reitmeier, and a platoon of other reporters were working with the police, and Ike White, the *World*'s famous lone-wolf star reporter, was working against them, with a squad of special undercover agents. Fred Sturtevant, a celebrated rewrite man, was welding the gross crude output into an artistic whole, and the circulation department was having such a picnic that there must have been a substantial psychological resistance to Ned's story, with its possibility of putting an abrupt end to the frenzy. Roeder, however, was beginning to think well of it, and that Monday night he told Ned to hand over his precious photograph to the art department, so that it could have an engraving ready. "It was a good day's work, kiddo," he said. "Thanks."

Ned was so full of his story that even though it was after midnight, when he got home to Flatbush, he awakened his father and told him about it. "Why didn't you grab the fellow and bring him in?" Frederick Sherwood Brown said. "That's what I would have done." He then went back to sleep.

The mystery continued to sell unparalleled multitudes of newspapers all the next day—Tuesday, June 29th. A *World* editorial that morning stated that in offering a reward the

paper was acting simply as a minister of justice, without ul-
terior object. The *Journal* editorialized in the afternoon,
"The only reason why every crime is not detected is that
society does not employ the best order of brains in its work.
. . . The *Journal's* offer should bring to the investigation
of this mystery intellects and intentions not usually given to
this kind of work." To offset the *World's* two-men-on-a-
ferry story, Tuesday's *Journal* splashed a report by one
Charles Anderson, of No. 7 Bowery, that he had seen two
men on a Mount Vernon trolley car on Sunday afternoon
loaded down with bundles wrapped in the fateful red oilcloth with gold stars. The resourceful *Telegram,* ever on the
lookout for a sporting angle, promoted the candidacy of "a
heavy bettor named McManus, who has not been at the
track for five or six days," under a headline that read:

RACING MEN
WILL VISIT
THE MORGUE

The *Evening World,* in its Night Extra, which was rela-
tively safe from Hearst plagiarism, offered a stimulating
speculation by still another medical man, under the headline

WAS IT CANNIBALISM?

DR. FRANK FERGUSON, THE PATHOLOGIST
IS INCLINED STRONGLY
TO THAT BELIEF

The same paper also presented an exclusive interview with
former Police Inspector Alexander S. Williams, who said,
inter alia: "The motive was revenge. . . . More than one
person committed the crime. . . . It was probably done by
a German."

Ned felt that the former Inspector was getting warm. But
there was nothing more he could do about the case himself.

Ike White and Roeder had vetoed the idea of going straight
to 439 Ninth Avenue and "arresting" Mrs. Nack and the
man with the black mustaches before somebody had positively identified the torso as Guldensuppe's. It would have
been easy to visit the Murray Hill Baths, collect a couple of
the big Dutchman's colleagues, and take them to the
morgue, but this would have been hard to keep quiet from
the competition. Roeder therefore waited until Tuesday
night and then got a man named Joseph Kavenagh, a Murray Hill rubber who was off duty, to accompany him to the
"storehouse," as the gay police reporters called the morgue.
In consequence, the Late Edition of Wednesday's *World*
had a technical scoop—a brief story on the second page
with the headline

ANOTHER IDENTIFICATION

DEAD MAN SAID TO BE WILLIAM
GILDENSUPPER, A TURKISH
BATH ATTENDANT

The story under this reported that two detectives had left
Police Headquarters at one-thirty that morning looking for
a suspect; they were "acting on information given by Joseph
Kavenagh, of 29 Madison Street, Hoboken." At the Murray Hill Baths, some cautious person in charge had informed the *World* that Gildensupper (the name was spelled
a half dozen ways in the newspapers when the story first
broke) had not worked there in three months.

The *World* of Thursday, July 1st, proudly claimed credit
for this first revelation of the torso's identity, which it had
printed with little display and less conviction. The reason
for its original lack of enthusiasm was that on Tuesday
night, while Roeder was squiring Kavenagh to the morgue,
another identification of the torso had been made, this one
seemingly more plausible and circumstantial, and the direc-
tors of the *World*'s board of strategy had fallen for it. A
cabinetmaker named Theodore Cyklam, who, like the al-

ready forgotten Mr. Lutz, had injured the index finger of his left hand (an occupational disfigurement, since a cabinet-maker uses it to hold every nail he drives), had disappeared from his home in College Point. (The locale jibed beauti-fully with the *World*'s pet exclusive story about the two men and the wagon on the Greenpoint ferry, which carried traffic to and from College Point. Louis Zimm, the superin-tendent of the factory employing Cyklam, and three fellow workmen had appeared at the morgue and sworn, after looking at the torso and its scarred forefinger, that it was Cyklam, or part of him. It was therefore Cyklam's picture, sketched by a *World* artist "from full and detailed descrip-tion given to the *World* by Louis Zimm," that appeared on the first page of Wednesday morning's paper, instead of Guldensuppe's, reproduced from the photograph snatched by Ned Brown.

Wednesday morning's *Herald,* although it didn't have the murdered man's name, profited by a quick tip from its man at Mulberry Street to head its main story:

MURDERED BY JEALOUS HUSBAND

"It was reported early this morning that the victim of the murder had been identified . . . and suspicion pointed to a jealous husband," the text below this stated. "It was said that the man was a shampooer in an uptown Turkish bath house. This man, it is said, had been living with a baker's wife."

Mrs. Nack's legal spouse, Herman Nack, was, in fact, the driver of a bakery delivery wagon, but he had not particu-larly resented it when his wife left him, and after the identi-fication of Guldensuppe he considered himself lucky to be all in one piece. He nevertheless enjoyed the eminence of a putative master criminal for at least one day.

MURDER MYSTERY SOLVED
BY THE JOURNAL

an eight-column streamer across the front page of that newspaper bragged on Wednesday, and more headlines dropped away beneath it:

MRS. NACK IDENTIFIED;
HER HUSBAND HELD
BY THE POLICE

MRS. MAX RIGER RECOGNIZES THE
MIDWIFE AS THE WOMAN WHO
BOUGHT THE OILCLOTH IN ASTORIA

STOREKEEPER FOUND BY EVENING
JOURNAL REPORTERS AND
TAKEN TO POLICE
HEADQUARTERS
WHERE SHE
TELLS HER
STORY

MRS. NACK IS AT ONCE ORDERED
UNDER ARREST BY THE AUTHOR-
ITIES WHEN MRS. RIGER'S
STATEMENT IS
COMPLETED

HERMAN NACK IS RUN DOWN AND
HANDED OVER TO THE POLICE
BY TWO JOURNAL REPORT-
ERS WHO FIND HIM
ON HIS BAKERY
WAGON NEAR
HIS WIFE'S
HOME

The *Journal*—by its own account, at least—had unraveled the whole mystery; it had had the body identified by Guldensuppe's colleagues, had interviewed Mrs. Nack and scared the devil out of her, and had put the police wise to the whole solution, all on the previous day, but had refrained from saying anything about it at the time, for reasons it didn't go into. Nearly half of its Wednesday front page was given over to an idealized sketch of Mrs. Nack's head, which made her look rather like Pallas Athena. The caption under it read, with what papers would now consider reckless disregard of the law of libel, "Mrs. Nack, Murderess!"

After tracing the bakery wagon driven by Herman Nack all night, *Journal* reporters overtook it at 11:15 this morning at the corner of Fortieth Street and Ninth Avenue [part of the *Journal* eulogy of the *Journal* ran].

It bore the sign of the Astoria Model Bakery, owned by Joseph B. Schaps of Astoria, L. I.

Nack was on the driver's seat. The two *Journal* representatives tried to climb up on the steps of the wagon, but Nack pushed them off.

He then whipped up his horse and dashed through Fortieth Street to Tenth Avenue.

He turned down Tenth Avenue, with the two *Journal* men in close pursuit. They watched for a policeman, but saw none until they reached the corner of Tenth Avenue and Thirty-third Street.

They managed to attract the policeman's attention, and he joined in the pursuit.

The wagon was overtaken in another half block, and then another struggle ensued.

Nack was desperate, and with his whip beat off the two *Journal* men.

He was ghastly white and seemed determined to escape arrest at all hazards. He fought with desperation.

Finally, the policeman, who belonged to the West Thirty-seventh Street station squad, climbed up on the opposite side of the wagon and subdued Nack.

The two men from the *Journal* helped the policeman to

overpower the desperate driver, and he was at once taken to the West Thirty-seventh Street station in his wagon.

There he proved to know nothing at all about the murder. The *Evening World,* chronicling "The Arrest of Supposed Murderer of William Guldensuppe (Nack)," gave all the credit to detectives, and didn't even mention the horsewhipped *Journal* reporters. It published a picture of Mrs. Nack and one of Guldensuppe, which, Ned was delighted to see, it had reproduced from his trophy. It also carried a long, if not entirely veracious, story of Mrs. Nack's love life, obtained by detectives from her and from neighbors of hers on Ninth Avenue. She said that she had quarrelled with Guldensuppe and that he had gone away, but that she did not believe he was dead. She had had telegrams from him on Sunday and Monday, she said. The name of a third man, known familiarly as Fred, crept into the stories of both the *Journal* and the *Evening World.* He was the man who had had the fight with Guldensuppe.

Guldensuppe's legs turned up on the same day, Wednesday, floating into a dock at the Brooklyn Navy Yard. And on the following day a notice appeared on the bulletin board in the *World*'s city room announcing an award of $5 to E. G. Brown, for outstanding work on the Guldensuppe murder case.

During the next few days, it became clear that Fred, and not the complaisant husband, was the man in the case. Fred's real name was Martin Thorn, the police learned. "Thorn" being a Germanization of "Torzewski." Thorn was born in Posen, in German Poland, and was a journeyman barber—a silent, moody kind of man, whom other men shunned and who, like Guldensuppe, lived in part off women; the rubber had been a genial *maquereau,* the barber a somber one. Guldensuppe had driven Thorn away, but the latter had sneaked back to see Mrs. Nack during the rubber's working hours. Once Mrs. Nack's picture had appeared in the newspapers, a woman in Woodside, Long Island, identified her as the stout woman who, with a male companion, had rented a house from her in what was then a sparsely settled neighborhood. The companion matched the description of Thorn. The house had outside drains, which leaked, and the neighbors' children now recalled that for two days the pipes had run "red water," which ducks had drunk with avidity.

Mrs. Nack was under arrest, but she refused to admit anything. Every policeman and every reporter in town, including Ned Brown, was out looking for Thorn, but nobody turned him up, and there was a report that he had got safely away on a ship to Germany. Actually, he was living in a cheap hotel on money he had obtained by pawning Guldensuppe's watch and clothes. He felt that his revenge on Guldensuppe would be incomplete if he kept it to himself, so within a few days of the identification of the fragments he walked into a barbershop where a man he knew was working, and told him the whole story—swearing him to secrecy, of course. The other barber, a man named Gartha, went home in a cold sweat and told his wife, who went straight to the police. Gartha made a date with Thorn at the corner of 125th Street and Eighth Avenue for nine o'clock on the evening of Tuesday, July 6th. Inspector O'Brien, disguised as a farmer, and about a hundred of his detectives, in various other disguises, kept it—each detective, to judge by subsequent newspaper accounts, trailed by a reporter. Thorn was waiting, and O'Brien arrested him.

The *Sun* of July 8th summarized the story Thorn had told to Gartha more or less as follows: Mrs. Nack had got tired of Guldensuppe (in the *Sun*'s version, Gieldsensuppe) and Thorn hated him. It was not long before they decided to get rid of him for keeps, and for that purpose they rented the house in Woodside, because it was a place where nobody knew them. Guldensuppe had been after Mrs. Nack to open a house of prostitution, so when the time came to do him in, she told him that there was just as much money in baby farming, and that, moreover, taking care of illegitimate children was a legitimate business. Then she said she knew of a good spot for a baby farm in Woodside, and lured Guldensuppe over there to look at it. It is a safe bet that Mrs. Nack packed a picnic lunch for the excursion.

Thorn was at the house when the couple got there, but Guldensuppe didn't know it. Thorn had bought a new revolver. He had a razor, too, and on the way over to Woodside he had bought a saw. The lovers had also laid in a supply of plaster of Paris, oilcloth, cheesecloth, cord, and other supplies they thought might come in handy. When Mrs. Nack and Guldensuppe arrived at the Woodside house, Thorn was hiding in a closet near the second-floor stair landing. He had taken off, and neatly hung up, his outergarments, because he didn't want to get blood on them, and he was standing in his undershirt and socks. When he heard the gate outside the house click shut—a prearranged signal—he made ready. Mrs. Nack suggested to Guldensuppe that while she went and had a look at the outhouse, he go upstairs and see what he thought of the arrangement of rooms; she was familiar with it already, she said. Guldensuppe went upstairs, and when he looked into a bedroom by the landing, Thorn opened the closet door behind him and shot him in the back of the neck. The rubber fell, almost certainly mortally wounded but still gasping—"snoring" was Thorn's word. Thorn dragged him into the bathroom, put him in the bathtub, and cut his throat with the razor; Ned Brown's deduction that the man in the morgue had been dissected alive was correct. After the butchery, Thorn ran hot water into the bathtub, washing a good deal of blood down the drain and making the puddle for the ducks. Then he encased the head in plaster of Paris, so that it would sink when he threw it in the river, but he failed to do this with the other pieces, an omission he later regretted. He and Mrs. Nack together tied up their neat bundles, lugged them to a trolley line, and took a car to the Long Island slip of the Greenpoint ferry. The head sank beautifully, but when they saw that the parcels containing the legs and the upper torso were floating, they decided to hold onto the one with the lower torso. The day after the murder, they hired a hack from an undertaker near Mrs. Nack's flat and drove to the Bronx, where they got rid of that bundle. They meant to live happily ever after, in a flat Mrs. Nack had rented at 235 East Twenty-fifth Street, but the excitement over the serialization of Gulden-suppe disconcerted them.

Thorn and Mrs. Nack were indicted for murder by a New York County grand jury on July 9th, but the indictment was found faulty, because the crime had been committed in Queens County. They were reindicted there, and in November Thorn was found guilty of murder in the first degree. He appealed, and was granted several stays, but in August, 1898, he was electrocuted in Sing Sing. Mrs. Nack, who had turned state's evidence against him, was permitted to plead guilty to manslaughter in the first degree. In January, 1898, she was sentenced to fifteen years in state's prison, which meant, with good conduct, nine years and seven months. The District Attorney defended this leniency on the ground that without her testimony it might have been difficult to es-tablish a corpus delicti, since Guldensuppe's head had not been found; William F. Howe, of Howe & Hummel, who was Thorn's attorney, was prepared to contend to the last ditch that the pieced-together headless body could have been that of anybody at all. Mr. Howe said that Mrs. Nack re-minded him of Lady Macbeth and all the Borgias rolled into one, and that she had hypnotized his client. "Martin Thorn is a young man of candor," he said. "From my first inter-view with him I found him saturated with chivalry—ready, if necessary, to yield his life as a sacrifice to the Delilah who has placed him in his present position."

Mr. Howe said this on November 11, 1897. By then, the Bellevue Hospital Medical School had been in session for a good month. But Edwin Gerald Brown, better known as Ned, had not reported for his sophomore year. In fact, he never has.

The Tale of the Murderous Philologist with but One Big Toe

AROUND 1840 America was swept by a fantastic fad called phrenology. It was based on the theory that the brain was composed of thirty-seven faculties, or propensities, each with an individual area. The more developed the faculty, the larger the area, which, it was clear, would produce a proportionate bulge of the skull. A study of the outside of the head told what ticked inside.

Understandably, the theory led to controversy—which made the fad grow. A pair of skilled operators, the Fowler brothers, set up a free show in New York with thousands of skulls on display. They called it the Phrenological Cabinet, and lecturers willingly phrenologized customers at three dollars a head, sending them home with attested charts personally signed by one of the Fowlers, Orson S., or Lorenzo N.

Phrenology prospered so in New York that applicants for jobs often had to have an okay from the phrenological brothers. By then, the Fowlers knew they had it so good that it was time to expand. They established phrenological cabinets in other cities and sent lecturers on the road with everything from plaster casts of the skulls of famous persons to simple printed charts.

"Let me," said Orson Fowler, "plant a course of lectures in a little village containing but a single tavern, two stores and a blacksmith's shop and a dozen houses, and they flock in from their mountains for ten miles in all directions and fill up any meeting place that can be found." Apparently, he was thinking of Appalachia, back when it was solvent.

Among those who embraced the new science was Edgar Allan Poe, that master of the macabre. Poe was so entranced by the bulges of idealism above his wide forehead that he forgot to check the bumps of destructiveness behind his ears, or the baser propensities at the back of his head. Walt Whitman was another convert. His huge, leonine head was so loaded with capabilities that he printed his phrenological chart in several editions of *Leaves of Grass.*

Cultured advocates of phrenology, who shunned the pitchman's approach of the Fowlers, made surveys of penitentiaries, particularly in New York State. By head bumps they classified prisoners from the totally incorrigible to those capable of varying degrees of reform, or even outright redemption.

In that final category, they found a man named Ruloff, who might very well have been labeled Exhibit A. His skull, massively shaped in all propensities, would have made the Fowlers drool on sight. But the prisoner was serving a limited term, so there was no way of obtaining his skull by any means, fair, foul, or Fowler.

The fanciers waited, yet never added Ruloff's skull to a phrenological cabinet. The fad died before he did, though both went out abruptly. Nobody was worrying about skulls any longer—the new scholars were more interested in brains, so Ruloff's was finally pickled in alcohol and placed on exhibit in the science museum at Cornell University.

Now, instead of looking at Ruloff's skull and wondering what went on inside it, you can look at his brain and wonder what went on outside it. Science has made great advances since phrenology was discredited.

Let's look into Ruloff's own case and see what was wrong there.

The Tale of the
Murderous Philologist
with but One Big Toe

CARL CARMER

THE Schutts were driving along the towpath one day and there walking beside the canal they saw a bright-faced young man who looked tired and hungry. They stopped and asked him about himself and he said his name was Edward H. Ruloffson, his home was Hammond River near St. John in New Brunswick, Canada, and he had come to the States to start his career. The Schutts were good people, so they took him into the wagon and they drove him home to Dryden. He turned out to be such a smart young fellow and so handy around the place they just kept him and sent him to school. It was only a short time before he had learned as much as the teacher knew, changed his name for some reason or other to Ruloff, and had a good job working in the drugstore. The Schutts got to be quite fond of him. So did their daughter Harriet, and the first thing the old folks knew

97

he'd up and married the girl. Then the happy couple moved over near Ithaca to a farm not far from Rogue's Harbor.

At first they seemed to be getting along all right. They had a baby, a little girl, and Ruloff was working steadily. Then one night folks nearby heard them quarreling. Some people say it was because he wouldn't let her go back to Dryden to visit her folks.

The next morning about ten o'clock Ruloff was over at the Robertson place, across the road from his own, asking for the loan of a horse and a democrat wagon because he wanted to take a box of books into Mottville. Tom Robertson said it was all right and when he saw Ruloff trying to lift a big wooden box onto the democrat he walked out and gave him a hand. It was mighty heavy, Tom said afterward, but he knew books were heavy so he didn't suspect anything.

Just as Ruloff took up the reins from the whip socket some school children who were out for noon recess asked for a ride and he let them climb up the back wheel and ride on top of the wooden box. Tom saw them pass over the top of the hill, the children playing on top of that box, and he said later he wouldn't forget it to his dying day, especially after he'd found out that almost certainly the corpses of Ruloff's wife and little girl were under the wooden cover they played on.

No one ever saw the box again. When people missed Mrs. Ruloff, her husband said she'd gone away to visit relatives in Ohio. Somebody told the Schutts about it over in Dryden but before any of them could get to Ruloff's place he had gone away and left no address. One of the Schutt boys started out on the trail and he caught up with his brother-in-law at Buffalo. Ruloff convinced young Schutt that he was on his way to join Harriet in Madison, Ohio, and persuaded him to go along as far as Cleveland by way of Lake Erie. Just before the boat left the dock, Ruloff gave young Schutt the slip and got off, leaving the boy to make the trip alone.

Strangely enough, Ruloff was on the boat dock at Cleveland when Harriet's brother returned from Madison where he found no trace of his sister. This time Ruloff said his wife had disappeared and he didn't know where she was. With apparent willingness he returned to Ithaca where an aroused countryside saw to it that he was arrested and tried. Since the death of his wife could not be proved, the most serious crime for which he could be indicted was abduction. That was sufficient, however, to bring him a sentence of ten years in Auburn prison.

Ruloff enjoyed those ten years. The prison library was well supplied with Greek and Latin classics and finally people who had discovered his interest in languages brought him other volumes. His mind was sharp and retentive and he knew more about languages than most scholars in America when he was released.

Unfortunately for him his old neighbors' minds were also retentive and as the time for his liberation drew near their wrath surged up again.

No sooner had the prisoner been set free than he was re-arrested for the murder of his child. The trial of this case occasioned a Court of Appeals judgment famous in American jurisprudence: "Absence in and of itself is not sufficient in a criminal case to establish death." Even while the court was debating this "corpus delicti" decision, however, Ruloff was escaping. He had won the affection and loyalty of the jailer's son, Albert Jarvis, and the two of them were bouncing along snowy roads behind a team of galloping black horses.

No one knows why Ruloff gave himself up a few months later. Perhaps he had advance knowledge of the Court of Appeals decision. At any rate, he surrendered himself while the judges were still debating and was immediately lodged in the Ithaca jail. But the escape cost him more dearly than he was for a long time to realize. The extreme cold of that winter night froze off the big toe of his left foot, a fact that was to have its sinister influence after many years had passed.

But Ruloff had overlooked an immediate danger. One

day many citizens of Ithaca and Dryden received a printed poster which read as follows:

Shall the Murderer Go Unpunished?

Edward Ruloff will soon gain his freedom unless prompt and effective measures are taken by the people to prevent it. . . .

Shall these things be? Shall this monster be turned loose to glut his tiger appetite for revenge and blood? . . . In the name of humanity, in the name of the relatives of the murdered wife, whose heartstrings have been lacerated by the fiend in human shape, in the name of the murdered wife and child, whose pale ghosts call to you from the silent tomb to do your duty, we ask you, shall the murderer go unpunished? . . . Will you allow this man who bears the mark of Cain upon his brow to go forth in this community and add fresh victims to the grave? No, you will not! You cannot!

We call on those who wish justice done to the murderer to meet at the Clinton House in Ithaca on Saturday, March 12, 1859, at 12 o'clock noon. It will depend on the action you take that day whether Edward H. Ruloff walks forth a free man or whether he dies the death he so richly deserves.

At the meeting scheduled on the poster, plans were made for constructing a battering ram and raiding the prisoner's cell. The ram was completed on the very day that Sheriff Robertson got wind of the conspiracy and spirited Ruloff away to Auburn prison for safekeeping. So great was the mob's disappointment that Sheriff Robertson lost his job at the next election.

Little is known of the twenty years of Ruloff's life between his escape and the sequence of strange events which led to his death. Young Albert Jarvis, the jailer's boy, stayed with him, believing in him implicitly, and a man named Dexter joined them. It is said that the three committed various crimes, mostly burglaries, in New England, and that

Ruloff served short sentences in various prisons for his part in them. When, however, he posed in a New Hampshire town as an Episcopal minister, graduate of Oxford, while he planned the robbing of the town bank, an irate judge sent him to prison for ten years. He escaped after three months.

Ruloff had not forgotten his scholarly gifts when he left Auburn. On the contrary, he had developed them until he could speak fluently in Hebrew, Greek, Latin, French, and German. Gradually his interest in philology supplanted his taste for crime and for several years he lived in New York City, first on Delancey Street and later on Third Avenue, as a studious, industrious, well-behaved citizen. During his first prison term he had begun work on a volume showing the common origin of all languages. This he entitled *Method in Formation of Language* and pushed to its conclusion as rapidly as his painstaking scholarship would allow. He convinced his two associates-in-crime that the publication of the work would be an event of such importance in the book world that it would not be necessary for any of them either to work or to steal again, and both of them were overjoyed when Ruloff told them he expected to get financial backing for his project at a convention of the American Philological Association at Poughkeepsie in 1867.

The distinguished faculty of the new college founded at Poughkeepsie by Matthew Vassar and the visiting philologists from other American seats of learning were greatly impressed at their meeting by one Professor Edouard Leurio who presented his erudite theories in a manuscript— *Method in Formation of Language*. Not one of them suspected as he listened to the suave flow of the professor's sentences that the speaker was a convicted felon, the probable murderer of his own wife and child, a masquerader under an alias, a scholar whose learning had been acquired in an institution of reform rather than of education. But when the professor asked for money to enable him to publish his contribution they politely informed him that there were neither precedents nor funds for such an enterprise.

Ruloff left Poughkeepsie in a towering rage. Jarvis and

Dexter were taken aback. They had supposed the publication of the work a certainty. Now they began to doubt its worth, and their leader decided on a last desperate venture to obtain for his researches their rightful recognition before the world.

One dark midnight soon thereafter three burglars entered the Halbert Shoe Store in the city of Binghamton, New York. Two clerks, Burrows and Merrick, who were sleeping on the premises, gave battle and one of them, Merrick, was mercilessly shot to death by the leader of the bandits. All through the early morning hours Burrows and a posse of townspeople sought the criminals. When sunlight came two of the latter were plainly visible floating lifeless on the clear waters of the Susquehanna. Their bodies were so bruised that many thought they had been beaten unconscious by the man whose murderous crime they had witnessed before they were thrown into the deeps of the river to drown.

About midnight of that day an officer accosted a courteous elderly gentleman who was carrying a brief case and whose only irregularity of conduct seemed to be that he was crouching in an uncomfortable position in an outhouse near the city limits of Binghamton. The gentleman willingly accompanied the constable to the sheriff's office where he explained that he was a traveling scholar somewhat embarrassed by a lack of funds. The sheriff at once apologized for delaying him and the benignly smiling gray-haired student had turned to go when a man whose memory had been groping back through twenty years noticed a depression in the left shoe of the sheriff's guest, just over the big toe.

"Aren't you Ruloff?" said the man.

"Yes," said the scholar promptly, and he went on to talk of the injustices that had been done in the past to a man whose only interest was in the classics and philology. He spoke so charmingly and convincingly that he was soon shaking hands with the sheriff and the other men in the office and they were all bidding him Godspeed.

He had been on his way again an hour or so before investigators at the scene of the murder reported that one of the burglars had left behind a pair of shoes, the left of which showed a distinct indentation over the big toe. Frantic pursuers soon caught the fugitive, who was walking briskly along the railroad tracks in a direction away from Binghamton.

Soon, though Ruloff defended himself at his trial with all his famous cunning, he was reposing behind prison walls again, reading and rereading his favorite poem, *The Prisoner of Chillon,* sending out appeal after appeal that his life might be spared in the interests of classical learning. A popular movement to gain him a reprieve gained such momentum among the sentimental and the pious scholarly that it would have succeeded had it not been for the insistence of New York's Governor Hoffman that the law take its course.

But Ruloff was executed, hanged on a sunny, mid-May morning at the last public hanging in Binghamton. I talked with a farmer who saw it and he told me that when they asked Ruloff if he wanted a minister to pray for him on the scaffold he said no, but if they wanted one up there to pray for the crowd it would be all right with him. And when the hanging was delayed a little past eleven o'clock in the morning, which was the time set, he complained, saying, "Hurry it up. I want to be in hell in time for dinner." The hanging was unusually gruesome, the farmer said, because, with characteristic bravado, Ruloff had put his right hand in his pocket before the trap was sprung. The fall jerked the hand free, he said, but Ruloff, still apparently conscious, put it back in his pocket.

After he was dead his body was displayed in its coffin outside the prison for a while. Then authorities from Cornell took it to extract the brain which they preserved in alcohol and displayed at the university. Scholars later stated that it weighed almost seven ounces more than the average, a half ounce more than that of the great Thackeray, five ounces more than that contained in the massive head of Daniel Webster.

No sooner had the body been buried than with the speed of modern tabloids sensational books began to appear purporting to reveal the truth about Ruloff and his crimes. *The Veil of Secrecy Removed* (published in Binghamton) stated that it was "The Only True and Authentic History of Edward H. Ruloff," but *The Man of Two Lives,* published by the American News Company in New York in 1871, also claimed itself reliable. As a matter of fact, no one has ever known definitely what happened to Ruloff's wife and child, though for a long time there was a rumor that the child was alive and dwelling in Pennsylvania. And no one has ever known what went on inside the massive convoluted brain at which curious visitors now stare without remembering.

The Case of the
Little Exterminator

GILLES DE LAVAL, Baron of Retz, who flourished from 1396 to 1440, is generally regarded as the prototype of the story-book Bluebeard who murdered seven wives and was aiming at Number Eight when she looked into the forbidden chamber and saw the heads of One to Seven inclusive. Gilles was definitely noted for his blue beard, though whether it came by that color naturally or was dyed to suit his whim, history does not relate.

However, due to the baron's wholesale lady killing, the term "Bluebeard" has been applied to similar operators ever since. Two other Frenchmen, Henri Desire Landru and Dr. Henry John Felix Marcel Petiot were modern counterparts of the original Bluebeard, even to having their crimes catch up with them. Perhaps it was their fate that produced the gruesome riddle, "Which is the better death sentence, to be burnt at the stake or have your head cut off?"

The answer is to be "burnt alive;" because, as every riddle-ridden child knows, a "hot steak" is better than a "cold chop." By that token, Gilles de Laval was more fortunate than his successors, for he went out by bonfire. Petiot and Landru succumbed to the persuasion of the guillotine.

All three were opportunists, for they took advantage of wartime excitement to go quietly about their lethal trade. Laval operated in his castle while the French were busy fighting the English in Normandy. Landru reached his zenith in a musty villa just outside of Paris, during World War I; Petiot thrived within the limits of the metropolis itself, during the German occupation in World War II. They all came to abrupt ends—largely because they persisted in their murderous ways even after they must have known that they were under suspicion.

Other so-called Bluebeards who flourished in various times and climes fell victims to the same error. They never seemed to learn the lesson of dropping out of sight when the going became too rough. Always their ego would crop up through their aliases and they would haunt their old stamping grounds or stay too long in one place.

There was, however, one notorious exception—a little man who chose a remote setting for his operations, intending, apparently, either to flourish in obscurity or gradually work his way into the bigger time. Which, nobody knows. The sudden gathering of war clouds threatened his career rather than furthering it. Still, as you will see, he proved equal to the situation.

The Case of the Little Exterminator

ARCHIE McFEDRIES

THE Four Horsemen of the Apocalypse were thundering over Europe in May, 1916, the twenty-second month of the First World War, and news of the casualties on the Serbian front was filtering in to the hamlet of Czinkota, Hungary. The grim tidings about the wounded and the dead came by post from a Central Powers notification headquarters in Budapest, addressed to Adolph Trauber, the village constable.

For some weeks now, Trauber, a mild, lumbering man of German extraction, had been fearing the worst. He had written a letter to his close friend, a little man named Bela Kiss, who had gone off to war a few months after the outbreak of hostilities in the summer of 1914, but the letter had been returned without explanation. And now, one fine afternoon when the village of Czinkota was slumbering in the warm

spring sunshine, Trauber, his hands trembling, opened a letter advising him that Bela Kiss had been killed in battle and
interred in a military cemetery.

Trauber, a very emotional man, brushed away a tear.
Then he went to the home of Maria Kalman, a widow who
had kept house for Kiss in a two-story structure of gray
stone, obscured from prying eyes by a high wall and towering trees, on the edge of the hamlet. The Widow Kalman, a
scrawny little woman with a pinched face, matchstick legs,
and large feet, walked with the constable to the blacksmith
shop and there stood, with a catch in her throat, while
Trauber affixed the name of Bela Kiss to the village's honor
roll.

The dread tidings soon spread through the hamlet, and
the peasants who labored in the vineyards came in from the
fields and gathered in little knots in front of the honor roll.
Everybody had liked Bela Kiss, a small, stubby man of forty-
two with a round, yellowish face, high cheekbones, and a
coal-black handlebar mustache. Eccentric and mysterious
though he had been, Kiss had, after first putting in an appearance in Czinkota in the spring of 1912, quickly become the most popular man in the region—kindly, solicitous, generous to a fault. And now the little man was
gone.

Kiss had, with his wife, first come over the horizon one
Sunday morning, from just where nobody ever seemed to
know, at the wheel of a splashy red roadster that roared
through the dusty main street, scattering the chickens and
the geese, screeching to a stop at the gray stone house. The
peasants, standing in their doorways, knew instinctively that
a man apart had appeared in their midst.

Kiss seemed to be a basically shy and retiring man, except
when he heard that some villager was ill or in need. Then
he was always on the job with advice, assistance, and, if
need be, cash. His wife, Maria, who was about fifteen years
his junior, was a gregarious person. She hired two local
servants, a laundress-cook and a maid-of-all-work, and, ac-

cording to the servants, was a fine person to work for. The servants didn't sleep in. Bela Kiss didn't like anybody but himself and his wife in the house at night.

Although nobody in Czinkota had any idea what Kiss did for a living, whatever it was obviously paid him handsomely. Kiss was in residence most of the time, leaving only occasionally in his little red car. When he was away overnight, Maria would remain in the house alone.

Not long after the Kisses had settled down, Trauber decided to pay his respects and inquire if there was any way he could be of service to them. Kiss, dressed in a wine-red smoking jacket, navy blue velvet pants, and puffing on a long, curved meerschaum pipe, received Trauber in his study on the second floor. The study was richly furnished, and Kiss had a pot of incense burning on his desk.

Trauber, who was neither a brilliant nor a stupid man, but something in between, noticed several charts hanging on the walls. "I see you are interested in astrology," he said to Kiss. "Ah, yes," answered Kiss, his voice a deep rumble, his eyes glowing. "The planets guide me through life, as a compass guides a sailor."

There wasn't any way that Kiss could think of, offhand, whereby Constable Trauber could be of service. "Of course," said Kiss, "you might keep an eye on things during those times when I am absent."

There was, it turned out, something for the constable—and, in fact, the whole village—to keep an eye on during those times when Kiss was absent. Maria Kiss, it developed, had a lover—an artist fellow named Paul Bihari. Bihari was quite dissimilar to Kiss; he was tall and lean, unkempt, talkative, and, judging by his frayed clothes, insolvent. But he had something that Kiss didn't have: youth. He was in his middle twenties.

Bihari, whose home was in Budapest, always appeared in Czinkota when Kiss was away, and he always disappeared just before Kiss returned.

Late one afternoon in late November, when the wind was

whistling up the Danube, a wagon drew up to the Kiss place and the man driving it deposited two metal drums, each about three feet high and a foot and a half in diameter. When one of the servants dropped into the wine shop after work, the vintner asked:

"What is he doing with those drums?"

The servant shrugged. "He puts them in a room next to his study on the second floor."

"What's in that room?"

"Nothing. Nothing but the two drums."

"Didn't you ask him what he is going to use the drums for?"

"Yes."

"And what does he say?"

"He just looks at me and runs his tongue over his lips and says nothing."

One morning, just before Christmas, when the servants reported for work, the Kiss place was ominously silent. Peeping into the master's study, the servants saw Kiss sitting at his desk, his head buried in his arms, sobbing. "Oh, Master, what is wrong?" asked one of the servants. Kiss looked up, blinked, got hold of himself and showed the servants a letter.

The epistle, on the monogrammed stationery of Maria Kiss, disclosed that Maria had fallen in love with Bihari, the artist, and had run off with him. Kiss stood there, looking at the servants as they digested the tidings, then snatched the letter, kissed it tenderly, and threw it into a roaring fire in the grate.

Bela gave the servants their notice; he wanted nothing, nobody, to remind him of his dear wife. The servants, understanding, said they would clean up the place before departing. The one who had always dusted the room where the two drums were tried to get in now. The door was locked. Before she could ask Kiss to unlock the door, she heard his voice from behind. "You needn't bother," Kiss was saying, "going in there."

Soon the tongues in the hamlet were clacking about poor Bela Kiss and his faithless wife. On Christmas morning, Kiss appeared at the door of Constable Trauber, his eyes as sad as a doe's, laden with brightly wrapped packages. "These," he said, "are presents I had bought for my wife. Since she is gone, I thought perhaps your family could use them. Merry Christmas." The constable, touched, invited Kiss in for a drink, but the sad little man just lowered his head and trudged away.

The winter winds blew hard in January and February, and the peasants huddled around their coal stoves, and all was dark and silent in the home of Bela Kiss. Nobody had laid eyes on him since he had left the presents at Constable Trauber's on Christmas morning.

The constable, wondering about Kiss, went out to the little man's place and forced an entrance. The house was dark and cold, and Trauber shivered at the sound of his own footsteps as he walked up the stairs to the second floor.

When the constable opened the door of Bela's study, which was plunged into semi-darkness by the drawn drapes, he was startled to hear the sound of sobbing. Trauber became aware of a figure hunched over the desk. Drawing the drapes aside so that the daylight dissipated the gloom, Trauber saw that the figure was nobody but little Bela.

"Kiss!" said Trauber. "You have been here all the time!"

Kiss struggled to his feet. The constable saw that he was skin and bones. "Kiss!" said Trauber. "What has happened to you!" Kiss pointed to the astrological charts on the wall, then to some charts that he had been working on at the desk. "I am to die by starvation," he said. "The stars have willed it."

"You can't starve yourself to death, Kiss. No woman is worth it!"

The little man shook his head sadly. "Nobody will ever know," he said, beating his breast like a ham actor, a catch in his voice, "how I miss her."

The constable stepped forward and took Bela by the

shoulders. "Kiss," he said, "you are going to listen to me. I am going to send a housekeeper in to take care of you."

Next morning, the Widow Kalman, a friend of Trauber's family, appeared at the door of Bela's place carrying a beat-up suitcase and a bag of groceries. "I have come to live here and take care of you," she announced to Kiss.

"But I want to be alone with my grief," Bela protested.

The Widow Kalman pursed her lips, squared her shoulders, and brushed past Kiss. She was soon bustling around the kitchen, whipping up a big pot of soup. The Widow Kalman was a superb cook and her employer's appetite picked up remarkably. In a few weeks Kiss was a changed man: all filled out, with a spring in his walk and a sparkle in his eyes.

By May, a year after he had first put in an appearance in Czinkota, Bela Kiss had apparently recovered from the shock of losing his young wife. One day he summoned the Widow Kalman to his study, ran his tongue over his lips, and told her that it wouldn't be necessary for her to sleep in any more. "I am well enough to take care of myself at night, thanks to you," he said, giving the woman a quick little smile.

Next day Kiss roared off in the red car. He returned two days later with a woman who, judging from her luggage, had apparently come to stay awhile. She was a dumpy doll in her middle fifties with washed-out blue eyes and faded blonde hair. In introducing the housekeeper to the new arrival, Kiss just mumbled the guest's name so that the Widow Kalman didn't catch it.

"What did you say the lady's name is?" the housekeeper later asked the little master. Kiss shot a heavy look at the woman and closed the subject before it was really opened.

After the Madam, as Kiss began to refer to the guest, was in residence for eight days, the same wagon drew up and delivered another one of those metal drums. Kiss instructed the delivery man to take the drum up to the second floor, where he unlocked the door to the secret room and rolled in the drum. Mrs. Kalman, catching a glimpse inside that room for the first time, saw the two other drums there. When the delivery man left, Bela asked the housekeeper, "Where is Madam?"

"Out in the garden, Master, picking some flowers."

Kiss walked closer to the Widow Kalman, put his forefinger to the lower lid of one of her eyes, lowered the lid and looked under it. Now he took the widow's pulse and began to make a ticking sound with his tongue. "My," he said. "I have been making you work too hard. You must take a holiday for a few days." Before the Widow Kalman, a bear for work, could protest, Kiss handed her a week's wages in advance and sent her packing.

When, a week later, the Widow Kalman returned from her holiday, the Madam was not on the premises. "Where is the Madam?" the housekeeper asked the master.

"Who?"

"The Madam?"

"Oh, *her*," said Kiss. "Why, she left."

"It must have been sudden," said the Widow Kalman, feeling a vague uneasiness about the way Kiss was standing there looking at her. "There was," said Kiss, speaking, as it was to turn out, the absolute truth, "a death in her family."

The Widow Kalman looked questioningly at Kiss as he ran his tongue over his lips and elevated his gaze until he was looking just over her head. "By the way," he was saying, still not looking directly at her but reaching into a vest pocket, "I bought a little present for you in Budapest."

"A present for *me?*" asked the widow, pleasantly surprised.

Kiss handed her a ruby ring. "Oh, how can I thank you, Master!" asked the widow, overcome by the little man's generosity. "It's just like the one that the Madam wore that I admired so much."

"Yes," said Kiss. "That's why I bought it for you."

The Widow Kalman was about to go on with her duties when Kiss told her to sit down. "I'm afraid you must think I am a bad man," he said.

"Why no, Master, I think nothing of the kind."

Kiss sighed. "I have a failing," he said. "You must know by now what it is."

"The women?"

"Yes. I just can't live without women. One after the other." Kiss got up, clasped his hands behind his back, and began to pace up and down. "Some men are cursed by a craving for drink," he said. "Others by a craving for women. I do hope you will forgive my feelings about women."

The Widow Kalman, feeling sorry for her little employer, told him that she understood.

Kiss got into his little red car and went off on another trip. When he returned, he was accompanied by one of the largest women the Widow Kalman had ever seen. The new arrival, who was in her forties, and whose name the Widow Kalman didn't catch, was almost six feet tall and must have weighed close to three hundred pounds. "A friend of mine," Kiss explained to the housekeeper. "She will be with us for a little while."

A few days later, Kiss again became alarmed over the state of the Widow Kalman's health. This time, while she stood by, he sat at his desk, the incense burning, and cast her horoscope. Finished, he looked up at her anxiously. "You'll have to go away—at least fifty miles away," he said. "The stars are highly unfavorable to you in this locality for at least another week. Here is a week's pay."

The day after the housekeeper left, the man who delivered the drum drove up to Bela's place with another one. Kiss was waiting for him. The drum the man had brought was the same size as the three others—about three feet high and half that in diameter. "You have made a mistake," Kiss said, peering at the drum. "I distinctly told you that I wanted a larger one this time."

"I know," said the man, "but this is all I could deliver to you in a hurry—and you said you were in a hurry."

"How soon can you get me the bigger one?"

"It will take a few days."

"All right," said Kiss. "But get it here as soon as you can."

"Do you want this one, then?"

Kiss hesitated briefly. Then, as if he had just thought of something, said, "Yes. Yes, of course. I can always use an extra drum."

The man asked Kiss what he was doing with all the drums. "Experimenting," answered Bela.

When the Widow Kalman returned, she asked where the fat lady was.

"Who?"

"The fat lady."

"Oh, *her*," answered Kiss. "She had to leave."

A few days later the housekeeper was in the village, doing the marketing, when a shopkeeper said to her, "That is a strange man you work for." The Widow Kalman told the shopkeeper to keep a civil tongue in his head. Her employer, she said sharply, was a wonderful man.

One summer evening Constable Trauber cycled up to the Kiss place. The Widow Kalman, having just finished the supper dishes, was leaving for the day. "Is the master at home?" asked the constable. "Yes," replied the housekeeper, "he's in the garden, smoking his pipe."

When Trauber approached him, Kiss extended his hand and invited the constable inside for a drink. Trauber, feeling the importance of his mission, wasn't thirsty. He had received a letter from Charles Nagy, Chief of Detectives of the Budapest Police. Nagy was circularizing all the constables in Hungary, seeking to locate two Budapest widows—one named Schmeidak, the other named Varga—who had, in recent months, dropped from sight.

Trauber was dropping in on Kiss simply as a matter of routine, for he had heard that Bela had had two lady visitors recently. One of the missing women, Trauber told Kiss, had weighed about three hundred pounds. Chief Nagy had traced both women to the flat of a man named Hofmann, near the Margaret Bridge in Budapest, but by the time the police had gone to the flat, Hofmann had vanished. Nagy feared that both women had met foul play at the hands of Hofmann.

"Why would Hofmann have killed the women?" asked Kiss, puffing his pipe, deep in thought.

"For money," answered Trauber. "Both women drew all their funds from the bank before they disappeared."

"But why," asked Kiss, blinking as he stared at the constable, "does the Chief of the Detectives in Budapest think this man Hofmann took those two women out of Budapest to kill them?"

Chief Nagy's reasoning was that Hofmann was an alias and that the killer, whatever his real name, lured his victims out into the country somewhere, there to murder and dispose of them with comparatively little risk of being detected.

Kiss began to laugh. "Constable Trauber," he said, "you may be looking at the murderer." Trauber didn't quite understand. Kiss, still laughing, explained that he had recently entertained two ladies who fitted the descriptions of the missing women. "My last guest," said Bela, "was so big and so fat that I had trouble disposing of the body." Bela almost broke himself up laughing and presently the constable joined in the macabre joke.

Now, suddenly growing serious, Kiss said, "Come upstairs with me. I want to show you something."

Kiss unlocked the door to his secret room. There, in a row, stood four metal drums, three of the same size, the fourth somewhat larger. There was a poker standing in a corner of the room and Bela took it and began to tap the drums, one by one. "Hear?" asked Kiss. "They're all filled with liquid. Can you guess what kind of liquid?"

Trauber hesitated to answer. The constable had heard that Kiss had been getting the metal drums and he had wondered, in a vague sort of way if Kiss could, by chance, be engaged in the manufacture of illicit spirits.

"I see that you can't guess what is in the drums," said Kiss. "Well, let me show you." Bela removed the lid of one of the smaller drums. "See for yourself," he said. "Petrol." And petrol it was.

It seemed that a man who was indebted to Kiss couldn't pay off with anything but gasoline. The farsighted Kiss had been happy to accept the liquid exchange. "Petrol," he explained to Trauber, "will be worth more than money one of these days."

Trauber knew that the little man had something there. The clouds of World War One were already low in the sky and, once war broke out, gasoline would become practically unobtainable for civilian use. A man with several drums of the stuff in reserve would be in a uniquely favorable position, not so much because of the monetary value of the fuel but because possession of it would enable him to wheel around the countryside at will in case of emergencies.

After replacing the lid on the drum of petrol, Kiss tipped the next drum and Constable Trauber could hear it gurgling. Now Kiss tipped the third drum, and the fourth, and they gurgled, too. "Now," said Kiss, looking Trauber straight in the eye, "you know my secret. I shall have to ask you to keep it. I don't want to be robbed."

As Trauber was leaving the house, Kiss handed him two keys. "One of these," he explained, "is the key to this house, and the other will let you into that room where I store the petrol."

"But why are you giving these keys to me?" asked the constable.

Bela looked earnestly at Trauber and placed his hands on the constable's shoulders. "In the event of my death, I wouldn't want my wife or that fellow she ran off with to lay hands on that valuable petrol," he said. "I would want you to have it as a present for your kindness to me. So keep the keys, to be used only in the event of my death."

When, in August, 1914, the war broke out and Hungary went in on the side of the Central Powers, Bela Kiss was a very busy little man, dusting around in that red car, at all hours of the day and night, as often as not with a woman at his side. The Widow Kalman, still the faithful, unsuspecting servant, was getting bigger and better holidays-with-pay from her solicitous master. The wagon kept creaking up every week or so with another drum for the master and by late summer there were about a dozen metal containers in the drum room.

Late one afternoon, when a summer storm was brewing, Kiss sent the Widow Kalman home early. He and the latest Madam, who had arrived the previous day, would, he said, fix supper for themselves.

Less than an hour later, when the storm seemed to be veering off in another direction, the Widow Kalman, loath to shirk her duties, returned unexpectedly to the Kiss house. The master didn't seem to be around; neither did the latest Madam.

Up on the second floor, the Widow Kalman heard sounds coming from the drum room. Putting an ear to the door of the room, she thought she heard the master humming. She went down to the kitchen and began to prepare supper.

About an hour after she had returned, the housekeeper, still in the kitchen, heard descending footsteps and Kiss popped his head in the doorway. "Ah," he said, smiling, "so you have returned. Wonderful woman, where would I find another so faithful?"

"Supper is almost ready," the Widow Kalman said to Kiss. "Where is the Madam? I haven't seen the Madam since I returned."

"Oh," said Kiss, "she left." He ran his tongue over his lips. "It was quite unexpected."

Kiss ate a hearty supper. "Did you wonder where I was when you returned?" he asked the Widow Kalman when he completed his meal.

"Yes. But I looked around and heard you in the drum room."

"Yes," said Kiss. "I went in there right after Madam left."

"How did Madam leave?"

"A friend of hers just happened to be passing this way and stopped for her."

One bleak morning in November, when Hungary was so

short of manpower that it was scraping the bottom of the barrel, an army car drew up to the Kiss place. Two grim-faced soldiers clumped in, without knocking, and told Kiss, who was just sitting down to a steaming breakfast, that he would have to accompany them to Budapest at once.

"What for?" asked Kiss, blinking.

"For the army. You are to be examined and inducted."

"But I am too old. I am forty-two."

"The age limit has just been raised to forty-five."

"But my heart is bad."

"The doctors will decide that."

"Very well, I'll come tomorrow," said Kiss, glancing up toward the second floor. "I have affairs to straighten out."

"You will come with us at once. You will be permitted to return for three days after you are inducted and examined."

Outside the house, Kiss got into his little red car. He said to the two soldiers, "I'll follow you into Budapest."

"No," countered one of the soldiers, "you'll ride with us."

At the recruiting station, Bela Kiss was found to be as sound as a metal drum. The Central Powers weren't horsing around with any delays in the fall of 1914. By midafternoon Kiss had not only passed his physical but was in uniform and, over his vociferous protests about not being allowed to return to Czinkota for three days, as promised, was on his way to the front.

After going to the front, little Bela wrote regularly to Constable Trauber, solicitously inquiring about the health of practically everybody in the hamlet. And then, in May, 1916, Trauber received notification that Bela had been killed in action and the villagers, saddened, told one another what a wonderful little friend Bela Kiss had been.

Bela's name had no sooner appeared on the honor roll than, late one afternoon, two soldiers drove into town, on the prowl for petrol. Petrol was in short supply at the front and the Army was scouring Eastern Europe for it. The two soldiers sought out the constable since he would be likely to know what was going on in his bailiwick. Trauber, who hadn't gotten around to removing the drums from that secret room in the Kiss place, patriotically escorted the soldiers there. They found seven drums in the room.

The two soldiers were rolling out the drums when the first soldier said, "It feels like there's something besides petrol in these drums. Something solid and heavy."

So the two soldiers turned one of the drums upright and removed the lid. They found themselves looking at a naked lady, kneeling in the liquid. Constable Trauber, peering into the drum, sniffed the fumes that were rising from it. "Alcohol," he said. "A woman's body preserved in alcohol."

Nagy, the Budapest detective chief, took over. One of the drums—the one containing petrol—Kiss had used to deceive the constable. In each of the other six drums there was a woman's naked body, nicely preserved in alcohol after she had been strangled by a length of silken cord.

In a locked drawer of the little monster's desk, Nagy found scores of letters from women all over Eastern Europe. They had answered advertisements that Kiss, under the alias of Hofmann, had placed in newspapers all over Hungary. He had palmed himself off as a lonely widower, seeking companionship. It was the old story of a scoundrel preying on the gullible sex. The widows, most of them without relatives who would wonder about their disappearance, had succumbed to the Kiss blandishments, turned over their savings, and then, for their trust and their trouble, wound up in a drum.

When Nagy learned from the man who delivered the drums that Kiss had bought more than a score of the containers, he ordered his men to tear up the countryside. Several more were found buried in desolate spots, each containing the remains of a naked, garrotted lady. One drum contained the corpse, nicely preserved in the alcohol, of Bela's faithless wife. The lady's lover popped up in another drum.

The technique of the drums was something new to the police. It had enabled Kiss to work in leisure, secreting and preserving the bodies of his victims until the time was propitious to slip a drum into that little red car and drive somewhere, in the dead of the night, and bury it.

Bela Kiss seems to have thought more of some of his victims than of others. He simply dumped some of them out of the drums, buried them in the earth, and, possibly in a burst of economy, used the drums over again. Every once in a while, a peasant plowing the field that summer would come upon the skeleton of a garrotted lady. All told, little Bela had run up a score of twenty-three ladies and one gentleman. The trouble was the Allies had killed him—apparently—before justice could catch up with him.

Starting life as a tinsmith, the diabolical Kiss had craved better things. He had, for several years before appearing in Czinkota, swindled gullible women. Apparently, though, he had really cared for the girl he married and the thought of murder had first inhabited his skull when he found that his young wife had an intrigue going with the artist.

After stowing his wife and her lover away in the drums, Kiss, no doubt surprised and delighted at his new-found talent, decided that it would be safer to murder his victims than have them walking around the streets of Hungarian cities. He had dabbled in astrology, and so he incorporated that ancient science into his scheme to deceive Constable Trauber when he went on that deceptive fast and reduced himself to skin and bones. He had diverted any possible suspicion by the classic though dangerous technique of showing him the dummy drum, then giving him a key to the drum room, knowing that Trauber, an honorable and gullible man, would not use it.

One day in 1919, a friend of one of Bela's victims, the fat lady, who had seen the man while he was romancing the lady in Budapest, under the alias of Hofmann, popped into Chief Nagy's office all out of breath. "That little fiend Kiss!" said the fat lady's friend. "I just saw him walking across the Margaret Bridge."

"You're sure?"

"As God is my judge."

Nagy was still trying to decide whether or not the informant had seen Kiss, or somebody who looked like him, when,
two afternoons later, one of his detectives walked in, eyes
glowing. "Two different people," the detective told Nagy,
"tell me they have seen Bela Kiss right here in Budapest."

Nagy, now suspecting that Kiss was alive, lit out for Belgrade and walked into the hospital where Bela Kiss had
"died" three years before. There he immersed himself in the
records of the warriors who had left the infirmary in boxes.
The hospital record of Bella Kiss, the stubby, forty-two-
year-old brunette, showed that Bela had been twenty-one
years old, a six-footer, and a blond. Now Nagy knew how
three persons had seen a dead man alive on the streets of
Budapest. Kiss, the artful dodger, had switched identifications with a fatally wounded man on the battlefield, gotten himself marked down for dead, and, under the alias of
the dead man, had been sprung from the army when the
war was over.

But if Nagy was elated by what he discovered in the infirmary records, his elation was not to last very long. Bela
Kiss, perhaps with an extra sense that warned him of danger, vanished from Budapest.

Years passed. Nagy and detectives of police departments
all over the Continent picked up suspects, only to release
them.

Then one day in 1925 the French Sûreté snared a deserter from the Foreign Legion. The deserter began to
spin some tales about a fellow Legionaire named Hofmann
—a stubby little man with coal-black eyes, a fine mustache
and a way of running his tongue over his lips—who, when
things were dull in the African Desert, would regale his
comrades with stories of how he had made a career of gar-
rotting the ladies.

When the Sûreté passed the deserter's story along to
Nagy, Nagy pounced on certain little tidbits that only he
and the arch-killer could possibly have known. Thus Nagy
decided that he had, at long last, the lead he needed. The

fly in the ointment was that Kiss, cunningly enough, had, in enlisting in the Foreign Legion, chosen a region of asylum where he was beyond official jurisdiction. But Nagy got in touch with the Legion anyway. He learned that, not long after the desertion of the man who had blabbed to the French Sûreté, Kiss had deserted, too.

Sir Basil Thomson, one of the greatest superintendents Scotland Yard ever had, regarded Bela Kiss as the most cunning man in the annals of modern murder. Sir Arthur Conan Doyle, the creator of Sherlock Holmes, always suspected that Bela Kiss, what with Europe being too hot for safety, had, after deserting the Foreign Legion, emigrated to the United States.

Through the years, the membership of The International Association of Chiefs of Police, which embraces practically every police department of importance in this country, occasionally wondered, when a widow or two dropped from sight after advertising in a matrimonial magazine, if little Bela Kiss was still around, and up to his old tricks.

There was a flurry in The New York Police Department in 1932 when Detective Henry Oswald of the Homicide Squad, known to the newspapers as Camera Eye because of his singular ability for never forgetting a face, barged into his office, went through the files, and pulled out a picture of Kiss that had been forwarded by the Budapest Police, where the dossier on Bela is still open. "By God," said Oswald, "I *thought* so!"

"Thought what?" asked another detective.

"I saw a man coming out of the subway at Times Square last night and his face has been haunting me ever since." Oswald showed the picture from Budapest to the other dick. "I'll bet a month's pay," he said, "I saw Bela Kiss last night."

But if Detective Oswald had seen Kiss, who would then have been in his fifty-eighth year, he was not to set eyes on the little man again. If Bela is still alive, he would be over

ninety years old. Yet more than one big-city detective, talking shop with his colleagues in the back room after the
day's hunting is done, still speculates on the fascinating possibility that little Bela may be sitting in a bus or a subway,
a derby clapped on his head, his hands folded in his lap,
looking just over the heads of the people sitting across
the aisle.

The Rock
Island Express

THE Night Express stood panting in the Philadelphia train shed while the conductor consulted his gold-cased watch. "Dispatches for Washington," he told the engineer. "That's what's holding us. Due to leave at ten fifty and it's ten fifty-five already. You'd think we were waiting for the President of the United States!"

Down the platform, a porter was helping some passengers put their luggage on the last car. There were four: three men, one much taller than his companions, and a woman.

"Anyway, those folks are lucky," decided the conductor. "They wouldn't have caught the Washington sleeper if we had pulled out on time."

Just then the railway superintendent trotted out with the dispatches and a package addressed to "E. J. Allen, Willard's Hotel, Washington." "All aboard!" the conductor called, and swung himself up the steps of the nearest car as the train chugged from the depot into the February night.

In the rear car, the tall man retired to his berth. When the conductor arrived, the bearded man nonchalantly produced two tickets and gestured to the closed curtains of the berth. "One is for my friend. He was feeling ill, so he turned in early."

When the conductor went forward, Mr. Allen stepped to

the back platform and closed the door behind him. It was an open platform, as they all were in the year 1861, yet he stayed there, staring back into the darkness as the train sped through Chester, Wilmington, and on to the Susquehanna River, where Mr. Allen caught guarded flashes from the right of way and answered them with blinks from a lantern of his own.

In Baltimore, the Washington sleeper was detached and hauled cross-town by horses to another depot. There it was hooked to a train to Washington, where it arrived at six in the morning, with Mr. Allen still keeping vigil on the rear platform.

A welcoming committee greeted the tall passenger, "Good morning, Mr. President." And so Abraham Lincoln was brought safely and secretly to the nation's capital through strife-torn countryside.

Mr. Allen went to Willard's Hotel and picked up the de-coy package that had held the Night Express in Philadelphia long enough for the President to slip on board. He dumped the dummy dispatches into the waste basket, stretched out on the bed, and went to sleep. It was fortunate, perhaps, that no one witnessed that, for E. J. Allen was in reality Allan Pinkerton, head of an organization so untiring that in later years it became known as "The Eye That Never Sleeps."

During the Civil War, Pinkerton took to the saddle with General McClellan and brought in valuable reports from enemy territory. After the war, the Iron Horse rolled westward. Close on its wheels came the train robbers, many of them malcontents who had already come under Pinkerton's scrutiny.

Hard on the heels of the train robbers came the Pinkertons—and Allan again hit the saddle along the outlaw trail with his sons, William and Robert. Their job now was the protection of property more than persons. But murder is a common adjunct to robbery. William Pinkerton—or "Big Bill," as he then was known—could cope with that too.

The Rock Island Express

CLEVELAND MOFFETT

THE through express on the Rock Island road left Chicago at 10:45 P.M., on March 12, 1886, with twenty-two thousand dollars in fifty- and one-hundred-dollar bills in the keeping of Kellogg Nichols, an old-time messenger of the United States Express Company. This sum had been sent by a Chicago bank to be delivered at the principal bank in Davenport, Iowa. In addition to the usual passenger coaches, the train had two express cars: the first, for express only, just behind the engine; and, following this, one for express and baggage. These cars had end doors, which offer the best opportunity to train robbers. Messenger Nichols was in the first car, and was duly at his work when the train stopped at Joliet, a town about forty miles west of Chicago. But at the next stop, which was made at Morris, Harry Schwartz, a brakeman, came running from Nichols' car crying, "The messenger is dead!"

The messenger's body was found lying on the floor of the car. The head had been crushed by some heavy weapon, and there was a pistol wound in the right shoulder. Apparently he had been overcome only after a hard fight. His fists were clenched, and the hands and fingers cut and scratched in a curious way, while under the nails were found what proved to be bits of human flesh. The pistol wound was from a weapon of .32 caliber; but it was not the cause of the man's death. This, unmistakably, was the blow, or blows, on the head, probably after the shot was fired. All who knew messenger Nichols were surprised at the desperate resistance he seemed to have made, for he was a small, light man, slightly more than five feet five in height, and weighing only one hundred and thirty pounds.

The express car was immediately detached from the train and left at Morris, guarded by all the train crew except Schwartz, who was sent on with the train to Davenport. After the first cursory inspection no one was allowed to enter the car where Nichols lay; and nothing was known precisely as to the extent of the robbery. The safe door had been found open and the floor of the car littered with the contents of the safe.

A force of detectives, including Pinkerton operatives, arrived at Morris on a special train from Chicago a few hours later. Search parties were at once sent out in all directions along the country roads, and up and down the tracks. Hundreds of people joined in the search, for the news of the murder spread rapidly through the whole region, and not a square yard of territory for miles between Morris and Minooka station was left unexplored. The ground was covered with snow, but the keenest scrutiny failed to reveal any significant footprints, and the search parties returned after many hours, having made only a single discovery. This was a mask found in a cattle-guard near Minooka—a mask made of black cloth, with white strings fastened at either side, one of which had been torn out of the cloth as if in a struggle.

Meantime William Pinkerton himself made a careful investigation of the car. His first discovery was a heavy poker, bearing stains of blood and bits of matted hair. It was hanging in its usual place, behind the stove. From this, Pinkerton concluded that the crime had been committed by a railroad man, his reasoning being that the poker could have been restored to its usual place after such a use only mechanically and from force of habit and that an assailant who was not a railroad man would have left it on the floor or thrown it away.

Coming to the safe, Pinkerton found that the twenty-two thousand dollars were missing, and that other papers had been hastily searched over, but left behind as valueless.

Among these was a bundle of canceled drafts that had been roughly torn open and then thrown aside. Pinkerton noticed that a small piece of one of these drafts was missing, as if a corner had been torn off.

All the train hands were immediately questioned, but none of their stories was in any way significant, except that of Newton Watt, the man in charge of the second car. He said that while busy counting over his way-bills and receipts he had been startled by the crash of broken glass in the ventilator overhead, and that at the same moment a heavily built man, wearing a black mask, had entered the car and said, "If you move, the man up there will drill you." Looking up, Watt said, he saw a hand thrust through the broken glass and holding a revolver. Thus intimidated, he made no attempt to give an alarm, and the masked man presently left him under guard of the pistol overhead, which covered him until shortly before the train reached Morris, when it was withdrawn. He was able to locate the place where the crime must have been committed, as he remembered that the engine was whistling for Minooka when the stranger entered the car. This left about thirty minutes for the murder, robbery, and escape.

Returning to Chicago, Mr. Pinkerton investigated Watt's character, and found that he had a clean record, was regarded as a trusty and efficient man, and had three brothers

who had been railroad men for years and had always given
perfect satisfaction. Watt's good reputation and straightfor-
ward manner were strong points in his favor, yet there was
something questionable in his story of the mysterious hand.
For one thing, no footprints were found in the snow on the
top of the car.

Brakeman Schwartz, the only man on the train who had
not yet been questioned, "deadheaded" his way, in railway
parlance, back from Davenport the following night on conductor Danforth's train, and reported to Pinkerton the next
morning. He was a tall, fine-looking young fellow, about
twenty-seven, with thin lips and a face that showed determination. He was rather dapper in dress, and kept his gloves
on during the conversation. Pinkerton received him pleasantly, and, after they had been smoking and chatting for an
hour or so, he suggested to Schwartz that he would be more
comfortable with his gloves off. Schwartz accordingly removed them, and revealed red marks on the backs of his
hands, such as might have been made by fingernails digging
into them.

"How did you hurt your hands, Schwartz?" asked Pinkerton.

"Oh, I did that handling baggage night before last," explained Schwartz; and then he related incidentally that on
the way back to Chicago, Danforth, the conductor of the
train, had discovered a valise that somebody had left in a
washroom. Later in the day Pinkerton summoned the conductor, who said that the valise was an old one, of no value;
and he had thrown it out on an ash-pile. The only thing he
had found in the valise was a piece of paper that attracted
his attention because it was marked with red lines.

Examining this piece of paper carefully, Pinkerton saw
that it had been torn from a money draft, and at once
thought of the package in the express messenger's safe. Now
no one can tear two pieces of paper in exactly the same way;
the ragged fibers will only fit perfectly when the two original
parts are brought together. There remained no doubt, when

this test was made in the present case, that the piece of paper found on conductor Danforth's eastbound train had been torn from the draft in the express car robbed the night before on the westbound train. The edges fitted, the red lines corresponded, proving that piece of paper had been carried from the one train to the other. Apparently someone connected with the crime of the previous night had ridden back to Chicago twenty-four hours later with conductor Danforth.

Pinkerton at once ordered an inquiry regarding the passengers who had ridden on conductor Danforth's train between Davenport and Chicago on the night following the murder. The valise was found on the ash-heap where the conductor had thrown it, and in the course of the next few days the detectives had accounted for all passengers on conductor Danforth's train, with the exception of one man who had ridden on a free pass. The conductor could only recall this man's features vaguely; and, while some of the passengers remembered him well enough, there was no clue to his name or identity. As it appeared that no other of the passengers could have been connected with the crime, efforts were redoubled to discover the holder of this pass.

So great was the public interest in the crime and the mystery surrounding it that three separate, well-organized investigations were undertaken. The Rock Island Railroad officials, with their detectives, conducted one; a Chicago newspaper, the *Daily News,* with its detectives, another; and the Pinkertons, in the interest of the United States Express Company, a third.

Pinkerton already had concluded that the crime had been committed by railway men. The railway officials doubted this, and an incident occurred which turned the investigation in an entirely new direction and made them discredit Pinkerton's theory entirely. This was the receipt of a letter from a convict in the Michigan City penitentiary, named Plunkett, who wrote the Rock Island Railroad officials, saying that he could furnish them with important information.

Edward St. John, the general manager of the road, went in person to the penitentiary to take Plunkett's statement, which was in effect that he knew the men who had committed the robbery and killed Nichols, and was willing to sell this information in exchange for a full pardon, which the railroad people could secure by using their influence. This they promised to do if his story proved true, and Plunkett then told them of a plot that had been worked out a year or so before, when he had been "grafting" with a "mob" of pickpockets at county fairs. There were with him at that time "Butch" McCoy, James Connors (known as "Yellow-hammer"), and a man named "Jeff," whose surname he did not know. These three men, Plunket said, had planned an express robbery on the Rock Island road, to be executed in precisely the same way, and at precisely the same point on the road, as in the case in question.

The story was plausible, and won St. John's belief. It won the belief, also, of Melville E. Stone of the *Daily News.* Detectives were instructed to go ahead on new lines, regardless of trouble or expense. Their first step was to capture "Butch" McCoy, the leader of the gang. "Butch" was a pickpocket, burglar, and all-around thief, whose operations kept him traveling all over the United States.

Stone finally decided to start on a personal search for McCoy and his associates. With Frank Murray, one of the best detectives in Chicago, and other detectives, he went to Galesburg, where the gang was said to have their headquarters. None of the gang was found, but they learned that "Thatch" Grady, a notorious criminal and buddy of "Butch" McCoy, was in Omaha. So they hurried to Omaha, only to find that Grady had gone to St. Louis. Then Stone and his detectives went to St. Louis hot on the scent, and spent several days in that city searching to no avail.

After going from one city to another on various clues, the detectives finally brought up in New Orleans. They had spent five or six weeks of time and a large amount of money, only to find themselves absolutely without a clue. They were

very discouraged when a telegram from Pinkerton told them
that "Butch" McCoy was back in Galesburg, where they
had first sought him. Proceeding there, they traced McCoy
into a saloon, and three of them, John Smith, representing
the Rock Island Railroad; John McGinn, for the Pinkerton
Agency; and Frank Murray, working for Stone, captured
him with drawn revolvers.

St. John and Stone were confident now that the whole
mystery of the express robbery would be solved and the
murderer convicted. But McCoy showed on trial that he had
left New Orleans to come North only the night before the
murder and had spent the whole of that night on the Illinois
Central Railroad. It also appeared that McCoy's associate,
Connors, was in jail at the time of the robbery, and that the
man "Jeff" was dead. So the whole Plunkett story was ex-
ploded.

Meanwhile the man who had ridden on the free pass, and
given the detectives so much trouble, had been accidentally
found by Jack Mullins, a brakeman on conductor Danforth's train. He proved to be an advertising solicitor, employed by none other than Melville Stone, who would have
given a thousand dollars to know what his agent knew; for
the advertising man had seen the conductor bring out the
valise containing the all-important fragment of the draft.
But he had not realized the value of the news in his possession, and Pinkerton took good care not to tell him. One hint
of the truth to the *Daily News* people, and the whole story
would have been blazoned forth in its columns, and the
murderer would have taken warning. Not until he had seen
the man safely on a train out from Chicago did Pinkerton
breathe easily; and it was not until months later that Stone
learned how near he came to getting a "scoop" on the whole
city and country.

The identification of the pass-holder removed the last possibility that the valise had been taken into the train by any of
conductor Danforth's passengers. And yet the valise was
there! In the course of their examination two of the passen-

gers had testified to having seen Schwartz enter the wash-room during the run. Brakeman Jack Mullins stated that he had checked there twice that night, that the second time he had noticed the valise, but that it was not there when he went in first. Other witnesses in the car were positive that the person who entered the room last before the time when Mullins saw the valise was Schwartz. Thus the chain of proof was tightening, and Pinkerton sent for Schwartz.

After talking with the brakeman in a semi-confidential way, the detective began to question him about Watt, his fellow trainman. Schwartz said he was a good fellow, and, in general, spoke highly of him. Pinkerton seemed to hesitate, and then said:

"Can I trust you, Schwartz?"

"Yes, sir."

"Well, the fact is, I am a little suspicious of Watt. You see, his story about that hand overhead does not exactly hang together. I don't want to do him any wrong, but he must be looked after. Now, my idea is to have you go about with him as much as you can, see if he meets any strangers or spends much money, and let me know whatever happens. Will you do it?"

Schwartz readily consented, on the assurance that the railroad people would give him leave of absence. The next day he reported that Watt had met a man who wore a slouch hat, had unkempt red hair, and in general looked like a border outlaw. He had overheard the two talking together in a saloon on Cottage Grove Avenue, where the stranger had discussed the murder of Nichols in great detail, showing a remarkable familiarity with the whole affair. Schwartz had a sort of Jesse James theory (which he seemed anxious to have accepted) that the crime had been committed by a gang of Western desperados and that this fellow was connected with them.

Mr. Pinkerton listened with interest to all this, but was less impressed than Schwartz imagined, since two of his most trusted "shadows," who had been following Schwartz, had given him reports of the latter's movements, making it plain that the red-haired desperado was a myth, and that no such meeting as Schwartz described had taken place. Nevertheless, professing to be well pleased with Schwartz's efforts, Mr. Pinkerton sent him out to track the fabulous desperado. Schwartz continued to render false reports. Finally, without a word to arouse his suspicion, he was allowed to resume his work on the railroad.

The "shadows" put upon Schwartz after this reported a suspicious intimacy between him and Watt, and a detective of great tact, Frank Jones, was detailed to get into their confidence if possible. He was given a "run" as brakeman between Des Moines and Davenport, and it was arranged that he should come in from the west and lay over at Davenport on the same days when Schwartz and Watt laid over there, coming from the east. Jones played his part cleverly, and was soon on intimate terms with Schwartz and Watt, taking his meals at their boardinghouse and sleeping in a room adjoining theirs. They finally came to like him so well that they suggested his trying to get a transfer to their "run," between Davenport and Chicago. This was successfully arranged, and then the three men were together constantly, Jones even going to board at Schwartz's house in Chicago. About this time Schwartz began to talk of giving up railroad work and going to live in Kansas or the far West. It was arranged that Jones should join him and Mrs. Schwartz on a Western trip. Meantime Schwartz applied to the company for leave of absence, on the plea that he wished to arrange some family matters in Philadelphia.

William Pinkerton, being informed by Jones of Schwartz's application, used his influence to have it granted. When the young man started East he did not travel alone. All his movements were watched and reported, nor was he left unguarded for a moment, day or night, during an absence of several weeks, in New York, Philadelphia, and other eastern cities.

To one unfamiliar with the resources and organization of a great detective system it is incomprehensible how continuous shadowing day after day and week after week, through thousands of miles of journeying, can be accomplished. The matter is made none the simpler when you know that there must be a change of shadows every day. However adroit the detective, his continued presence in a locality would soon arouse suspicion. The daily change of shadows is easy when the man under watch remains in one place; for then it is only necessary to send a new shadow from the central office early each morning to replace the one who "put the man to bed" the night before. But it is very different when the subject is constantly traveling about on boats or railways, and perhaps sleeping in a different town each night. Without the network of agencies, including large and small bureaus, that the Pinkertons had gradually established all over the United States, the shadowing of a man in rapid flight would be impossible. As it was, nothing was easier. Schwartz spent several days in Buffalo, where his actions were reported hour by hour until he bought his ticket for Philadelphia. As he took the train a fresh shadow took it too, securing a section in the same sleeping car with him, and taking his meals at the same time Schwartz took his, either in the dining car or at stations. No sooner had the train left the station than the Pinkerton representative in Buffalo reported by cipher dispatch to the bureau in Philadelphia, whither Schwartz was going. The exact form of the dispatch, which well illustrates a system in constant use in the Pinkerton bureaus, was as follows:

R. J. LINDEN,
    441 CHESTNUT STREET,
      PHILADELPHIA, PA.

Anxious shoes sucker Brown marbles man other dropping eight arrives put grand fifty marbles articles along or derby coat ship very tan seer wearing these have and is ribbon ink dust central Tuesday for dust to rice hat and and paper vest yellow ink get must jewelry morning depot on.

                                  D. ROBERTSON.

In dispatches of this sort important information regarding criminals is constantly flashing over the wires, with no danger of any leak.

The result of the shadowing in Schwartz's case was conclusive. No sooner was the brakeman out of Chicago than he began spending money far in excess of his income. He bought fine furniture, expensive clothing, articles of jewelry, presents for his wife, and laid in an elaborate supply of rifles, shotguns, revolvers, and all sorts of ammunition. The shadows found that in almost every case he paid for his purchases with fifty- or one-hundred-dollar bills. As far as possible these bills were secured by the detectives from the persons to whom they had been paid, immediately after Schwartz's departure. It will be remembered that the money taken in the robbery consisted of fifty- and one-hundred-dollar bills.

In addition to this, it was found that Schwartz had a wife and child in Philadelphia, whom he had deserted. This gave an opportunity to take him into custody and still conceal from him that he was suspected of committing a higher crime. The Philadelphia wife and child were taken on to Chicago, and Schwartz was placed under arrest, charged with bigamy.

William Pinkerton went to the jail at once, and, wishing to keep Schwartz's confidence as far as possible, assured him that this arrest was not his work at all, but that of detectives Smith and Murray, who were, as Schwartz knew, working in the interests of the railroad people and of the Chicago *Daily News*. Pinkerton told Schwartz that he still believed that Watt was the guilty man, and promised to do whatever he could to befriend Schwartz. The latter did not appear to be very much alarmed, and said that a Philadelphia lawyer was coming on to defend him. The lawyer did come a few days later, when a bond for two thousand dollars was furnished for Schwartz's reappearance, and he was set at liberty. Matters had gone so far, however, that it was not considered safe to leave Schwartz out of jail, and he was immediately rearrested on the charge of murder.

Whether because of long preparation for this ordeal or because he was a man of strong character, Schwartz received this blow without the slightest show of emotion, and went back into the jail as coolly as he had come out. He merely requested that he might have an interview with his wife as soon as possible.

Pinkerton had evidence enough against Schwartz to furnish a strong presumption of guilt; but it was all circumstantial, and, besides, it did not involve Newton Watt, whose complicity was more than suspected. From the first, Pinkerton had been carefully conciliatory of the later Mrs. Schwartz. At just the right moment he got her under his direction, and by taking a train with her to Morris, and then on the next morning taking another train back to Chicago, he succeeded in preventing her from getting the advice of her husband's lawyer, who was meantime making the same double journey on pursuing trains with the design of cautioning her against speaking to Pinkerton. She had come to regard Pinkerton more as a protector than as an enemy, and he, during the hours they were together, used every device to draw from her some damaging admission. He told her that the evidence against her husband, although serious in its character, was not, in his opinion, sufficient to establish his guilt. He told her of the bills found in Schwartz's possession, of the torn piece of the draft taken from the valise, of the marks on his hands and the lies he had told. All this, he said, proved that Schwartz had some connection with the robbery, but not that he had committed the murder, or done more than assist Watt, whom Pinkeron professed to regard as the chief criminal. The only hope of saving her husband now, he impressed upon her, was for her to make a plain statement of the truth, and trust that he would use this in her husband's interest.

Mrs. Schwartz at last admitted that her husband had found a package containing five thousand dollars of the stolen money under one of the seats on conductor Danforth's train, on the night of his return to Chicago. He had kept this money and used it for his own purposes, but had been guilty of no other offense in the matter. Mrs. Schwartz stuck resolutely to this statement, and would admit nothing further.

Believing that he had drawn from her as much as he could, Pinkerton now accompanied Mrs. Schwartz to the jail, where she was to see her husband. The first words she said, on entering the room where he was, were: "Harry, I have told Mr. Pinkerton the whole truth. I thought that was the best way, for he is your friend. I told him about your finding the five thousand dollars under the seat of the car, and that that was all you had to do with the business."

For the first time Schwartz's emotions nearly betrayed him. However, he braced himself, and only admitted in a general way that there was some truth in what his wife had said. He refused positively to go into details, seemed very nervous, and almost immediately asked to be left alone with his wife. Pinkerton had been expecting this, and was prepared for it. He realized the shock that would be caused in Schwartz's mind by his wife's unexpected confession, and counted on this to lead to further admissions. It was, therefore, of the highest importance that credible witnesses should overhear all that transpired in the interview between Schwartz and his wife. With this end in view, the room where the interview was to take place had been arranged so that a number of witnesses could see and hear without their presence being suspected; and the sheriff of the county, a leading merchant, and a leading banker of the town, were waiting there in readiness.

As soon as the door had closed and the husband and wife were left alone, Schwartz exclaimed:

"You fool, you have put a rope around Watt's and my neck!"

"Why, Harry, I had to tell him something, he knew so much. You can trust him."

"You ought to know better than to trust anybody."

The man walked back and forth, a prey to the most violent emotions, his wife trying vainly to quiet him. At each affectionate touch he would brush her off roughly, with a curse, and go on pacing back and forth fiercely. Suddenly he burst out:

"What did you do with that coat—the one you cut the mask out of?"

"Oh, that's all right; it's in the woodshed, under the whole woodpile."

They continued to talk for over an hour, referring to the murder and robbery repeatedly, and furnishing evidence enough to establish beyond any question the guilt of both Schwartz and Watt.

Meantime Watt had been arrested in Chicago, also charged with murder, and in several examinations had shown signs of breaking down and confessing, but in each instance had recovered himself and said nothing. The evidence of Schwartz himself, however, in the interview at the jail, taken with the mass of other evidence that had accumulated, was sufficient to secure the conviction of both men, who were condemned at the trial to life imprisonment in the Joliet penitentiary. They would undoubtedly have been hanged but for the conscientious scruples of one juryman, who did not believe in capital punishment.

About a year after the trial Schwartz's Chicago wife died of consumption. On her deathbed she made a full confession. She said that her husband's mind had been inflamed by the constant reading of sensational literature of the dime-novel order; and that under this evil influence he had planned the robbery, believing that it would be easy to intimidate a weak little man like Nichols, and escape with the money without harming him. Nichols, however, had fought like a tiger up and down the car, and had finally forced them to kill him. In the fight he had torn off the mask that Mrs. Schwartz had made out of one of her husband's old coats. It was Watt who fired the pistol, while Schwartz used the poker. Schwartz had given Watt five thousand dollars of the stolen money, and had kept the rest himself. He had carried the money away in an old satchel bought for the purpose. A most unusual place of concealment had been chosen, and one where the money had escaped discovery, although on several occasions, in searching the house, the detectives had literally held it in their hands. Schwartz had taken a quantity of the cartridges he bought for his shotgun, and emptying them, had put in each shell one of the fifty- or one-hundred-dollar bills, upon which he had then loaded in the powder and the shot in the usual way, so that the shells presented the ordinary appearance as they lay in the drawer. The detectives had even picked out some of the shot and powder in two or three of the shells; but, finding them so like other cartridges, had never thought of probing clear to the bottom of the shell for a crumpled-up bill.

Thus about thirteen thousand dollars lay for weeks in these ordinary-looking cartridges, and were finally removed in the following way: While Schwartz was in jail, a well-known lawyer of Philadelphia came to Mrs. Schwartz, one day, with an order from her husband to deliver the money over to him. She understood this was to defray the expenses of the trial and to pay the other lawyers. Superintendent Robertson remembers well the dying woman's emotion as she made this solemn declaration, one calculated to compromise seriously a man of some standing and belonging to an honored profession. There was a flush on her face, and her eyes were bright with hatred as she declared that not one dollar of that money was ever returned to her, or ever used in paying the costs of her husband's trial. Nor was one dollar of it ever returned to the railroad company, or to the bank officials, who were the real owners.

The End of
the Borden Case

THERE is an echo effect in styles of murder. As everyone knows, one neat strangling sometimes produces a veritable rash of similar deeds. A bomb is often followed by several others.

But sometimes the most remarkable parallels occur continents and decades apart. Take the Lizzie Borden case. There *was* a coincidence—if it was a coincidence—that was truly remarkable.

On July 19, 1860, Inspector Jonathan Whicher of Scotland Yard decided to arrest sixteen-year-old Constance Kent for the atrocious murder of her young stepbrother, Francis Saville Kent. The murder weapon had disappeared. So also had a nightgown worn by Constance. Circumstances automatically cleared the household maid, and a story about a mysterious prowler was unconvincing.

On the very day when Inspector Whicher took his bold step, a daughter was born in the family of a very prosperous undertaker in Fall River, Massachusetts. Her name was Lizzie Borden.

In England, Constance Kent was rapidly cleared of the outrageous charges and, sorrowing, she took to a convent, while Inspector Whicher was all but cashiered from the Yard. It was whispered that Constance's father, Samuel Saville Kent, was the secret slayer. Then, five years later, Constance emerged from seclusion, confessed the murder, and admitted that she had burned the blood-stained nightgown.

Meanwhile, in Fall River, Mass., Lizzie Borden's mother had died. Her father, Andrew Jackson Borden, married again, presenting Lizzie and her elder sister, Emma, with a stepmother at the exact time when Constance Kent was being sentenced to life in an English prison.

When Lizzie was thirty, her father gave her a trip to Europe as a birthday present. In England, Lizzie found everyone agog over another murder, the Maybrick case. By then, Constance had been released from prison and disappeared into new seclusion, but her history had been reviewed in connection with the current murder.

When Lizzie returned to America, she found the Maybrick case was a big topic, even in Fall River. There was little or no mention of Constance Kent. But Lizzie knew about her.

Two more years passed. Then, on a hot summer day in 1892, a double murder in Fall River inspired the song of the year:

> Lizzie Borden took an axe
> And gave her mother forty whacks
> And when she saw what she had done
> She gave her father forty-one.

Why Lizzie? The murder weapon had disappeared. Lizzie had burned a dress. The maid was automatically cleared. There was, naturally, the usual talk of a prowler, but— Lizzie, of course, denied it all.

It was the Kent case all over, with the stepmother as the target. Nobody apparently had heard of the Kent case—except perhaps Lizzie Borden.

The End of
the Borden Case

EDMUND PEARSON

ON that day in August, 1892, when the investigation began, Mr. Borden lay horribly murdered in his own house, in
broad daylight. Upstairs was the body of his wife, slain with
the same weapon and by the same person. The woman had
been killed soon after breakfast; the murderer had then
waited in the house from an hour and a half to two hours,
until the old gentleman returned from town, and then killed
him within fifteen minutes of his return; within five or six
minutes from the time when he was speaking to his younger
daughter; and, *according to her own account,* when she was
not more than thirty or forty feet distant.

Both husband and wife had been killed by repeated and
savage blows of a hatchet, which caved in their skulls, and
with Mr. Borden, rendered the victim unrecognizable. Mrs.
Borden had been surprised and attacked as she was making

145

up the bed in the guest room; her husband, while he was taking a nap on a couch downstairs.

There were two possible explanations, and only two. One was that some mysterious murderer, coming from the outside, and acting upon a motive which nobody could plausibly suggest, had entered the house unseen by its three inmates; killed Mrs. Borden without being heard or seen; remained hidden in those small, closely connected rooms for at least ninety minutes, and then killed Mr. Borden and escaped still unseen. The suggested motive was homicidal mania, which seems improbable, since careful selection was made of two victims, while two other easier ones were spared; or else a business quarrel with Mr. Borden—evidently a grave one, since it led *first* to the slaughter of poor harmless Mrs. Borden.

The other explanation, which seemed, at first thought, even more wildly improbable, was that the murders had been done by an inmate of the house. There were only two: Miss Lizzie Borden and the servant, Bridget Sullivan. Miss Emma, the elder sister, was out of town on a visit; and the guest, Mr. John Vinnicum Morse, brother of Mr. Borden's first wife, was elsewhere in the city about his own affairs.

Of the two women thus left in the house, no suspicion of anything more than guilty knowledge has ever been attached to the servant. She had no motive whatever for the crimes; she was exonerated by the statements of the woman who was actually accused; and it is altogether probable that she knew nothing whatever about the murders. She was never shaken in her story that she was at work in the rear of the house at the time when Mrs. Borden was killed, and that she was in her own room, on the third floor, at eleven o'clock, when the attack was made on Mr. Borden.

This leaves Miss Lizzie Borden. What cause had the police for arresting her? First, as to motive, the ill-feeling in the family was notorious in Fall River; the two daughters hardly spoke to their stepmother, and avoided eating their meals with her and with their father. There had been for many years quarrels about money; the daughters feared that they were to be disinherited in favor of the second wife. The old people had been violently sick that same week, and three witnesses swore at the inquest that Miss Lizzie had tried to buy prussic acid at a pharmacy. She had made dire predictions to a friend, only the night before the murders, that she feared disaster to her father.

On his return from town, a quarter of an hour before his death, she told him that Mrs. Borden had had a note from some friend and had gone out on a sick call. At that moment, the dead body of her stepmother was lying on the floor upstairs, and *in sight* from the head of the staircase which Miss Lizzie had just descended. Moreover, neither the sick friend, the sender of the note, the messenger who brought it, nor the note itself could ever be found, and her story was uncorroborated when she was on trial and in jeopardy of her life, when confirmation of the tale would have been of supreme value to her attorneys.

Three days after the murders, she burned a dress, which was pretty conclusively shown to be very like the one she wore when the murders were committed. The inference was that the dress bore bloodstains, or the signs of attempts to remove such stains.

Finally, she told flatly contradictory stories about herself at the time of her father's murder, at last settling on the ridiculous assertion that she had gone to the barn loft—which, on a sultry August morning, was hotter than Gehenna—and had remained there, eating pears and *looking for sinkers for a fishing line* for twenty minutes—just long enough to allow the mysterious murderer to kill her father and escape.

She told these and various other stories to neighbors on the day of the murder and at the inquest, but at the trial availed herself of her right not to go on the witness stand. Hence she never explained the contradictions and absurdities in her early accounts, nor showed any anxiety to clear herself of suspicion. She accepted the advice of her astute attorney, and remained content with letting the State prove her guilt, if it could.

This, the State was unable to do within the restrictions of

a capital trial, and against the rulings of a hostile court. No witness could testify that he saw bloodstains on Miss Borden's clothes, her face, or her hands; and three or four persons saw her within half an hour of her father's death. This apparently had great weight with the jury; far greater weight than it deserved. She herself had given the alarm of the murders, calling upstairs to Bridget. The State was never able to produce any weapon that could be established as the one used by the murderer.

It did, however, offer a hatchet found in the cellar, whose blade fitted the wounds. The handle had recently been broken, and the head was covered, not with the ordinary drifting dust of a cellar, but with ashes, as if it had just been washed and rubbed in the ashes.

The previous good reputation of the accused woman, contrasted with the brutality of the murders, made a conviction very doubtful. This difficulty was increased by the fact that she was an active church member and worker in religious societies. There was something of an attempt to overbear the Court by sectarian activity. A deputation of pastors called on one of the judges before the trial; what to say or to do, it is hard to imagine. They were not thrown out, as they deserved to be. And the prisoner was constantly escorted and supported in court by a pair of officious and meddlesome clergymen.

Three judges presided at the trial, and made two rulings which practically insured an acquittal. One was to exclude her contradictory evidence at the inquest, the other was to refuse to admit the testimony of three witnesses to the attempt to buy prussic acid the day before the murders.

Finally, the charge to the jury was delivered by one of the justices—who, like Mr. Borden, was an elderly man with grown daughters—and who, it has been said, was so shocked at the thought of parricide that his feelings overcame his reason. It has always been the belief, in legal circles that the charge was agreed upon by the three justices, but was altered overnight by the one who delivered it, and, in the process, still further strengthened in the prisoner's favor.

At all events, as it was delivered, it amounted to an argument for the defense, and almost a direction to acquit. Doubtless, the jury, sober, middle-aged men, scandalized at the possibility of convicting a "respectable" woman of such fiendish crimes, were immensely relieved to be told by the learned judge (whose integrity was unquestioned) that the accusation was absurd.

The case had also been tried out of court, by newspapers and by public opinion. Emotion ruled many people; they decided that "a woman couldn't do such a thing" and shut their eyes to facts. The extremely grave evidence about the attempt to buy poison, for instance, was ignored by many of the newspapers, and even today is often unknown to those who have discussed the case. It is probable that the public hysteria was not without influence on the jury.

The story runs that, as the jury filed out, with the extraordinary charge in their ears, the prosecutor turned to his assistant and expressed himself in some such vigorous terms as Washington used at the battle of Monmouth.

Those who observed the defendant at the trial—and reporters were there in swarms—saw, for the most part, what they went to see. Some of the newspapers had apparently gauged public opinion; decided that the theory of guilt was unpopular and shocking; that the Government's case was weak in one or two essentials, and that it was wise policy to support the defense. Their reporters therefore pictured the prisoner as an injured innocent; "a noble Christian woman" undergoing martyrdom. The police were described as persecutors; the District Attorney as a brutal inquisitor.

The truth was that the police, when the murders were discovered, had been fearful to take the logical step of an arrest, and had been negligent, if anything, in the interests of justice. The social position of the suspect had insured her more than her share of consideration. There were present at the trial, however, discerning men who, without predetermination as to guilt or innocence, looked at the prisoner to see if the crimes seemed impossible for a person of her appearance. Some of these have said that they understood what was meant when, the day after the murders, a relative of Mr. Borden gave out an interview to the press, in which Miss Lizzie was described as "haughty and domineering" and of "a repellent disposition." This relative had also said, very pointedly:

"I am positive that Emma knows nothing of the murder."

Observers remarked that Miss Lizzie's iron will and determination were also apparent; there were, in fact, incidents recorded in which she had said that she never failed in anything she undertook. One of the most definite bits of testimony, as to her feeling toward her stepmother, was a remark to a dressmaker, in which she objected to the word "mother" as applied to Mrs. Borden; described that lady as "a mean, good-for-nothing thing," and said that she never took her meals with the older people if she could help it. Of course, by itself, this is far from proof of a murderous temper, and defendant's counsel dismissed it all as girlish petulance. Miss Lizzie was then thirty-two.

After the acquittal, after the cheers had died down and the kissings were over, the Misses Borden returned to their home and spent a merry evening with their friends, looking at the dozens of newspapers with their pictures of everybody in the case. Newspaper illustrations were new and very crude, but even the minor witnesses had been pictured in all the papers.

The sisters were free and independent women now, and able to afford themselves a more modern and spacious dwelling than the small house whose antiquated arrangements had been one of the causes of quarrel with their tight-fisted father. Soon they moved to a better street and bought a larger and more comfortable house—the one in which Miss Lizzie died. It is in a pleasant situation, with a garden, a lawn, and trees. There was space, in later years, when the horse and carriage gave way to a motor car, for a large and rather extravagantly glazed garage.

The estate was named Maplecroft. As the years went by, there was neither peace nor happiness within or without. Her church had supported Miss Lizzie enthusiastically during her months of imprisonment and the days of her trial, but it is said that her one attempt to return to it was never repeated. Many, although not all, of her friends now began to look the other way. They were not convinced by the verdict.

Her oldest and best friend never saw her again after the day when she appeared in court, an unwilling witness for the State. This was the lady whose testimony about seeing Miss Lizzie burn the dress led the Grand Jury to vote an indictment, and cut heavily against the prisoner at the trial. It was to this lady that Miss Lizzie uttered, on the night before the murders, her forebodings of evil for the house of Borden. Her listener became convinced that the prophetess knew well whereof she spoke.

The visits of the sisters to summer resorts elsewhere in the state were never repeated, when their identity became known. Miss Lizzie's frequent trips to Boston, for shopping and the theater, did not always bring joy to the hotel she visited. Care had to be used. Shopping was done in Boston rather more than in Fall River. A man who had good opportunity for observing told me that in thirty years following the acquittal, only twice had he seen the celebrated lady on the streets of her native city.

Her brief but odd friendship wih Miss Nance O'Neil, the actress; her extreme fondness for dogs, birds, and all animals; her many kindly acts to her servants and to the poor are all familiar matters to her townsfolk. Her house was well curtained and guarded; the blithe book agent, the bond salesman, and the reporter never passed the servants, nor were they admitted into the presence of the mistress of Maplecroft.

No collection of *Bordeniana* is complete without mentioning the legend of the expressman and the fable of the kitten. The latter shall come first, as the briefest and the more disagreeable and apocryphal. According to this, the defendant in the celebrated murder trial, some years before that event, was one day annoyed by a kitten which was running about the house. Taking the kitten under one arm and seizing a hatchet in the other hand, she disappeared into the cellar, where the chopping block was kept. After a brief absence, she returned upstairs, remarking grimly:

"There, I guess we won't be troubled by that animal any more!"

This is repeated, with shuddering horror, wherever her name is mentioned; I have heard it, at second hand, from an alleged eyewitness. Yet I cannot think it anything but a slander. Her love for animals, which was so well illustrated in her will, seems to me conclusive on this point.

The other legend is more pleasing. There came one day to the house (whether the humble old home on Second Street or the more spacious Maplecroft, I do not know) an express messenger, bringing in his wagon a wooden box for Miss Borden. She met him inside and asked him to open the box for her. He started to tear off the top with his hands, when Miss Lizzie remarked:

"Wait a minute. I'll go down cellar and get the hatchet."

She was gone but an instant, but when she reappeared the man was not there. Wondering, she ran to the window and looked down the street. Far away and already vanishing in a mighty cloud of dust went the express wagon at top speed; the driver was standing up and lashing at his horse, in terror for his life.

Three or four years after the acquittal (in February, 1897, to be exact) there occurred something that belongs to fact and not legend. It is duly recorded in the local press. I think it may account for the coolness of some of her friends in later years, and for the social ostracism which was not wholly the fancy of newspaper reporters. In that month, a firm of silversmiths and jewelers in Providence took out a warrant for the arrest of Miss Lizzie Borden, charging her with the theft of two pictures, one of them a painting on porcelain called "Love's Dream." The warrant was never served, the charge was never met, and the case was settled out of court.

This was an odd incident in the life of a woman possessed of a fortune of two or three hundred thousand dollars. I fancy that some of her friends, who thought that the accusation of murder had been triumphantly refuted, had their faith sorely shaken at this time. They must have recalled the burglary in her father's house, a year before the murders, and Mr. Borden's abandonment of the investigation.

In the story of the spiritualistic séance at the home of Mr. Morse's nephew, we return once more to rumor and gossip. According to this tale, that quaint old gentleman, John Vinnicum Morse, was himself present on the evening when ghostly aid was invoked. The control told them to hunt for certain bloodstained handkerchiefs, hidden by the murderer of Mr. and Mrs. Borden as he fled from town on the fatal morning. The search was to be made under some stones beside a road leading out of Fall River. The hunt was made; the handkerchiefs were found; and Lizzie's innocence established. Q.E.D.

How do such yarns begin? A newspaper man was sent to inquire about this one, and he talked with the tall and venerable John Vinnicum Morse, in person. That gentleman informed him that no handkerchiefs had been found, no search had been made, and no séance had ever been held. He added, so says my informant, the reporter:

"Young man, if you want to know my opinion, I do *not* believe that that young woman is guilty."

For a few years, neither rumor nor fact concerning the Borden household agitated Fall River. Then, about 1904, another addition was made, not to gossip, but to veritable history. A local newspaper office received a curious postcard message. The communication was to this effect:

Miss Emma Borden of French Street has left for California. She is threatened with lung trouble, and her friends are much worried.

The message was unsigned, and the writing unfamiliar to the editors of the paper. The card had been addressed to them and then enclosed and mailed in an envelope. The newspaper was one that had been friendly to Miss Lizzie, but the editors were, nevertheless, a little disquieted. They recalled the predictions of disaster made the night before the slaughter of Andrew Borden and his wife, and wondered if the axe were now being whetted for Miss Emma. They telephoned to the house and managed to speak to the younger daughter. She confirmed the report that her sister was leaving town, but denied all the rest of the message. She was reticent as to Miss Emma's address and the cause of her departure.

This was the beginning of the separation and estrangement of the sisters. The exact reasons for it are unknown, except to a very few. It has been, of course, the subject of gossip; some of it possibly mere scandalmongering. Miss Emma Borden had gallantly come to the aid of her sister, in the trial, and testified in her behalf. It was thought that her sense of loyalty led her to take a very liberal view of the restrictions of her oath as witness.

The attorneys for the Commonwealth did not share the opinon already quoted that Miss Emma was without any knowledge of the murder. They held that she was in no doubt whatever about the identity of the assassin. They hoped that the horror of the killings would affect her—as the weaker-willed of the two sisters—and cause her to make admissions which would tend to clear up the mystery. This never happened.

One of these attorneys, on entering the Borden house for the first time, found a book of recipes and prescriptions. He took it up, and it fell open in his hand—at a passage devoted to the subject of prussic acid. It is also said that there was evidence of an earlier attempt to procure this poison, earlier than the one made in Fall River the day before the murders. This took place in New Bedford, and again the clerk in the pharmacy identified Lizzie as the applicant.

In Fall River, suspicions have been directed toward a number of people as accessories or accomplices: the neighbor and family physician, Dr. Bowen; Bridget Sullivan; and John Vinnicum Morse. I think all these suspicions were unjustified. Of Dr. Bowen, it was alleged that he alone really knew and sympathized with the woman whose life with her father and stepmother was so unhappy. When he came to the house on that morning, he helped her conceal the evidence; ran out, in fact, with the bloodstained hatchet under his coat! This is moonshine. All that is positively known of Dr. Bowen is that he did not profit financially by any services he may have rendered his neighbor.

The famous quatrain, beginning:

> Lizzie Borden took an axe
> And gave her mother forty whacks

is probably the most celebrated piece of doggerel about any American crime. It can be sung, if one likes, to the tune of "Ta-ra-ra-boom-de-ay." It has gone around the world: I have seen it printed in a newspaper of Durban, Natal.

Not so pungent, and not so widely known, is the more charitable set of verses by A. L. Bixby, entitled "To Lizzie." I suppose they were printed during the trial. Two stanzas will indicate their flavor:

> There's no evidence of guilt,
>   Lizzie Borden,
> That should make your spirit wilt,
>   Lizzie Borden;
> Many do not think that you
> Chopped your father's head in two,
> It's so hard a thing to do,
>   Lizzie Borden.
>
> You have borne up under all,
>   Lizzie Borden.

> With a mighty show of gall,
>   Lizzie Borden;
> But because your nerve is stout
> Does not prove beyond a doubt
> That you knocked the old folks out,
>   Lizzie Borden.

The deaths of the two sisters, their reunion in the Fall River cemetery, and the terms of their wills attracted wide attention. Miss Lizzie's bequests were to cousins, to friends, servants, and old schoolmates. Miss Emma made similar bequests, and left $100,000 to charitable institutions, in varying amounts of from three to ten thousand dollars. Two or three clauses in Miss Lizzie's will were of interest. She wrote:

"I have not given my sister anything, as she had her share of her father's estate, and is supposed to have enough to make her comfortable."

Miss Lizzie's largest public bequest was of $30,000, together with shares of stock in a manufactory, to the Animal Rescue League of Fall River. She also left $2,000 to the Animal Rescue League of Washington, D. C.

Miss Emma's favored charities were homes for the aged, rescue missions, nursing associations, the Salvation Army, the Girl Scouts, a Boys' Club, and so on, but she also remembered the animals: $5,000 to the Massachusetts Society for the Prevention of Cruelty to Animals; the same amount to the Animal Rescue League of Providence; and to the Animal Rescue League of Fall River, $20,000, as well as a fifth share of the residue of her estate.*

It is thus apparent that human sentiments toward animals found expression in about the same terms from each sister. Miss Lizzie wrote in her will:

> I have been fond of animals and their need is great and there are so few who care for them.

---

* There were newspaper reports of a plan, by relatives in the West, to contest Miss Emma's will. The plan was afterward reported as abandoned.

The fact that both sisters remembered the stray dogs and cats and suffering horses is worth consideration, since amateur psychologists have been inclined to make deductions from the last will of Miss Lizzie. They recalled a story of O. Henry,* in which an astute detective decided, from his militant affection for a dog, which of two men was guilty of murder.

Of course, to the Freudian, or pseudo-Freudian, the kindlier the deed the darker and more degrading the suspicion which it should provoke against him who does the deed. But if kindness to dogs and birds is indicative of a murderous disposition, what a carnival of secret homicides must have stained the soul of the late president of the Society for the Prevention of Cruelty to Animals.

I have heard that one of America's foremost novelists disbelieved the possibility of Miss Lizzie Borden's guilt, and argued in her defense. A friend of mine, who is a lawyer, thinks that such a belief is consequent upon the novelist's profession. He says:

"Of course, Mr. Tarkington was accustomed to look for what is probable and convincing. The grossly improbable facts, which constantly occur in real life, are abhorrent to the artistic conscience of the writer of fiction. He is bound to discard them as impossible."

It might be added that the author of detective novels and mystery plays is another kind of writer who is also in danger of disqualification when it comes to the solution of a murder problem in real life. His first axiom in the construction of his plot is that, whoever is guilty, the generally suspected person *must* be innocent. Second, comes his invariable presentation of the police as ruffians, hounding the defenseless along the path to the scaffold or the electric chair. Third, the villain or second villain of the piece always is the hectoring District Attorney. The State is presented as always wrong; the prisoner always right.

The murderer of the Bordens undoubtedly had a bad hour between the two killings. It is the thought of that hour,

* "The Theory and the Hound."

and the iron courage which sustained it, which sets this crime apart from all others. Bridget would not discover the body of Mrs. Borden: she never went into the guest room. Mr. Borden seldom went there. Yet Bridget must be out of the way for the opportunity to kill Mr. Borden. (If, indeed, his death was part of the original plot, and not the necessary result of the first murder, as Banquo's followed King Duncan's. The attempted poisoning of both husband and wife suggest that both victims had been marked down.)

Moreover, Mr. Morse, out on his morning errands, must not return too soon. By noon, inquiries would begin as to Mrs. Borden. Bridget's disappearance upstairs, at 11 A.M., was apparently not an invariable habit. Miss Lizzie tried to send her downtown, shopping. In the end, fortune served, for Bridget went upstairs, and Mr. Morse stayed away until nearly noon.

How far the events of that morning were planned and how far they were chance will never be known. Like the old Scottish lady, who waited impatiently for the Day of Judgment when the whole matter of the Gowrie Conspiracy would be clear, we shall have to be content with conjecture.

Many persons in Fall River believe that Bridget had guilty knowledge, and that she retired to Ireland "with a fortune." The luck that gave Miss Lizzie fifteen or twenty minutes clear, with neither Bridget nor Mr. Morse about, is used as an argument in Miss Lizzie's favor. But it is an even more incredible instance of luck for an "outside" murderer, since he had to count not only on the absence of Bridget and Mr. Morse, but also upon the absence of Miss Emma, and upon avoiding Miss Lizzie herself, at the time of the first murder, when she was in the house, and upon the truly miraculous chance of her going to the barn loft on that preposterous errand of the sinkers, for precisely the time he needed to slaughter Mr. Borden.

The most charitable explanation, consistent with known fact, might acquit her of the actual commission, but it cannot clear her of guilty knowledge. The house is small; and the neighbors were near, and—as it was proved—lynx-eyed, and quick to see a stranger, or any unusual event in the street.

A friend of mine has an ingenious theory that the murders were committed by a Chinaman, one of Miss Lizzie's Sunday-school pupils. This obliging Christian convert, overcome with grief at hearing of his teacher's sad life at home, decided to remove her parents, brighten her life, and enrich her with $250,000 all at one—or two—strokes. It was to be his good deed for that day. How he got in, or out, is not explained, nor have I heard that Miss Lizzie had a Chinese student at all.* I think that he was born of my friend's fancy —invoked probably by his recollection of the fact that hatchets were favorite weapons in those carefree days when the Hip Sing and On Leong tongs were carrying on their warfare.

The prosecutor believed that Mr. Morse's visit precipitated the murders; that Miss Lizzie overheard a conversation between her father and Mr. Morse to the effect that her father had been to see his lawyer. To her this meant a new will, which would disinherit his daughters in favor of the second wife. She determined on instant action, and, when the poisoning attempt of Tuesday failed, and when on Wednesday the attempt to buy prussic acid also failed, the hatchet was resorted to on Thursday. Miss Emma's absence may have been chance or scheme; it was fortunate for both sisters.

Aside from all other suspicious circumstances, the two facts that seem to clinch the argument are the story about the note, and the first version of her absence from the house during her father's murder. As to the note, it is incredible, if such a thing were sent, that nobody should have come forward, or been found, who dispatched it or who brought it. If there were no note, she told a lie, and why should she do that except to conceal guilt?

* A correspondent now tells me that he had heard that she did teach a Chinese class in Sunday School.

Her first story about absence from the house was that she came back from the *yard,* on hearing a groan or distressed noise from her father. This placed her within twenty feet of the murderer and his victim, with the victim still able to groan, yet it was apparent that he died without waking, almost at the first blow. And yet the murderer escaped unseen by her! The yard is very small; a narrow driveway to the barn.

She soon saw that this story would not do, and altered it to put herself in the barn loft at the time of the murder; omitted all reference to being called into the house by the groan; and represented herself as coming in casually and discovering the murder by accident. Here was not confusion of words, but two totally different stories.

Imagine a woman of sullen disposition, jealous and moody; the daughter of a stern, rather tyrannical old man. Add, if they are of importance, smoldering and repressed sexual emotions. They are, of course, tremendously important to the Freudians, who will jeer if such guesswork is not assumed as fact and trumpeted as such. (These emotions were not altogether repressed, if gossip be trusted.) Give her a great determination to put things through; never to own defeat in the long run. Still, perhaps, we are far from imagining a woman who could slay two persons—one of them her father—hack their heads to bits with a hatchet, between breakfast and luncheon, and still be in condition, when the neighbors arrived, to discuss which undertaker should be called in.

Here her character becomes a mystery. Her lawyers and friends never permitted the suggestion of insanity. The old solution of our grandfathers: that she "had not the fear of God before her eyes, but was moved and seduced by the instigation of the Devil," seems to us an unsatisfactory formula. But some of us, who see its limitations, and discard the absurdities of the witch hunters, complacently swallow the hocus-pocus of St. Freud, the hunter of complexes. A little learned babble about phantasies, frustrations, and inhibi-

tions sounds very impressive to those who are quick to recognize the absurdities in the older demonology.

The psychoanalyst might have discovered, if he had had
his innings, that, at the age of eight, Miss Lizzie liked to play
that she was Mary, Queen of Scots, and with this he could
have done much—without explaining wherein this differed
from every other little girl. Sir James Stephen wrote that
"such a thing as atrocious wickedness is consistent with
good education, perfect sanity, and everything, in a word,
which deprives men of all excuse for crime." My New England neighbors used to say that "some folks are downright
cussèd."

Wherein lies wisdom? Make your choice. There is no
doubt that the scheme of thought that comes to us tricked
out in new phrases and heavily ornamented with sex sym-
bolism, is the popular one today.

To suggest a theory of how the crimes may have been
committed, and to explain away all the physical difficulties,
one might speculate in some such fashion as in this which
follows.

The murders, in all probability, had long been considered; they had been definitely planned for a few days before
the crime. The weapon was at hand—a hatchet found in the
cellar. She darted up to the guest chamber as soon as Mrs.
Borden went there the second time, and killed her in a few
seconds. Bridget did not hear the noise of the fall of the
body either because she was in the barn or yard, gathering
the materials for the window washing (as we know she was
doing that morning) or because of the passing of a wagon
at the time. Another reason why Bridget did not hear the
sound has been suggested: that Mrs. Borden was already
on her knees tucking in the bedclothes. A still simpler and
better one than all these is that there was no fall. At the first
blow she slumped to her knees; after that, with the repeated
blows, her body straightened out at length.

Mr. Borden came in, and fell asleep the moment after he
lay down; he was not well, and it was a hot day. She had

kept the hatchet concealed in some paper in her own room, or elsewhere, after the first murder. Few, if any, drops of blood fell on her at that time—such an attack, from behind, does not necessarily send any blood to the rear. There is no jet of blood, unless an artery is severed. Bram, on the *Herbert Fuller,* slew three persons with an axe, and did not seem to acquire bloodstains. Constance Kent had a blood-stained garment, but it passed the examination of the police. At all events, there was no trouble after the first murder: she had at least an hour, clear, to remove any traces of blood.

After her father had fallen asleep—to continue these conjectures—Bridget was upstairs, and it needed only a few seconds to deal the ten blows which were inflicted on the second victim. She may have held a newspaper, or his coat, before her, for, in this instance, the murderer stood in a shower of small drops of blood. If not, the few drops which fell on her face, hair, or hands were soon removed. She hurried to a mirror, examined herself for stains, and cleansed them at the kitchen sink. There were one or two spots on her blue dress, and these she discovered a day or two afterward (as with Constance Kent's nightdress), and burned the garment the following Sunday.

The hatchet was washed at the running tap in the kitchen sink; taken down cellar; the handle broken by a blow on a chopping block; and the head covered with ashes—as it was found. All this could be done in seven or eight minutes; she had twelve or fifteen. Then she called upstairs to Bridget:

"Come down quick; Father's dead; somebody came in and killed him."

And those who think that she would have been highly agitated when the neighbors came in simply do not understand her. They are "trying to read their own emotional natures" into a very different character.

The Ghost from the Grave

MOST men who murder their wives are natural fiction-eers. After years of telling tall tales to the little woman and gaining sympathy, the spouse slayer forgets what a chronic liar he has become. True, he may reach the homicidal stage only after his better half becomes bitter enough to doubt him, but by then he is usually so enamored by his gift at twisting facts that he blames her rather than himself.

The man who disposes of his wife loses his best audience and often his only sympathizer. All the folks who kept quiet, rather than be rebuked by the misguided woman in the case, now have their say. Right then, the calculating killer is out in the cold world on his own, and utterly unable to cope with it.

These gentry are then suddenly swept with horror, de-spair, remorse, and other emotions that they never before displayed. They attribute the unfortunate fate of their wives to mysterious prowlers, phantom attackers, guns that went off accidentally (sometimes twice), stoves that shouldn't have been left burning, giddy spells while driving along cliffs, sleeping pills taken during despondency, and similar womanly mistakes.

Of course there are times when the victim simply disap-pears, so what then? That is when ingenuity really comes to the fore. One man develops a quirk of dumping truckload after truckload of gravel upon an ever-growing pile until people wonder why anyone should be hoarding so much gravel, so they dig to the bottom and find—you guessed it!

Others have been swayed by the urge to start furnace fires in midsummer, forgetting that a smoking chimney will stand out like a beacon against the sultry sky. When the police make inquiries—as they so often do—the lonesome husband usually has some plausible answer, such as saying that his wife was away so long, he thought he ought to clear the moths out of the place before she came back. But alibis never seem to account for the charred remains that the police find when they poke about the dead coals.

Some may have gotten away with it, like the man whose wife walked out of taproom after taproom, always proclaiming loudly, "This time I'm going for good!" One wintry night, she really went for good, but not for long. Come springtime, the ice went out from a local pond, and her body bobbed serenely to the surface, along with a load of iron weights that had proven too few to guarantee a permanent submergence. But her husband denied everything beyond identifying the body, which left him free to marry another woman whom he had met in the meantime and who was standing hopefully by.

That is one sweep of the pendulum. Let us follow its swing to the opposite extreme. And here, surprisingly, we find the strange case of a grief-stricken husband so distressed by the doubts of others that he seeks solace from the world beyond.

The Ghost
from the Grave

WALTER B. GIBSON

JOHN Astor Harrison Blake McCormick had a line of talk as impressive as his string of names. He particularly impressed Mrs. Ida Kimball Matheson as they dined at the Scenic Café in Seattle, Washington, with Mrs. Anna Dumas, the mutual friend who had introduced them. The Matheson lady listened in rapt amazement to McCormick's adventures during the Klondike gold rush of a dozen years before, when he had fought his way back over the White Pass from Dawson, carrying six thousand dollars in gold in his money belt.

"Nobody ever had adventures like that in White Cloud, Michigan," said Mrs. Dumas. "Did they, Jennie?" Then, as Mrs. Matheson shook her head, Mrs. Dumas turned to McCormick and explained: "Ida never did like her name, so we called her Jennie. She and I were school chums, back in White Cloud. This is her first visit to Seattle."

McCormick cocked his head and gave Jennie an apprais-
ing survey through his gold-rimmed glasses. He already
knew that this slightly plump and rather attractive lady from
White Cloud was a widow whose only son was dead. He was
also sure that Jennie had some money from her former marriage. Now, as Jennie blushed at the sudden gleam in Mc-
Cormick's eyes, he returned a bland smile that disarmed
her.

"It's been a pleasure meeting you, Mrs. Matheson—or
may I call you Jennie?"

Jennie's nod accompanied her blush. Her friend Anna
promptly stated, in approval: "Mr. McCormick is in the loan
business, Jennie. He's pretty busy, but I'm sure he can find
time to show you around. Could you, John?"

John McCormick not only could, but did. He and Jennie
took trips to Bremerton, Everett, and Tacoma. Amid new
tales of adventure, McCormick asked Jennie to tell him
some more about herself. All she could say was that her father, William Kimball, had been a hard-working farmer
with half a dozen daughters to raise. Jennie had been married off in her early teens to "Mr. Matheson" as she termed
her late husband, in a listless, impersonal tone.

Also a farmer, Mr. Matheson had gone into the saloon
business, which made more work and longer hours for Jennie. But Mr. Matheson hadn't been idle either. When he
died, he had left his widow property in excess of $60,000,
which included some choice real estate in Grand Rapids,
Michigan.

Something more than a beautiful friendship had developed between McCormick and Jennie when the Seattle loan
shark saw the White Cloud widow off to Michigan, from the
Northern Pacific depot. Following that, McCormick pinned
his future on a direct-mail campaign. His letters, beginning
"Dear Jennie" caused the White Cloud mail carrier to beat
a path through snow and ice to the homestead where Jennie
lived with her parents, Mr. and Mrs. William Kimball. In
turn, Jennie coined a nickname for her Gay Blade in Seat-

tle. She addressed McCormick as "Dear Artle" without spec-
ifying what whimsy had inspired such a handle.

While McCormick's correspondence thrived, his loan
business fell off. About a year after his meeting with Jennie
Matheson, John McCormick decided to pull up stakes and
head east. To Anna Dumas, McCormick confided that he
planned to marry her old school chum.

"I knew it that first night!" enthused Mrs. Dumas. "I just
knew you would fall in love with Jennie."

"For sixty thousand simoleons," returned McCormick, in
an off-guard mood, "I could fall in love with anybody.
That's ten times what I brought back from Yukon, and living in White Cloud can't be tougher than coming over the
White Pass."

"You can't mean it!" exclaimed Mrs. Dumas in sheer
horror. "You can't be marrying Jennie just for her money."

"Why not?" retorted McCormick with a cryptic smile and
a cocky eye-glint. "I've got to collect for the time I spent
writing all those letters, don't I?"

That was the sort of statement that might some day be
used against John McCormick. For the moment, Anna
Dumas could only mutter: "There's many a true word
spoken in jest." With that, she crawled into her shell like a
Dungeness crab, deciding that McCormick could go his own
rakish way, which he did. The old Klondike prospector beat
his way over the Rockies by Pullman to Minneapolis, where
Jennie, eager to greet her east-bound Romeo, arrived to
meet him.

McCormick blew the cash left over from his train fare on
a grand dinner in a swank restaurant, and slipped a handsome tip to the orchestra to play the current song hit "Rings
on My Fingers" in honor of the bride-to-be. He then agreed
to spend a week in White Cloud, getting acquainted with
Jennie's folks.

The result ran true to form. Pa Kimball was immediately
suspicious of the smooth character who had conquered the
Klondike single-handed and still bragged about his belt-load

of gold. But Ma Kimball accepted McCormick at face value, which included his pink cheeks, youthful smile, and birdlike gaze. When McCormick failed to receive some overdue remittances from Seattle, he borrowed a few hundred dollars from Jennie and took her to Detroit, where they were married on June 4, 1914. As Mr. and Mrs. Astor H. McCormick, a name which gave distinction and offered good business prospects, they went to Grand Rapids.

There, Astor H. decided to open a loan office, using the $6,000 which presumably he had never spent. He suggested that Jennie put up an equal sum. Once she agreed, McCormick discovered that his Seattle interests were not yet liquidated, so Jennie had to kitty in with the whole $12,000. The cash was put in a joint account, but only McCormick drew upon it, as Jennie soon learned.

Within a few months, Jennie began questioning her husband's disbursements. The result was a series of quarrels which drove Jennie into a hysterical mood. Neighbors who heard shrieks from the McCormick apartment by night, began to sympathize with Jennie by day. When McCormick stayed out nights, rather than stir up Jennie's nerves, she suspected that other ladies in Grand Rapids might be catching the glint of her husband's roguish eyes. Jennie became the victim of what the neighbors classed as a "persecution complex," and opinion promptly swung to McCormick's side.

Jennie then hired a private detective named E. J. Nichols, who called at the loan office under an assumed name and let slip that he wanted money for a little fun his wife wasn't to know about. That made McCormick and Nichols hail fellows at their first meeting. A few days later, they took a train from the Union Station on the Père Marquette Railway and went to Detroit to see a ball game. McCormick was actually a baseball fan and anxious to watch the great Ty Cobb, then at his peak. But when McCormick tossed away $200 betting on the fourth-place Tigers, Nichols found out where some of Jennie's money was going.

E. J. learned more that night, when McCormick took him

on the rounds of the Detroit dives and fleshpots. Back in Grand Rapids, Nichols put in a fast report to Jennie Mc-Cormick, before the joint bank account ran out. Jennie promptly made out two checks: One to E. J. Nichols for investigation rendered: the other to an attorney named Arthur F. Shaw as a retainer. Sensing that the game was up, McCormick grabbed the remaining money, filed suit for divorce on grounds of mental cruelty, and headed for Seattle.

Attorney Shaw notified the Seattle authorities and Mc-Cormick was arrested. Jennie started West with her attorney to recover the money, but on the way she became softhearted and wired ahead for her husband to be released. McCormick was not in Seattle when Jennie arrived there. Investigation proved that he had been married before in Kansas, and that McCormick's famed trip to the Klondike had been for the purpose of abandoning his five children. He'd managed, however, to keep this checkered past a secret, particularly from people like Anna Dumas.

Hardly had Jennie McCormick returned to Grand Rapids, before who showed up but the missing Astor H., ready to consider a reconciliation. The money was gone, but Jennie forgave her wayward husband. She believed him when he promised to be true to her alone. Her full control of the exchecquer left him no other choice. Also, Jennie was a lot softer than the Klondike, so it wasn't surprising that McCormick had returned to work his present claim.

The McCormicks took a second honeymoon and were basking pleasantly in Charleston, South Carolina, when word came that Jennie's mother was ill. The Kimballs had moved to Ladysmith, Wisconsin, to be with another married daughter, Ruey Hewitt, whose husband, James, was in the meat business. So the McCormicks hurried to Ladysmith and all of Jennie's misgivings faded when John Astor H. said he liked the town and wanted to settle there.

To him, Ladysmith had something of that old Yukon spell, so he said. Situated at the foot of Flambeau Falls, after which it had originally been named, the town was successively called Warner, Corbett, and finally Ladysmith, in honor of a Mrs. E. D. Smith, whose husband had induced the Manasha Wooden Ware Company to open a branch there. Trappers and lumbermen still came into town and meanwhile Ladysmith had become an important railroad junction. It was the county seat of Rusk County, but had a population of only a few thousand, which offered a chance to "grow with the town," as McCormick put it. His idea was to open a grocery store, so Jennie bought a building on Worden Avenue and a bungalow-type house a few blocks away. By the time winter set in, McCormick was a storekeeper by day and a homebody by night.

In February, 1915, Jennie began to suffer attacks of indigestion. Far from griping at his wife's ill-health, McCormick played the contrite husband to perfection. He cooked Jennie's meals, did her housework for her, and still put in his full hours at the store, where he had hired a neighbor, Frank Cowin, as clerk.

The McCormicks had no telephone, so between times, John would go over to Ned Hand's livery stable, where Doc Enger, the local veterinarian, had an upstairs office. Using Enger's phone, McCormick frequently called Dr. L. M. Lundmark, the physician who was treating Jennie's mysterious malady, its symptoms running the gamut of extreme headaches, severe abdominal pains, and a chronic irritability which Dr. Landmark diagnosed as "neurasthenia." Among the medicines which he prescribed was lactate pepsis, with one-sixtieth grain of strychnine, to be taken in capsule form.

Despite McCormick's care and the choice foods which he brought home and prepared for Jennie's meals, the patient had lost forty pounds by mid-July. This didn't please Mrs. Hewitt, nor another sister, Mrs. Kinchella, who had come on from California for a visit. They insisted that Jennie have a trained nurse and after McCormick pleaded evasively about "expense" and insisted that he would willingly continue his "self-sacrifice," the sisters finally won their point by threatening to act as volunteers. A nurse, Laura Holter, was brought from Minneapolis and she took over McCormick's chores, cooking included.

Jennie McCormick promptly began to get better. Within a week, her stomach pains were gone and she was able to eat and retain solid food, something she hadn't managed with John's home cooking, tasty though it had been.

On July 27, McCormick had a heart-to-heart chat with his wife, while Miss Holter was absent. The discussion turned to Jennie's will.

"Your parents are wonderful folks, Jennie," complimented McCormick. "I'm sure you want them to be happy in their old age. That's why you're leaving all your money to them, isn't it?"

Jennie nodded in reply.

"Maybe you ought to turn over all your money to them now," suggested McCormick, "and let them take care of you instead."

"How ridiculous!" Jennie exclaimed. "They wouldn't know how to handle money. Why, they'd be helpless!"

"You mean they *will be* helpless," corrected McCormick gently, "if anything should happen to you, dear Jennie. Then they will have the money, but no one to look out for them."

As he stressed the term, "Dear Jennie," McCormick saw tears well in his wife's eyes.

"They say you can't teach an old dog new tricks," he said, "but you taught me to jump through the hoop, Jennie, and I like it. You could never change Pa Kimball, though. Suppose Ma should drop off suddenly, like we were afraid she might, last fall. Pa would be lost, because he's too old. Of course Ruey's husband is doing better; he might handle things better—"

"No better than you can!" interrupted Jennie, with a flash of her old indignation. "You're proven yourself a good manager, Artle. I'll fix it so everybody will know it—if the time should come!"

Jennie's way of "fixing" it was to make out a new will, naming husband John as the sole heir to her estate which still totalled $40,000. The new will was all signed and put away when Laura Holter returned.

Jennie's recovery now became quite rapid, and she insisted to Miss Holter that "Artle" was responsible. Some credit was due Miss Holter, for her close watch on Jennie's diet. But McCormick was so solicitous toward his wife's welfare that the claim seemed sound. On Monday, August 9, McCormick came home for midday dinner and found Jennie seated on the front porch. She had been writing notes on a pad of paper which now lay beside her, while Miss Holter was in the kitchen frying a batch of pan fish.

Husband and wife were chatting pleasantly, when the nurse arrived with a pail, intending to fetch water from a neighbor's pump. McCormick obligingly took over the task, so that Miss Holter could assist Jennie to an outhouse behind the bungalow, the Chick Sale style of architecture being still the vogue in Ladysmith. When they returned to the house through the kitchen door, the pail of water was beside the stove where the fish were sizzling in their pan. Miss Holter helped Jennie into the combination dining and living room, and their arrival roused McCormick, who was resisting the heat by reclining, shirt-sleeved, on the couch.

On the table was a tray in which Miss Holter had placed two large capsules of the sort prescribed by Doctor Lundmark. The nurse brought a glass of water, so that Jennie could swallow the capsules, which were taken before meals. The fish dinner followed and McCormick topped the meal with a cigar, which he considerately smoked on the front porch, rather than upset Jennie's delicate stomach with the fumes.

Sudden shrieks brought McCormick rushing indoors. Jennie was shrieking: "I'm burning up! I'm burning up inside!" Miss Holter was trying to hold Jennie as she writhed, but it took McCormick's added strength to get her to the couch. There, Jennie's screams were dwindling to moans, when the nurse brought a glass of whisky. At sight of it, Jennie shrieked anew: "No, no! It will burn me—it will burn me. Take it away—let me die!"

A telephone had recently been installed in the McCormick homestead. Grimly gesturing to it, Miss Holter told McCormick: "You'd better phone Dr. Lundmark, and hurry!" McCormick did that, while the nurse was getting a camphor preparation, with which she rubbed Jennie's head. Except for an occasional piercing shriek, Jennie was now moaning constantly, the burden of her theme being: "I'm going to die—die—die—"

McCormick heard Dr. Lundmark drive up and rushed out to the front porch to beckon the physician into the house. Two neighbors, Mrs. Martin Cowin and Mrs. Margaret Kurz, had heard the intermittent screams and were peering, half-troubled, half-curious, from their homes. A workman on the street watched Dr. Lundmark stride hastily into the McCormick house. McCormick himself was too distraught to notice these people. But from that moment on, they kept eyeing the house, wondering what might happen next.

Results were rapid. Jennie's moans subsided while McCormick was telephoning members of her family. Dr. Lundmark pronounced the woman dead; then, puzzled by the circumstances, he turned to Miss Holter and inquired as to the symptoms that caused the sudden demise. Anybody but a trained nurse might have garbled the answer, but Miss Holter was as straight to the point as a hospital report. She laid the cause to the capsules, since they were the only thing that Jennie had taken internally, other than the fish dinner and its fixings, which McCormick and Miss Holter both had eaten.

"Impossible!" returned Dr. Lundmark with an emphatic head-shake. "The strychnine content was too slight. We'd better look around for something else that she might have taken independently."

McCormick was the first person to look around; in fact,

he'd started already. Dr. Lundmark saw McCormick start out through the kitchen, and suddenly the physician decided to follow him. The trail led to the outhouse and there, McCormick met Lundmark as he arrived. Noting the physician's inquiring glance, McCormick shrugged and said: "I was just wondering about poor Jennie poisoning herself. You know, she'd kind of halfway threatened to do it, but I didn't take her seriously. Right now, I thought I had a hunch, but I guess I was wrong. I'd better get back to the house to meet the family."

Abruptly, McCormick left the rear premises, but Dr. Lundmark remained there. On a hunch of his own, the physician began a diligent probe with suitable garden implements and from the depths, he excavated a small bottle which bore a label from White Cloud, Michigan. This bottle contained crystals which were later identified as a form of strychnine. The visits of both McCormick and Lundmark to the preserves out back were witnessed by the curious neighbors and the man working in the street. But only Laura Holton and Ruey Hewitt—first of Jennie's relatives to arrive— were present in the bungalow when Dr. Lundmark showed his find to McCormick.

"It's just as I thought. I suspected that Jennie might have taken something with her," said McCormick, with a nod. "She was acting very moody on the porch, but she covered it up when Miss Holter came out. I'm sorry you found that bottle, though. It's kind of too bad, Doc, that people will think that poor Jennie did away with herself."

Some people didn't think that way and one was Ruey Hewitt. She was quite convinced that McCormick himself had administered the fatal dosage. Dr. Lundmark preferred to reserve decision until the state chemist had tested the crystals in the White Cloud bottle and performed an autopsy on Jennie's body. Meanwhile, McCormick was left alone with his grief, and Miss Holter.

"We won't be needing Jennie's medicine any more," said McCormick sadly. "You'd better throw out those capsules."

"It's the customary thing," agreed the nurse, "except that Dr. Lundmark might want them."

"If he did, he'd have said so," returned McCormick. "He messed into about everything else while he was here."

So the capsules were thrown out, an unfortunate oversight in the light of the state chemist's report. The autopsy showed that Jennie McCormick had absorbed one and one-half grains of strychnine, equivalent to the amount in ninety of the capsules that Harry Speidel, a Ladysmith pharmacist, had made up at Dr. Lundmark's prescription. Also, the crystals in the White Cloud medicine bottle proved to be a form of strychnine sulphate.

As a result, an inquest held by Coroner O. B. Ellingboe of Rusk County brought the verdict that Jennie McCormick had come to her death by strychnine poisoning delivered by some person or persons unknown. It didn't name McCormick; in fact, the verdict almost suggested his innocence. Perhaps he'd really tried to cover his wife's suicide, by disposing of the bottle.

Then McCormick blithely produced the will in which "Dear Jennie" left him her full fortune. At that, Pa Kimball stormed that his attorneys would not only contest the will, but would prove that a man "couldn't get away with murder." The attorneys were building up a case, but it was the sort that would bog down when it met a head-on test. For up to that point, no one could offer direct proof or tangible evidence that John A. H. B. McCormick had committed a single criminal act toward his wife's death or the appropriation of her wealth.

However, Pa Kimball's emphatic soundoff and the reverberations it stirred from Jennie's sisters, accomplished one result. It made McCormick brood, which in turn disturbed his sleep. He was an unhappy man toward the end of September, muttering to sympathetic customers that "if only Jennie had realized how her family would act, she would have done something to prevent it." The notion became an obsession with McCormick. Soon he was saying: "Jennie *must* have known what they'd do to me!"

Then, in ardent, prayerful whisper, McCormick would add: "I know my dear Jennie will find some way to tell us." He tried this number on the Ladysmith ladies who patronized his Worden Avenue store and found that it impressed them. So on the night of Thursday, September 23, the grieving husband had a dream. It couldn't have occurred on a better night, because the Ladysmith weekly newspaper, the *News,* was published on Fridays and McCormick was able to catch that week's edition by getting down to the office when it opened.

"I saw Jennie last night, in a dream," McCormick told the attentive editor. "She was angry, the way her family has acted. She asked if I remembered that she'd been writing on a tablet, the day she died. When I said yes, she told me that I'd find a note on the tablet, explaining everything. When I asked where the tablet was, she beckoned me to the extension table in the living room. We were trying to draw it open, when I woke up."

The editor frowned, a trifle puzzled. This wasn't stop-press news. But McCormick had more to tell him.

"That was our dinner table," McCormick explained. "We'd open it up and put in leaves, when any of Jennie's folks came for dinner. It was a long while since we'd opened up that table. I guess poor Jennie would not have understood that her family wouldn't come to see me again. After I woke up, I looked at the table and I noticed it hadn't been pushed tight shut. There was just a little crack, like somebody had tried to close it alone. So I opened the extension and on the cross-piece I found this!"

Triumphantly, McCormick produced the very pad that he had mentioned, but again the editor of the *News* was disappointed. He saw that the pad was blank and said so.

"Yes, it looks blank," McCormick agreed. "So probably Jennie changed her mind and tore up the note that she had written. But if you look close, you'll see the impression of what Jennie wrote. It goes through several pages, so it's pretty readable."

It was readable enough for the *News* to print it in that day's edition. There was only one word that puzzled the editor. He asked: "Who is Artle?"

"Artle," replied McCormick as the clincher, "is myself. You know, my wife's real name was Ida, but she called herself Jennie. She thought it was fun making up names for people and mine was Artle. We'd been laughing about it, those few days Jennie was feeling better. Miss Holton will remember."

The note, as it appeared in the *News,* ran approximately as follows, allowing for a few discrepancies in spelling, due to the difficulty of deciphering the impression:

Dear Artle
I will son be gone. I cant stand this pain. Dont wory you will be better off. Good-by Dear

> *Jennie*

I cant get well God will forgive me

Besides running the suicide note, the *News* went all out for "Dear Artle" in an editorial stating that an innocent man, accused of a fiendish crime, was entitled to be set right before the community. Most of Ladysmith agreed, but a skeptical minority classed the "dream note" as inconclusive, on the assumption that Jennie had destroyed the original and therefore might not have gone through with her suicide.

Comparisons with Jennie's letters proved that the impressions were in her handwriting; on that, all were agreed. A further convincer was needed as to her suicide and it was furnished a few months later. McCormick decided to rent the residence that had become a "dream house" in the literal sense, but as the day approached, he confided in his clerk, Frank Cowin, that a certain regret had gripped him.

"I just can't bear to watch that furniture go out," McCormick told Frank. "Jennie chose most of it herself, like she did the house. It all seems like a part of her."

"Maybe I could help," the clerk suggested. "One of us has got to be here in the store. I can go over to your house."

"A good idea," agreed McCormick. "I don't want to be around if any of Jennie's relatives show up. By the way, the carpets are going out, too. So make sure that the moving men roll them properly."

Before closing time, Frank Cowin came dashing into the store waving a small sheet of paper and shouting: "Lookit, boss! Look what I found under the carpet in the bedroom. It squares you, alrighty!"

Frank's find was an actual note in Jennie's handwriting and it contained the significant statement: "I am to blame for all this. I took it all alone." Interpreting the first sentence to mean Jennie's suicide; the second a reference to the poison, this document—like the writing pad—was an exoneration for McCormick. The "carpet note" was also turned over to the authorities.

During the next year, McCormick became more and more firmly established as a Ladysmith merchant. On August 24, 1916, he was named executor of his wife's will. He left Frank Cowin to run the store and took an extended trip to Seattle, spending the estate's money lavishly. All the while, Pa Kimball fumed, but his daughter Ruey was more practical. Bit by bit, she was gathering material that might some day surprise the town of Ladysmith even more than the messages which McCormick had reclaimed from the dead hand of his poor Jennie.

Ruey Hewitt had found one staunch ally in Arthur F. Shaw, the Grand Rapids attorney who still regarded McCormick as a two-timing fortune hunter, and could produce some Seattle witnesses to prove it, including Jennie's old friend, Mrs. Anna Dumas. Added to that were the suspicions of the Grand Rapids neighbors and the testimony of detective Nichols, all indicating an early plot on McCormick's part, to acquire Jennie's fortune.

When Ruey checked the bottle from the old home town of White Cloud, she found it had originally contained nothing more deadly than cough syrup. She promptly gave that her own interpretation.

"It proves that Jennie didn't buy the strychnine crystals," Ruey told Shaw. "McCormick found that bottle and used it just to pin the guilt on Jennie."

"But where did he get the stuff?" queried Shaw. "Your father's attorneys have checked, and they say he didn't buy it in Ladysmith."

"He got it somehow," Ruey asserted. "Whether he begged, borrowed or stole—"

A sudden thought struck Ruey Hewitt, but she reserved it until her return to Ladysmith, where she promptly called on Dr. Lundmark. The physician shook his head when Ruey suggested that they start tracking down missing strychnine.

"If we only had those capsules," said Dr. Lundmark. "If we'd found them all loaded with strychnine sulphate, there would be some evidence of suicide, since your sister might have fixed them beforehand, without Miss Holter knowing it. But if they'd proven to be exactly what I prescribed, then it would point to McCormick's guilt. He alone would have had a chance to load them after Miss Holter had placed them on the dish."

"That's when he did it," argued Ruey, "and we can still prove it. All we have to show is how and where he got the poison."

"He doesn't handle it at his grocery store," declared Lundmark, with a tired smile, "and he certainly couldn't have stolen any from the drugstore. Besides, he never went anywhere except home. McCormick really was a homebody, you know."

"Not until he came to Ladysmith," retorted Ruey, "but I've got to admit that he was always there, the last month or so. I can hear his voice now, answering the phone, when I'd call to talk to Jennie."

"I called frequently, too," said Lundmark. "That was one reason he put the phone in, so I could keep close touch."

A sudden idea dawned on Ruey Hewitt.

"Tell me," she exclaimed, "do veterinarians ever give strychnine to horses?"

"Of course," replied Lundmark. "Large doses of it. They always keep such compounds in their office."

"And that's where McCormick called you from, a vet's office, before he put in his own phone. We're going to see Doc Enger, over Hand's livery stable!"

See Dr. Enger, they did. When he heard what they had in mind, the veterinary grimly pulled open a desk drawer, just below the phone that McCormick had so often used. There was the box of strychnine sulphate that Enger kept as an occasional horse remedy. There was still no proof that McCormick had tapped the supply, but that didn't bother Ruey.

"One thing is certain," Ruey said emphatically, "Jennie didn't take any of the stuff. She was never up in this office, not even once."

That find gave strength to the web of circumstance that the Kimball attorneys, largely through Ruey's efforts, had woven about McCormick. In April, 1917, the town of Ladysmith was startled by the charges that accompanied William Kimball's action to appeal the last will and testament of his daughter. It was charged that McCormick had married Jennie with the fraudulent intent of acquiring her property. It accused him of giving her the fatal dose of poison. It questioned the authenticity of the alleged notes which McCormick claimed had been written by Jennie before her death.

Ladysmith residents were skeptical, even contemptuous of Ruey Hewitt as a detective. Now, as affidavits and witnesses passed in parade, the skeptics sat in awe and the pink faded from McCormick's boyish cheeks. Judge James Wickam, of the Rusk County Circuit Court, found the mass of evidence so damaging that he did more than set aside the will. The jurist remitted the case to the county court and made a finding that charged McCormick with the murder of his wife. On the day when Judge Wickam gave his opinion,

April 28, 1917, John McCormick was arrested by Sheriff W. M. Dodson and held for further trial.

The big case opened on October 5, before Judge W. B. Quinlan. By then, McCormick had regained his sangfroid and was confident that his attorneys, L. E. Smith and Glenn Williams, would shatter the circumstantial evidence against him. District Attorney O. J. Falge was aided by former Attorney General L. M. Sturdevant, of Eau Claire, and the state's case closely followed the pattern set by the Kimball attorneys.

Beginning with an affidavit from Mrs. Anna Dumas, stating that McCormick had avowed he was marrying Jennie for her money, Falge described McCormick's defalcation of his wife's funds in Grand Rapids, followed by the reconciliation which had set him up in business, and finally enabled McCormick to talk his wife into making out a new will. McCormick smiled at this, regarding it as largely hearsay.

District Attorney Falge introduced Ruey Hewitt's well-supported claim that McCormick could have stolen the strychnine sulphate from Enger's office. Next, the D. A. reviewed the evidence according to Judge Wickam's finding, which in substance ran as follows:

Jennie McCormick, far from being in a suicidal mood, had been cheerful on the fatal day. Only in capsule form could the poison have been taken without some show of facial expression and Jennie had given no such display. There had been ample opportunity, however, for John McCormick to fill the capsules with strychnine and later dispose of the bottle in the outhouse where Dr. Lundmark had found it. According to three witnesses, McCormick had been seen going to the outhouse at a time which Judge Wickam regarded as "rather significant."

Judge Wickam had also raised a question as to the authenticity of the notes and the ways in which they had been found. It would have been impossible, he claimed, for Jennie to have taken poison and then hidden the notes in the places where they had been found. Why had she destroyed the original of the "dream note" and left only the impression? The jurist's answer was that the imprint strongly suggested deception. He was dubious too, about the "carpet note."

While the district attorney gave that summary, McCormick studied the jury with quick glances. He retained his smile, confident that he would never be convicted without much stronger proof as to the "deception" mentioned in Judge Wickham's opinion. The defense attorneys agreed with their client. They argued that the finding of the notes was actually in McCormick's favor: that he should be acquitted, not convicted, on the very thing that the prosecution valued above all else: circumstantial evidence.

To shatter Judge Wickam's criticism of the notes, the defense introduced two handwriting experts from St. Paul, Minnesota. These experts studied the pad impression and the fragmentary note, compared them with accepted samples of Jennie's handwriting and decided that they had actually been written by the dead woman. Such expert testimony, should it stand, could well offset any inconsistency on Jennie's part in writing them, as put forth by Judge Wickam.

Assisting the defense attorneys was a lawyer from Milwaukee named Albert K. Stebbins, who had come to Ladysmith on behalf of a casualty company which had bonded McCormick as executor of his wife's estate. As the defense counsel were congratulating their client on having his case as good as won, Stebbins began to look troubled. The state was calling its own expert witness, a man whom Stebbins recognized.

"It's John R. Tyrell," Stebbins told the others. "He examines documents for the Northwestern Mutual Life, in Milwaukee."

"All the better," put in McCormick. "We have two handwriting experts on our side already. This Tyrell makes three."

"He's more than a handwriting expert," returned Stebbins. "Why, he's been in the business twenty years or more. He's the fellow who went to New York to testify at the famous Molineux trial."

McCormick's bland face went ashen.

"Wasn't that a poison case?" he asked.

"Yes," replied Stebbins, "but Tyrell's job is mostly to uncover forgeries by persons faking medical examinations. I guess he won't matter. It's just a concidence that he handled a poison case before—"

Attorney Stebbins cut himself short as he looked at McCormick. Right then, Stebbins wished that neither he nor Tyrell had ever left Milwaukee. If ever a smug countenance had frozen in utter guilt, it was that of John McCormick. The biggest team of horses from Hand's Stable couldn't have dragged him back on the witness stand. But that wasn't going to be necessary. Tyrell monopolized what remained of the trial.

First, the document expert introduced a simple, but singular machine. It was a small funnel, rigged with wires, so that it balanced on a pencil point that extended straight down from its spout. Into this funnel, Tyrell dropped bits of gunshot, all of which had been accurately weighed and attested. With the wires, he ran the funnel back and forth across a pad of paper, the pencil point drawing a line with each trip.

Gradually the pencil strokes became stronger until they exactly matched the samples of Jennie's handwriting, as to darkness and thickness. At that point, which Tyrell classed as Jennie's "normal hand," the allotment of shot varied from six ounces to eight and three-eighths. When Tyrell removed the top sheet of the pad and showed the one beneath, the impression thereon was very slight. There was none on the third sheet of the pad.

While McCormick fidgeted, Tyrell went to work on an impression basis. To force an indentation to appear half a dozen sheets deep, as with the pad McCormick had "discovered" in his living room, Tyrell had to use nearly fifty-eight ounces of shot. Such pressure would never have been exerted by Jennie McCormick; in fact, it was doubtful if she could have applied it in her weakened state. Also, though matching Jennie's writing, the impressions lacked what Tyrell termed "her normal flow." The St. Paul experts agreed, once this point was raised.

Having shattered the "dream note," Tyrell went to work on Exhibit B, the note from under the living room carpet. He produced a highly magnified photograph with which the jurors could compare the "carpet note" under a powerful microscope.

"My tests with the impressions," Tyrell stated, "led to an immediate suspicion of this second note. It was faked well enough to pass ordinary muster, but under the test I gave it, the alterations are apparent."

The "carpet note" had been a portion of one of Jennie's "Artle letters" which McCormick had picked as suiting his requirements. But even after clipping it from the sheet, he had been forced to make changes. Its two most vital statements originally read:

"I am not to blame for anything. I told you all about it."

McCormick had worked on these chiding remarks, actually in Jennie's hand, first erasing the words "not," "you" and "it." He then altered "anything" to "all this" "told" to "took," "about" to "alone." He inserted a new "it" before the word "all" and the result was:

"I am to blame for all this. I took it all alone."

The jury was completely won by the convincing testimony of John F. Tyrell. The document expert was a middle-aged man, well described as a "gentleman of the old school" with a manner both authoritative and kindly, utterly dispassionate, as to the case on trial. He might have been exposing a child's prank, rather than a murderer's machinations.

The trial lasted sixteen days, but the jury was only out one hour. They brought in a verdict of guilty on the charge of first degree murder. McCormick, still protesting his innocence, was sentenced to life imprisonment in the Wisconsin

State Prison at Waupun. Until Tyrell's evidence, the jury—almost to a man—had been ready to believe that claim of innocence. McCormick's mistake had been to spoil what would have amounted to a perfect crime. He'd faked the notes to break a chain of circumstance that was actually too loose to incriminate him until he showed himself a fraud.

Under Wisconsin law, John McCormick shared in the estate of his dead wife Jennie and he used his portion of her fortune to fight for a new trial. It was granted and in January, 1924, more than six years after McCormick's original conviction, the trial was held at Chippewa Falls.

The judge and prosecutor were the same. So was the evidence and the trial again took sixteen days. To complete the train of coincidence, John McCormick was again convicted. He returned to his jail cell broken and morose. Two years later, he died there.

The She-Devil of Nagyrev

WHEN Johann Strauss immortalized the Blue Danube in his great waltz, he pictured its waters dancing on beyond gay Vienna, through rugged mountain passes, past picturesque towns and villages, beneath ancient walls of ruined castles, until it was welcomed by the striking skyline of exotic Budapest, the capital of Hungary.

Even Karl Baedeker and his successors, who compiled exacting guidebooks during that same period, agree that some stretches of the river capture the nuance of the waltz. But below Budapest the picture changes. There, Baedeker tells us, the river flows through the monotonous and dreary Hungarian plain. Passengers who made the 24-hour trip down to the Serbian border by steamboat in the early 1900's generally agreed that Baedeker was right and Strauss was wrong.

They also agreed that there was only one thing worse than a trip downriver from Budapest to Belgrade—a trip up the Danube from Belgrade to Budapest. According to the early Baedeker, fares were cheaper upstream, whether you bought a round trip or just a one-way ticket. Things were really that bad.

There was just one escape from that return trip up the Danube. A few hours upstream from Belgrade, you came to the mouth of the Tisza River, the Danube's principal tributary. There, you could switch to another steamer that beat its way up to Szegedin, the only big town on the Tisza. Unhappily, it was even slower going up the Tisza, and besides, it got you nowhere. Compared to the Danube, the towns were more insignificant, the scenery more monotonous and the banks more thinly populated. About the only thing to do was drop off somewhere and make the best of it.

That's what Susi Olah did, when she went up the Tisza. She simply picked an insignificant town and relieved the monotony by thinning the population still further. She took her time about the slaughter. In fact, she made it a life's work. It could be that we are misjudging Susi. Perhaps she merely wanted to see the Danube where it was really beautiful, up above Budapest. Maybe she just happened to take the wrong boat.

The She-Devil
of Nagyrev

AVERY HALE

WHEN, in the year of 1909, a square-faced, black-eyed woman of forty by the name of Susi Olah appeared in the Hungarian village of Nagyrev, there to minister to the populace as a midwife and nurse, only Providence could have foreseen the baleful forces that were about to be set in motion. Nagyrev, and its sister village of Tiszakurt, which connected with it by a creaky wooden bridge across the narrow Tisza River, was less than one hundred miles, but more than one hundred years, from Budapest, Hungary's sophisticated capital. Lying in the great grape-growing and wine-making region of Tiszazug, Nagyrev was a settlement of some fifteen hundred peasants who picked the grapes and then stomped on them and who walked with bare feet through earthen streets that found their way, without particular design, among huts of whitewashed plaster with thatched

189

roofs. There was no gas or electricity in either of the villages, and no plumbing or telephones, no doctor or priest. There was a store or two, and a village inn, with a bar, where the menfolk got drunk; here was a simple settlement, populated by simple, backward people. Simple, that is, until Susi Olah, the nurse and midwife, came along.

Aunt Susi, as the newcomer to the village was presently to be called, was a woman of impressive stature and, apparently, of impressive though clouded background. She stood almost six feet, weighed about two hundred pounds and was of belligerent mien; her eyes looked like a couple of black currants in an uncooked suet pudding, and she had a large hooked nose which, considered with her other attributes, somehow created the impression that her natural mode of transportation should have been a broom—an impression which, in the light of subsequent events, had a certain validity. Aunt Susi was supposed to have functioned in Budapest as a midwife and nurse, and she mentioned to the villagers that she was a widow. Nobody ever took the trouble to find out whether Olah had been her maiden name or the name of her departed husband; this was principally because Aunt Susi's activities in Nagyrev, over a period of twenty years, were eventually to become so fascinating to everyone who heard about them that what she had been and what she had done before putting in an appearance in the wine region became anti-climactic.

Most of the vineyards in the region were owned by nonresident aristocrats whose treatment of the peasants who worked their land would probably have induced apoplexy in a British or American labor leader. The peasants in Nagyrev and Tiszakurt were under-nourished, poorly clothed and housed, and half-frozen in the winter months. The arrival of an unwanted child in a household often marked the difference between a meager diet and semi-starvation for the entire family; a growing child or a mature person who became incapacitated for work in the fields became a burden; old people were, purely and simply, excess baggage.

Aunt Susi found this financial pinch operating to her professional detriment. There were three other midwife-nurses in the two villages. Aunt Susi soon learned that although there was plenty of work for her to do, especially as a nurse, she could not hope to get any pay, for the simple reason that the villagers were all in hock to her three competitors. This would never do. Never.

One winter's day in 1910, when Aunt Susi had been in the wine region for less than six months, she invited one of her rival practitioners—a Madame Nagy—over for a pot of tea and some homemade pastry. The day was so bitter that Madame Nagy was half stiff from cold when she arrived at the little whitewashed shack that Aunt Susi called home. But Madame Nagy was stiffer yet before another day had dawned; she was full of rigor and mortis. She had, it seemed, become violently ill with cramps and nausea after having left Aunt Susi's house. The coroner, a local character who knew nothing about medicine and who held his post because he was one of the few citizens of the region who could read and write, ascribed Madame Nagy's demise to pneumonia, and Madame Nagy was carried across the wooden bridge to Tiszakurt and tucked away in a burial ground on the edge of a forest outside the village.

One down, two to go. Another of the nurse-midwives, a Madame Szabo, found herself in possession of an invitation to take tea with Aunt Susi. She, like Aunt Susi's previous guest, died within twelve hours of thanking her hostess for a lovely time. The coroner, hearing that Madame Szabo had been alternately doubled up with cramps and straightened out with nausea, had no difficulty in determining the cause of death. Pneumonia, to be sure.

Two down, one to go. The remaining competitor, who was also a Madame Szabo, received an invitation to tea at Aunt Susi's, but gave the disconcerting reply that she didn't *like* tea. This seemed strange. Madame Szabo had been a tea drinker all her adult life. Was it possible that her sudden aversion to the beverage had any connection with

the fact that her two professional colleagues had partaken of
tea during what had subsequently turned out to be the final
repasts of their lives?

Aunt Susi was no woman to let an obstacle stand in her
way. If the second Madame Szabo did not take tea, surely
she took coffee. No, Madame Szabo did not drink coffee,
either. Wine, then? No, Madame Szabo had become, overnight, a teetotaler. Well, surely Madame Szabo ate pastry
and drank mineral water. Madame Szabo did, indeed, but
not Aunt Susi's pastry and mineral water.

Madame Szabo was impossible. She was just the kind of
suspicious, untrusting character who might have gone to the
police, to point out that maybe there was more than coincidence to the fact that two of her professional colleagues had
died after taking tea with Aunt Susi—had there been any
police to go to. The nearest police were away down in Szolnok, an eight-hour trip by steamer down the Tisza River.

Aunt Susi put Madame Szabo out of her thoughts. Apparently. Then one night in April of 1910, somebody, apparently a grateful patient, left a package of homemade
sweets on her doorstep. The sweets were the last things that
ever went down Madame Szabo's throat. Cramps and
nausea. Pneumonia.

Three down, none to go. With her three competitors out
of the way, Aunt Susi had the field to herself. There was
something about her, as she clumped slowly through the village, her arms folded across her ample chest, her little black
eyes rolling from side to side and missing nothing, that
caused the villagers to realize, quite suddenly, that a unique
personage was in their midst. The villagers were superstitious
in the extreme; they subscribed to legends of witches, goblins,
and other supernatural creatures who functioned best in the
dark of the moon—legends that had come down to them
from medieval times. They believed, too, that certain hu-
mans who walked the earth were possessed of supernatural
powers—the evil eye, the black curse, the power of life and
death, especially death. The villagers had never actually laid

eyes on a supernatural human being, but something told them they were looking at one as Aunt Susi would stalk into a sickroom and draw a bead on the patient.

Aunt Susi did nothing to dispel the illusion; in fact, she nurtured it. Another woman put the big question up to Aunt Susi one day: was Aunt Susi possessed of supernatural powers, or was she not? Aunt Susi had a mouth that was too small for her large face, and her mouth grew smaller at the question, smaller in smug satisfaction. Her whole attitude, without the employment of so much as one word of speech, seemed to be: "Why not put me to a test?"

The woman who put the big question to Aunt Susi had a child, a girl of ten who was a cripple. Pastor Franz, of the Calvinist church across the river in Tiszakurt—a gentle, naive man—had often come and prayed for the crippled child and nothing had ever happened. Would Aunt Susi consider coming to the mother's home and looking at the child?

Aunt Susi, after an hour with the crippled girl, told the child's mother she was afraid the child would be dead within a month. Aunt Susi had occult sources of information that forewarned her of impending deaths. The mother was later to say that her emotions were mixed when she received the news. She loved her daughter yet, if the child died, she would be spared passage through life as a cripple; her death would, moreover, lift the burden of having to feed, clothe, and shelter an unproductive member of the household.

Aunt Susi made several visits to the patient. Each time she called, she would reach into the folds of her garments and produce a small bottle. She would pour the contents of this bottle into a glass and instruct the child to drink it. The liquid gave the patient cramps and nausea.

The crippled girl died in agony one month, almost to the day, from the time Aunt Susi had made her dire prediction. Aunt Susi informed the coroner that death had resulted from pneumonia. The huge hook-nosed nurse and midwife took on added stature among the superstitious populace.

Pastor Franz, the minister across the river, heard about Aunt Susi's prediction. Since Pastor Franz was one of the few intelligent men or women in either Nagyrev or Tiszakurt, he couldn't shake off the feeling that Aunt Susi's prediction of the crippled girl's death had been based not on supernatural sources but on more earthly factors.

Pastor Franz had a long talk with the dead girl's mother, which served only to confirm his suspicions that something untoward was in the breezes. Then he called on Aunt Susi. Aunt Susi was openly hostile. Then she melted and suggested that she put on a pot of tea for Pastor Franz. The minister said no thanks, he really must be going. Next morning he took a river steamer to Szolnok and talked to the police who had jurisdiction over the region that embraced Nagyrev and Tiszakurt but who never went near the twin villages.

The police weren't too impressed by the minister's story. But they said they would look into the matter. About a month later, an officer called on Aunt Susi. She brewed him a pot of tea, and then showed him around her kitchen, where she kept bottles of medicines with which she ministered to the sick. The bitter medicine she had given the crippled girl? Aunt Susi grunted. A combination of salts and licorice water, which had made it darkish and bitter. The officer laughed and became confidential. Aunt Susi joined the officer in his laughter.

Word seeped through the village that a policeman had been questioning Aunt Susi about her mysterious powers and that the officer had gone away quite impressed. The fact that even the police, for whom the villagers had a vague respect, had doffed a plumed helmet to Aunt Susi only added to the woman's stature.

The day after the officer called, she dropped in on Pastor Franz. She suggested that the two of them had been involved in a misunderstanding. Pastor Franz, the trusting Christian, agreed. Well, then, why didn't the pastor come over to Aunt Susi's for some tea and some of her special pastry? Why not indeed!

Pastor Franz had never tasted such delicious pastry. Truth to tell, he made something of a glutton of himself. That was why, that night after he went to bed, he blamed only his own uncontrolled appetite when the pastry came back on him. It came back with a bang. The minister was jackknifed with cramps and wracked by vomiting. He had only one desire—to die. He wasn't obliged, but he dragged himself around half dead for several days. He kept reminding himself that one of the seven deadly sins was gluttony, and that he had been a sinner. He was too physically miserable and too repentant over having sinned to become in the least suspicious that Aunt Susi's delectable pastry might have been loaded.

There were, even as Pastor Franz was staggering back to normal after his sin, the births of three unwanted children in Nagyrev. Aunt Susi, officiating at the deliveries, predicted to the parents, for a fee, that the children would not live out the first week. And they didn't, either.

Across the river in Tiszakurt, there dwelled a large family that was burdened by the aged and infirm parents of the woman of the house. This woman approached Aunt Susi and, just to relieve herself of the suspense of knowing how long she and her husband would have to support her parents, inquired of Aunt Susi if she would question her mysterious sources and come up with an answer. Aunt Susi collected a fee and consulted the sources and received intelligence that was either very good or very bad, depending upon one's point of view. Both of the old people would depart the earthly scene before the moon was full, or in about three weeks.

Living not far from Aunt Susi was another man named Szabo. This Szabo, a widower with no children, wasn't exactly intelligent, but he wasn't stupid, either. He thought it was very odd that Aunt Susi's three competitors in the field of midwifery had all died of pneumonia within a short time of Aunt Susi's appearance on the Nagyrev horizon, and he thought it was strange, too, that Aunt Susi could call the shots on impending deaths the way she did. It would have been bad enough that Szabo entertained such thoughts and kept them to himself. But no. *He* had to go down to the village inn, get drunk, and begin talking.

Aunt Susi soon heard about brother Szabo's insinuating mutterings. She made it a point to become acquainted with the gentleman. She had him over for some of that brisk tea and delicious pastry. Szabo was not, all things considered, an unattractive man; that is to say, he owned almost an acre of vineyard all by himself, which placed him among the ten wealthiest residents of the community. Szabo, visiting back and forth with Aunt Susi, came to find that the lady, now that he had gotten to know her, wasn't at all like what he had thought she had been like when he had talked to the boys down at the inn. She was, on the contrary, quite the most attractive female he had ever laid eyes on. In fact, he had hopes of one day making Aunt Susi his wife.

The story of the romance between Aunt Susi and brother Szabo soon became a news item for the village. Aunt Susi's women friends were congratulating her on her upcoming nuptials when Aunt Susi rolled her little black eyes and let them in on a secret. Brother Szabo, as fine a man as he was and as much as Aunt Susi loved him, wasn't long for this world. Brother Szabo was suffering from a mysterious stomach disorder. He couldn't possibly withstand a series of violent attacks that would hit him, poor man, any day now.

After brother Szabo was laid away, Aunt Susi produced a little note by which her fiancé had left her his acre of vineyard. Everybody in the village—well, *practically* everybody —was happy that Aunt Susi had fallen heir to the land. Aunt Susi had been a resident of Nagyrev for two years now and had, by virtue of her untiring ministrations at childbirths and to the sick and the dying, carved a niche of her own in the hearts of the populace. Some of the menfolk occasionally discussed her at the village inn, and offered the opinion that she was an old fraud, but that's about as far as opposition to Aunt Susi now went. The womenfolk swore by her.

When, in 1914, five years after Aunt Susi had come to Nagyrev, the first world war broke out, the midwife-nurse was a bulwark of comfort to women whose husbands and sons left for the front. Some of the womenfolk, preparing for motherhood, were beset by the uncertainties of a future with an extra mouth to feed and a man away at the war. Aunt Susi told the pregnant women not to bother their heads about the future. She would fix everything. She had, she disclosed, contacts with sources that not only supplied her with predictions, but she was in touch with forces that could *control* the predictions. She could thus assure the expectant mother of an unwanted child that the child would not live.

While the mortality rate among newly born children has always been high in backward communities of Europe, it is doubtful if the Nagyrev-Tiszakurt infant death rate would have reached such unusual proportions had it not been for Aunt Susi's ability to contact the forces that controlled human destinies.

All the while, Pastor Franz was keeping one eye on Aunt Susi. He had originally been suspicious of her, then his suspicions had been allayed, and now he was suspicious again. But Pastor Franz was a practical man; he knew better than to raise a finger or a voice against the most popular figure in either of the villages. The villages were more remote than ever, now that the war was on. With the manpower shortage that comes with war, police would be practically unobtainable for an investigation in a remote settlement based on nothing more than vague suspicion, especially when they had investigated the same thing once before and gone away satisfied that nothing whatever was amiss. And if Pastor Franz didn't watch his own step very carefully, he might wind up as the very kind of a case history that had made him suspicious of Aunt Susi all over again.

It was in 1916, in the second year of the war, that Susi Olah, now forty-seven, took unto herself a spouse by the name of Julius Fazekas, a widower of about her own age and the proprietor of one of the handsomest blond mustaches in the wine region. Some of the more cynical observers among the over-draft-age men who were still collecting at the bar in the inn would have bet their drinking arms that what had really attracted Aunt Susi to brother Fazekas was not his mustache but three acres of fine land that he owned.

Three years after Aunt Susi's marriage, in 1919, the war ended and peace came to the villages of Nagyrev and Tiszakurt. Well, not *exactly* peace. The returning soldiers weren't, somehow, as welcome as they might have been. The women of the two villages, having worked overtime in the fields while the men were away at war, had looked forward to a measure of ease, however small, when the men came back. But *these* men, the beasts, drove the women harder than the women had driven themselves. They rooted the ladies out of bed before daybreak, handed them rakes, and bade them be off to the fields while they themselves lay around the house or went down to the bar at the inn.

Aunt Susi looked upon this situation with a contemplative gaze. Therein lay the germ of what was to become, in those two remote villages in central Hungary, a full-scale war of the sexes. Aunt Susi, thirsting for power, saw in the slave-driving and the beatings the very thing she needed to be a liberator of a downtrodden sex.

When Aunt Susie saw a woman with two black eyes and assorted cuts and contusions dragging herself to work in the fields, she would stop her and commiserate with her. What a pity, she would say, that the woman's brute of a husband had not been killed in the war. With that as a starter, Aunt Susi would reduce the situation to its fundamentals. The women of Nagyrev and Tiszakurt had made out all right while the war was on and the men were away. What was the difference now, except that the returned men for the most part were quarrelsome, unproductive burdens on the community? The ignorant peasant women, with generations of abject submission to male dominance instilled in them, had never dared to so much as think of objecting to anything a

man did. But now Aunt Susi unveiled new vistas to them—
and they were enchanted by what they saw.

It was in the year 1920, that about a score of the most
robust, and quarrelsome, members of the community died
suddenly and quite unexpectedly in the space of a few
months. The coroner who had first functioned when Aunt
Susi had come to the region eleven years before had in the
meantime become a coroner's case himself; Aunt Susi had
seen to it that a relative of hers through her marriage to
brother Fazekas had been appointed to preside over the
formalities surrounding death. The new coroner was just as
expert as the previous one had been in the field of diagnos-
tics. Although practically every death followed violent
cramps and nausea, it was ascribed to pneumonia.

There arose, in the spring of 1921, a new spirit in the
villages. As the women formed into rake brigades and
tramped to work in the fields their nut-brown faces, framed
in peasant shawls, shone with the light of emancipation. The
happiest women were, curiously enough, those who had just
lost their husbands and who might normally have been expected to be dark with bereavement.

Aunt Susi's husband, brother Fazekas, was not a discreet
man. He made the mistake of beginning to wonder why it
was that some of the most robust men in the villages were
dropping like flies—and he followed that up by the greater
mistake of giving voice to his wonderment in the presence of
Aunt Susi. Brother Fazekas quickly contracted pneumonia
and died.

As time passed, Susi Olah moved through the streets of
Nagyrev and Tiszakurt in a shimmering envelope of mysti-
cism. Men, women, and children had come to look upon the
hook-nosed midwife and nurse as the possessor of the power
of life and death. The women practically worshipped her;
the men were in fear of her. Even the boys who hit it up at
the inn had learned by this time to control their tongues;
there was, somehow, a high incidence of mortality among
those who dared to criticize Aunt Susi. Some husbands,

making a vague connection between pneumonia and brutality, even began to show slight signs of consideration toward their wives; every so often a woman would be heard to talk back to a man. It was an unheard-of condition.

Over in Tiszakurt, Pastor Franz, the first man ever to have become suspicious of Aunt Susi, was growing old with the years and with mortal dread. He suspected that Aunt Susi was brewing mysterious potions that were continuing to kill quarrelsome husbands, but how to prove such a terrible accusation? Pastor Franz was hanging on to his little church because he was infirm and had no place else to go in Hungary and because he prayed that someday he could somehow throw the light of truth and justice into the pall of mystery and evil that seemed to have settled over the community.

By 1929, ten years after the end of the war, about one hundred males in the two villages had dropped off after attacks of cramps and vomiting. If other male villagers suspected what was happening to their fellows (and they couldn't have been dumb enough *not* to have had definite thoughts in the matter) they were powerless to do anything about it. There were no police to turn to, no telephones to use, and they couldn't write. They were prisoners of a lethal conspiracy that they saw every time they looked into a pair of female eyes.

Aunt Susi, who was now rounding out her second decade in Nagyrev, had turned her sixtieth milestone and looked like something straight out of Frankenstein's laboratory. She had, since first appearing in the wine region, added about fifty pounds to her six-foot frame; her eyes were smaller and blacker than ever, all but obscured in folds of facial fat; her voice, coming out of that too-small mouth beneath the hooked nose, was strangely deep and forbidding; she seemed, somehow, literally to drip with evil.

Then, in July of 1929, somebody sat down in Budapest, some seventy miles away, and wrote a letter—a very nasty letter. The letter was addressed to the law-enforcement authorities in Szolnok, down the Tisza River from Aunt Susi's bailiwick. It was unsigned, and to this day nobody knows who wrote it. What the letter said, in effect, was that Aunt Susi had, over a period of twenty years, knocked off more than one hundred men and children and that if the authorities would go to the trouble of disinterring a body or two in the little cemetery on the edge of Tiszakurt they would find evidence to corroborate murder charges.

A couple of policemen were sent to Nagyrev, dressed in mufti and going under the cover of wine buyers. They soon settled on Pastor Franz as the man most likely to help them. Pastor Franz had, through the years, kept close tabs on the whole incredible series of events. He knew the names of the men who had died under circumstances that had struck him as mysterious, and he was able to trace for the investigators the human threads that had connected Aunt Susi with the deaths.

Aunt Susi, Pastor Franz believed, had, especially in the later years, employed confederates in the furtherance of her terrible deeds. She had been particularly close to several women, one of whom, a Mrs. Ladislas Szabo (that *name* again!) had seemingly divested herself of an elderly father and an unproductive uncle. The officers questioned Mrs. Szabo in her thatched hut and wrung a confession from her. What Mrs. Szabo did was to fill in the details of what Pastor Franz had outlined. Mrs. Szabo, it seemed, had been one of several lieutenants who had aided Aunt Susi in the furtherance of her occult activities. These women had been supplied by Aunt Susi with a syrup mixture which, when introduced into wine or coffee or food, in one large dose or several small ones, invariably induced what had come to be recognized as pneumonia.

On the basis of Mrs. Szabo's confession, Aunt Susi and about a score of other women she implicated were rounded up and put on the river steamer and taken to Szolnok for interrogation. During the eight-hour trip down the Tisza, Aunt Susi gave the dark-of-the-moon business to the other suspects; such was her power over them that when they reached Szolnok for questioning by the authorities they clammed up. Even Mrs. Szabo, the only one who had confessed, recanted her confession. There was nothing for the authorities to do but release the women—nothing, that is, except to plant detectives at strategic spots around the two villages to study, from a distance, the behavior of the women when they returned from their brief incarceration.

Aunt Susi and her co-conspirators waited for the fall of night. Then they headed straight for the graveyard on the edge of Tiszakurt. The moon was shining. Detectives watching the women saw them switching headstones, rude wooden markers, on many of the graves. The reason for this was obvious. Aunt Susi and her confederates, knowing that the authorities would probably get around to digging up the bodies of her victims, was shuffling the markers so that markers bearing the names of the victims would appear over graves of people who had died of natural causes. A fine, misleading trick—had it worked. The watching detectives were able to keep track of the headstones that were shifted. Then, when a corps of grave diggers were brought in from Szolnok, the police knew just where to have the boys start digging.

More than fifty bodies were disinterred. They were shot through with arsenic. In some instances, where the bodies had completely decomposed, it was possible to establish the presence of arsenic in the hair and in the finger and toenails.

A wholesale batch of police hit the villages to make wholesale arrests. A total of thirty-one women were arrested for murder. Aunt Susi—one of the truly outstanding archkillers in all criminal history—beat the law, in her own fashion, at the very end. She mixed herself a drink just as the police were heading her way and died before they got there. A search of her hut disclosed the source of the arsenic: flypaper. She had soaked the flypaper in water, then mixed the water with syrup.

Journalists from all parts of Europe converged on Szolnok to attend the trials of Aunt Susi's confederates. Making a murder charge stick after a period of years was quite a trick. Some of Aunt Susi's confederates beat the rap; others were not so lucky. Mrs. Szabo, Aunt Susi's chief lieutenant, and two other women were hanged; two more got life in prison, and six received sentences of from eight to twenty-five years. Another went insane.

And so the law bade a fond farewell to the villages of Nagyrev and Tiszakurt. Presumably the setting sun found the simple folk of Nagyrev and Tiszakurt returning, after twenty incredible years, to normal—if, that is, anybody could possibly qualify for normalcy after having been exposed to the presence of Aunt Susi Olah.

The Man Who
Came Back

CIRCUMSTANTIAL evidence!

The term frightens the average man. He sees himself in a situation that he cannot explain, where whatever he says may be used against him. He seldom realizes that circumstance is apt to work more in his favor than against him, that it is often an innocent man's greatest safeguard against false testimony. If he is like most people, he firmly believes that it would be better for a hundred malefactors to go free than to have one innocent man suffer.

Perhaps. But Horatio and his companions at the bridge were ready to die for Rome. Nathan Hale regretted that he had but one life to lose for his country. The defenders of Bataan were expendable. Always, it seems, the select few are willing to sacrifice themselves for the many.

Except in a courtroom, every precedent, every statute in the law books, every device from a writ of *habeas corpus* to a plea of *non compos mentis,* is invoked to nullify the opinions of veteran judges and the verdicts of sincere juries. Why?

One hundred and fifty years ago, a writer named Phillips, in an essay on the Theory of Presumptive Proof, said:

> "Circumstances, it is said, cannot lie. This is very true; but witnesses can. And from whom do you

205

obtain circumstances, but from witnesses? Thus,
you are liable to two deceptions: first, in the tale
told by the witness; and, secondly, in your own
application of those circumstances. Where a fact
is positively sworn to, as seen by the witness, the
conclusion or inference to be drawn from it, is
generally obvious. But, where the inference is to
be drawn from a long train of circumstances, it is
a matter of judgment; it is an exercise of the understanding; and, as all men do not understand
alike, very opposite conclusions are sometimes
drawn from the same shades of probability."

These comments by Phillips are part of the introduction
to an unusual book, *Famous Cases of Circumstantial Evidence,* published nearly a century ago. The case that follows
comes from that compendium, and is given *verbatim.* So incredible are the circumstances that even those willing to believe them will agree they are too fantastic to be duplicated.

Yet, around the year 1812, at the very time when Phillips
was penning his essay, almost the exact counterpart of this
case, which occurred in Denmark, was being repeated in the
State of Vermont.

The fact that such a thing could happen twice is enough
to make us shudder.

The Man Who Came Back

S. N. PHILLIPS

THE most striking case of circumstantial evidence in which the testimony against the accused was altogether fabricated by the accuser, is one taken from the Danish records, and which, from its impressiveness, has been made the subject of remark by both Danish and German writers. The unhappy fate of the clergyman, Sören Qvist, is familiar to his countrymen, though many generations have passed away since the events which are about to be related.

Sören was the pastor of the little village of Veilby, situated a few miles from Grenaee, in the Jutland peninsula. He was a man of excellent moral character, generous, hospitable and diligent in the performance of his sacred duties; but he was also a man of constitutionally violent temper, which he lacked the ability to restrain, and was consequently subject at times to fierce outbreaks of wrath, which were a scourge to his household when they occurred, and a humiliation to himself. Like most Danish clergymen of that day, he was a tiller of the soil, as well as a preacher of the word; and from the produce of his tithes, and the cultivation of his farm, realized a comfortable competence. He was a widower with two children—a daughter who kept house for him, and a son holding an officer's commission in the army. At Ingvorstrup, a village not far from Veilby, dwelt a cattle-farmer, one Morten Bruns, who, by means anything but honest and honorable, had acquired considerable property, and who was in ill repute as a reckless self-seeker and oppressor of the poor. This man Morten thought fit to pay court to the pastor's daughter, but his suit was rejected by both parent and child; and either the refusal, or the manner of it, so irritated the suitor that he swore secretly to be revenged on both.

Some months later, when the short-lived suit had been forgotten, the pastor, being in want of a farm servant, engaged Niels Bruns, a poor brother of the rich Morten, the discarded lover. Niels soon showed himself to be an utterly worthless fellow, lazy, impudent, and overbearing; and the result was a constant recurrence of quarrels and mutual recriminations between him and his master. Sören on more than one occasion gave the fellow a thrashing, which did not at all tend to improve the relations between them. These relations, however, were destined to come to a speedy close. The pastor had set Niels to dig a piece of ground in the garden, but on coming out he found him not digging, but leisurely resting on his spade and cracking nuts which he had plucked, his work being left undone. The pastor scolded him angrily; the man retorted that it was no business of his to dig in the garden; at which Sören struck him twice in the face, and the fellow, throwing down the spade, retaliated with a volley of abuse. Thereupon the old man lost all self-control, and seizing the spade, he dealt the fellow several blows with it. Niels fell to the earth like one dead; but when his master in great alarm raised him up he broke away, leaped through the hedge, and made off into the neighboring wood. From that time he was seen no more, and all inquiries after him proved vain. The above was the pastor's account of the facts.

Ere long strange rumors began to circulate in the neighborhood, and, as a matter of course, they reached the pastor's ears. Morten Bruns was known to have said that "he would make the parson produce his brother even if he had to dig him out of the earth." Sören was intensely pained at the calumny implied, and instituted at his own expense a quiet search after the missing man—a search which failed altogether. Even before that failure was known, Morten Bruns, in fulfillment of his threat, applied to the district magistrate, taking with him as witnesses one Larsen, a cottager, and a laborer's widow and daughter, on the strength of whose testimony he declared his suspicion that the pastor had slain his brother. The magistrate represented to him the risk he ran in making so serious a charge against the clergyman, and advised him to weigh the matter well before it was too late. But Morten persisted in his design, and the statements of the witnesses were taken down. The widow Karsten deposed, that on the very day when Niels Bruns was said to have fled from the parsonage, she and her daughter Else had passed by the pastor's garden about the hour of noon. When they were nearly in front of the hedge which encloses it on the eastern side, they heard someone calling Else. It was Niels, who was on the other side of the hazel bushes, and who now bent back the branches, and asked Else if she would have some nuts. She took a handful, and then asked him what he was doing there? He answered, that the pastor had ordered him to dig, but that the job did not suit him, and he preferred cracking nuts. Just then they heard a door in the house open, and Niels said, "Now, listen, and you shall hear a preachment." Directly after they heard (they could not see, because the hedge was too high and too thick) how the two quarreled, and how the one paid the other in kind. At last they heard the pastor cry, "I will

beat thee, dog, until thou liest dead at my feet!" Whereupon there were sounds as of blows, and then they heard
Niels calling the pastor a rogue and a hangman. To this
the pastor made no reply; but they heard two blows, and
they saw the iron blade of a spade and part of the handle
swing twice above the hedgerow, but in whose hands
they could not discern. After this all was quiet in the garden,
and, somewhat alarmed and excited, the widow and her
daughter hurried on their way.

Larsen deposed that on the evening of the day following
that of the disappearance of Niels, as he was returning home
very late from Tolstrup, and was passing along the footpath
which flanks the southern side of the pastor's garden, he heard
from within the garden the sound of someone digging the
earth. At first he was rather startled; but seeing that it was
clear moonlight, he determined to find out who it was that
was working in the garden at that late hour; whereupon
he slipped off his wooden shoes, climbed up the hedge, and
parted the tops of the hazel bushes so as to enable himself
to see. Then he saw the pastor in the green dressing-gown
he usually wore, and with a white nightcap on his head,
busied in leveling the earth with a spade; but more than
this he did not see, for the pastor turned suddenly round as
if some sound had struck his ear, and witness being afraid
of detection, let himself down, and ran away.

When the witnesses had thus deposed, Morten demanded
that the parson should be arrested. Wishing to avoid such
a scandal if possible, the magistrate, who was a friend of
Sören's, proposed that they should go together to the parsonage, where they would probably receive a satisfactory
explanation of the facts deposed to. Morten consented to
this, and the party set out. On approaching the house they
saw Sören coming to meet them—when Morten ran forward, and bluntly accused him of murdering his brother,
adding that he was come with the magistrate to make search
for the body. The pastor made him no reply, but courte-
ously greeting the magistrate, gave directions to the farm

servants, who now gathered round, to aid by all the means
in their power the search about to be made. Morten led the
way into the garden, and after looking round for some time,
pointed to a certain spot and called upon the men to dig
there. The men fell to work, and Morten joined them,
working with a show of frantic eagerness. When they had
dug to a little depth the ground proved so hard that it was
evident it had not been broken up for a long while. Sören
had looked on, quite at ease, and now he said to Morten,
"Slanderer, what have you got for your pains?" Instead of
replying, Morten turned to Larsen, and asked him where it
was that he had seen the parson digging. Larson pointed to
a heap of cabbage stalks, dried haulms, and other refuse,
and said he thought that was the place. The rubbish was
soon removed, and the men began digging at the soil beneath.
They had not dug long, when one of them cried out, "Heaven
preserve us!" and as all present crowded to look, the crown
of a hat was visible above the earth. "That is Niels's hat!"
cried Morten, "I know it well—here is a security we shall
find him! Dig away!" he shouted with fierce energy, and
was almost as eagerly obeyed. Soon an arm appeared, and
in a few minutes the entire corpse was disinterred. There
could be no doubt that it was the missing man. The face
could not be recognized, for decomposition had commenced,
and the features had been injured by blows; but all his
clothes, even unto his shirt with his name on it, were identified by his fellow servants; even a leaden ring in the left ear
of the corpse was recognized as one which Niels had worn
for years.

There was no alternative but to arrest the pastor on the
spot—indeed, he willingly surrendered himself, merely
protesting his innocence. "Appearances are against me,"
he said; "surely this must be the work of Satan and his min-
istry; but He still lives who will at His pleasure make my innocence manifest. Take me to prison; in solitude and in
chains I will await what He in His wisdom shall decree."

The pastor was removed to the gaol at Grenaee the

same night, and on the following day came the judicial examination. The first three witnesses confirmed their former
statements on oath. Moreover, there now appeared three
additional witnesses, viz: the pastor's two farm servants
and the dairymaid. The two former explained how on the
day of the murder they had been sitting near the open window in the servants' room, and had heard distinctly how
the pastor and the man Niels were quarreling, and how the
former had cried out, "I will slay thee, dog! Thou shalt lie
dead at my feet!" They added that they had twice before
heard the pastor threaten Niels with the like. The dairymaid
deposed that on the night when Larsen saw the pastor in
the garden, she was lying awake in bed, and heard the
door leading from the passage into the garden creak; and
that when she rose and peeped out, she saw the pastor, in his
dressing-gown and nightcap, go out into the garden. What
he did there she saw not; but about an hour afterwards she
again heard the creaking of the door.

When asked what he had to say in his defense, the pastor
replied solemnly, "So help me God, I will say nothing but
the truth. I struck deceased with the spade, but not otherwise than that he was able to run away from me, and out of
the garden; what became of him afterwards, or how he came
to be buried in my garden, I know not. As for the evidence
of Larsen and the dairymaid, who say that they saw me in
the garden in the night, it is either a foul lie or it is a hellish
delusion. Miserable man that I am! I have no one on earth
to speak in my defense—that I see clearly; if He in heaven
likewise remains silent, I have only to submit to His in-
scrutable will."

When, some weeks later, the trial came on, two more
fresh witnesses were produced. They declared that on the
oft-mentioned night they were proceeding along the road
which runs from the pastor's garden to the wood, when
they met a man carrying a sack on his back, who passed
them and walked on in the direction of the garden. His
face they could not see, inasmuch as it was concealed by the

overhanging sack; but as the moon was shining on his back, they could plainly descry that he was clad in a pale green coat and a white nightcap. He disappeared near the pastor's garden hedge. No sooner did the pastor hear the evidence of the witness to this effect than his face turned an ashy hue, and he cried out in a faltering voice, "I am fainting!" and was so prostrated in body that he had to be taken back to prison. There, after a period of severe suffering, to the intense astonishment of everyone, he made, to his friend, the district magistrate who had first arrested him, the following strange confession: "From my childhood, as far back as I can remember, I have ever been passionate, quarrelsome, and proud—impatient of contradiction, and ever ready with a blow. Yet have I seldom let the sun go down on my wrath, nor have I borne ill-will to anyone. When but a lad I slew in anger a dog which one day ate my dinner, which I had left in his way. When, as a student, I went on foreign travel, I entered, on slight provocation, into a broil with a German youth in Leipsic, challenged him, and gave him a wound that endangered his life. For that deed, I feel it, I merited that which has now come upon me after long years; but the punishment falls upon my sinful head with tenfold weight now that I am broken down with age, a clergyman, and a father. O Father in heaven! It is here that the wound is sorest."

After a pause of anguish, he continued: "I will now confess the crime which no doubt I have committed, but of which I am, nevertheless, not fully conscious. That I struck the unhappy man with the spade I know full well, and have already confessed; whether it were with the flat side or with the sharp edge I could not in my passion discern; that he then fell down, and afterwards again rose up and ran away —that is all that I know to a surety. What follows—heaven help me!—four witnesses have seen; namely, that I fetched the corpse from the wood and buried it; and that this must be substantially true I am obliged to believe, and I will tell you wherefore. Three or four times in my life, that I know of,

it has happened to me to walk in my sleep. The last time
(about nine years ago), I was next day to preach a funeral sermon over the remains of a man who had unexpectedly met with a dreadful death. I was at a loss for a
text, when the words of a wise man among the ancient
Greeks suddenly occurred to me, 'Call no man happy until
he be in his grave.' To use the words of a heathen for the text
of a Christian discourse, was not, methought, seemly; but
I then remembered that the same thought, expressed in well-
nigh the same terms, was to be met with somewhere in the
Apocrypha. I sought and sought but could not find the
passage. It was late, I was wearied by much previous
labor; I therefore went to bed, and soon fell asleep. Greatly
did I marvel the next morning when, on arising and seating
myself at my writing desk, I saw before me, written in
large letters in a piece of paper, 'Let no man be deemed
happy before his end cometh (Syrach xi. 34).' But not this
alone; I found likewise a funeral discourse—short, but as
well written as any I had ever composed—and all in my
own handwriting. In the chamber none other than I could
have been. I knew, therefore, who it was that had written
the discourse; and that it was no other than myself. Not
more than half a year previous, I had, in the same marvelous
state, gone in the nighttime into the church, and fetched
away a handkerchief which I had left in the chair behind
the altar. Mark now—when the two witnesses this morning delivered their evidence before the court, then my
previous sleepwalkings suddenly flashed across me; and
I likewise called to mind that in the morning after the night
during which the corpse must have been buried, I had been
surprised to see my dressing-gown lying on the floor just
inside the door, whereas it was always my custom to hang
it on a chair by my bedside. The unhappy victim of my
unbridled passion must, in all likelihood, have fallen down
dead in the wood; and I must in my sleepwalking have
followed him thither. Yes—the Lord have mercy!—so it
was, so it must have been."

On the following day sentence of death was passed upon

the prisoner—a sentence which many felt to be too severe, and which led to a friendly conspiracy on his behalf; and had it not been for his own refusal to be a party to anything unlawful, he might have escaped. The jailer was gained over, and a fisherman had his boat in readiness for a flight to the Swedish coast, where he would have been beyond the reach of danger. But Sören Qvist refused to flee. He longed, he said, for death; and he would not add a new stain to his reputation by a furtive flight. He maintained his strength of mind to the last, and from the scaffold he addressed to the bystanders a discourse of much power, which he had composed in prison during his last days. It treated of anger and its direful consequences, with touching allusions to himself and the dreadful crime to which his anger misled him. Thereafter, he doffed his coat, bound with his own hands the napkin before his eyes, and submitted his neck to the executioner's sword.

One-and-twenty years after the pastor, Sören Qvist of Veilby, had been accused, tried, condemned, and executed for the murder of his serving-man, an old beggarman applied for alms to the people of Aalsöe, the parish adjoining to Veilby. Suspicions were aroused by the exact likeness the beggarman bore to Morten Bruns, of Ingvorstrup, who had lately died, and also by the curious and anxious inquiries the man made concerning events long past. The pastor of Aalsöe, who had buried Morten Bruns, took the vagabond to his parsonage, and there the fellow, all unconscious of the portentous nature of the admission, acknowledged that he was Niels Bruns, the very man for whose supposed murder the pastor had suffered the shameful death of a criminal. Had his brother Morten survived him, it is pretty certain the truth, concealed so long, had never been known, as Niels had only returned to the district in the hope of profiting by Morten's death, the news of which had accidentally reached him. He professed—and, indeed, plainly experienced—the utmost horror on hearing the dreadful history of the pastor's cruel fate. It was all Morten's doing, he said; but he was so overcome by the terrible narrative that he could scarcely gather strength to reply to the questions put to him. The result of his examination and confession may be summed up very briefly. Morten had conceived a mortal hatred of Sören Qvist from the time that he refused him his daughter, and had determined on revenge. It was he who compelled Niels to take service with the pastor; he had spurred him on to the repeated offenses, in the expectation that violence would result, owing to the pastor's hasty temper; and had carefully nursed the feud which soon arose between master and man. Niels told him daily all that took place. On leaving the garden on that fatal day, he had run over to Ingvorstrup to acquaint his brother with what had happened. Morten shut him up in a private room that no one might see him. Shortly after midnight, when the whole village was asleep, the two brothers went to a place where the roads cross each other, and where two days previously a suicide had been buried—a young man of about Niels' age and stature. In spite of Niels' reluctance and remonstrance they dug up the corpse and took it into Morten's house. Niels was made to strip and don a suit of Morten's, and the corpse was clad, piece by piece, in Neils' cast-off clothes, even to the very earring. Then Morten battered the dead face with a spade, and hid it in a sack until the next night, when they carried it into the wood by Veilby parsonage. Niels asked what all these preparations meant. Morten told him to mind his own business, and to go and fetch the parson's green dressing-gown and cap. This Niels refused to do, whereupon Morten went and fetched them himself. "And now," he said to his brother, "you go your way. Here is a purse with a hundred dollars—make for the frontier, where no one knows thee; pass thyself under another name, and never set thy foot on Danish soil again as thou wouldst answer it with thy life!" Neils did as he was commanded, and parted from Morten forever. He had enlisted for a soldier, had suffered great hardships, had lost a limb, and had returned to his native place a mere wreck.

The Monster of Aurora

THERE are two schools of thought about the way to commit a perfect murder. One believes that the cover-up should precede the crime; the other recommends handling the ticklish details afterward. There are, of course, a few perfectionists who feel that equal attention should be paid to the preliminaries and the aftermath. But that, it seems to me, is likely to put too much strain on the culprit. Normally —or should we say abnormally—you have to prepare carefully or repair.

It is almost impossible to decide the merits or demerits of this question, because there is no way to keep a reliable score of perfect crimes. By definition, those that are perpetrated without a hitch are never recognized as murders. And unless we know the total to begin with, there is no way of calculating the percentage of those that missed.

However, a comparison of near-perfect jobs that failed to make the grade reveals some interesting facts. They seem to indicate that the cover-up work is more effective *after* the event than *before*.

In nearly every case the perfection of the crime itself is the flaw, since it narrows the search to the only person clever enough to perpetrate it. The farther back investigators go, the more details they encounter, the greater their suspicions grow, even to the point where they will reject an ironclad alibi as false.

In short, by planning too well beforehand, the slayer goes from the complex to the simple. He can't backtrack and change things once sleuths have begun to probe them. He, like his victim, falls in the toils of his machinations.

But in covering up *afterward,* the murderer moves from the simple—the crime itself—to the complex. He can superimpose some bigger and more baffling mystery upon the first, creating imaginary situations and even fanciful perpetrators, as occasion may demand. That course can lead even astute investigators into a maze of their own speculations, so that when they return to the starting point—the crime—it will seem rather inconsequential.

The murder may never be discovered if the *corpus delicti,* or "body of the crime" is not established and whatever circumstantial evidence there may be is unsupported. The while, a canny culprit can remain in complete control, creating more confusion by the smartest dodge of all—playing simple in a real dumb way.

But that course, too, has its hazards. The man who chooses it can never look back. His past is fixed and he must treat it as forgotten, banking on the fact that he thought of everything at precisely the right time. What's more, he must really think of everything, for in plotting the perfect crime, *almost* everything won't do.

The story that follows tells you why.

The Monster of Aurora

ALAN HYND

SHORTLY after World War I, a man named Warren Lincoln was very active in Chicago. Lincoln—a frail, bald-headed man of 45 with large, washed-out blue eyes—was a criminal lawyer who specialized in homicide cases. Once, in 1920, he got six murder acquittals in a row, and an alcoholic journalist in the pressroom of the Criminal Courts building abandoned a search for a misplaced corkscrew long enough to dub the little man "Scott Free" Lincoln.

Lincoln's success with juries was unofficially ascribed to three factors; ability to locate legal loopholes, a singularly guileless countenance, and the suspicion that he held frequent monetary conferences with witnesses, and even jurors, at night under a two-watt bulb.

In 1921, Lincoln felt a nervous breakdown coming on.

219

This condition was closely related to a tip that a reporter passed on to him. "If I were in your place, Lincoln," said the reporter, "I'd take to the hills. They're beginning to smell those last two acquittals of yours in high places."

Lincoln was not rich, but he was comfortably fixed. He gave up his practice, which had the effect of forestalling a possible investigation into his ethics, or lack of them. With his wife, Lina, he moved to a depressing little frame cottage on a monotonous street on the outskirts of Aurora, Illinois. There, theoretically, the peace and quiet was to have been good for his nerves.

Mrs. Lincoln wore rimless nose glasses. She was half a head taller than her husband, weighed 250 pounds, and looked like a W. C. T. U. worker, which she was. She was the kind of a woman who wanted everybody to be happy —her way.

Mrs. Lincoln had not always been the antithesis of all that was feminine. She had, in fact, been just the opposite when Lincoln had married her as a young girl. She had been a striking brunette, tall and statuesque. As the years had rolled on and she had become preoccupied with minding other people's business, grinding away at one cause after another, she had forgotten all about her personal appearance. The result was that when the metamorphosis was complete she had a shape like a sack of flour and a face that, from the other side of a dinner table, would have put the average man off his appetite.

Warren Lincoln, however, was quite contented. He had apparently passed that stage in life where the cosmic urge was of primary concern to him. He was an absent-minded sort of a man, and it is entirely possible that he still saw his wife, not as she was in actuality, but in idealized form, as she had been when he had first met her.

Whatever the truth of the matter, there was one thing that now interested Warren Lincoln more than sex, and that was sweet peas. He planted several beds of sweet peas in the back yard, and he delighted in mincing around the neighborhood, presenting little bouquets of his latest blooms to people he had taken a liking to. He was marched off to church every Sunday morning, where his wife contributed a rich alto to the choral effects, and he was made to attend prayer meeting on Wednesday night. Liquor and tobacco were forbidden, in or out of the house.

The Lincolns had a visitor in the summer of 1921. It was Mrs. Lincoln's brother—a booming big squared-faced ex-Boy Scout leader by the name of Byron Shoup. Shoup, a bachelor of 40, was hipped on keeping in condition. When he decided that he liked Aurora better than his native Nebraska and determined to stay with the Lincolns indefinitely, he sent for his athletic paraphernalia, which included Indian clubs, exercise rings and bars, and a punching bag. Even the more distant neighbors could hear the leathery rhythm of Shoup's punching bag, which he kept between two of Lincoln's sweet pea beds, at six o'clock every morning.

Shoup was a bully. He insisted that Lincoln take violent exercises. Lincoln was allowed to stop only when he collapsed one day.

These three—Lincoln, the frail little ex-lawyer, his domineering wife, and her athletic bully of a brother—made up a household, as need hardly be mentioned, where something had to happen, sooner or later. What did happen, however, was hardly in accordance with what seemed to be in the books. What eventually came about was a jigsaw murder mystery which, because of the improbable twists and turns that it took, and because of its fiction-like denouement, occupies, even today, a niche of its own in the hall of infamy.

Shoup, in his enthusiastic pursuit of the athletic life, trampled his brother-in-law's sweet pea beds. Lincoln was heard to put in a mild protest one morning. Later, there were screams from the cottage. The screams continued, intermittently, all day. By nightfall, Chief of Police Frank Michels, a casual man with a glazed uniform and a stringy mustache, knocked on the front door of the cottage to see what was wrong.

Mrs. Lincoln answered. Shoup stood right behind her. They refused to talk to the chief, or admit him. "I know something about the law," Mrs. Lincoln told the chief. "You can't enter this house without a warrant."

Chief Michels, whose long career as a cop had been principally devoted to traffic problems and Saturday night drunks, was vaguely disturbed. There was something forbidding about Mrs. Lincoln and her brother.

Mrs. Lincoln and Shoup became actively identified with a movement, in the spring of 1922, to close up every speakeasy in Aurora. They sniffed out the terrible places for parties of raiders. When Shoup wasn't helping his sister in prohibition work, he was practicing football tackling or wrestling holds on his brother-in-law.

Warren Lincoln, as an escape from home life made miserable by Shoup, took up secret speakeasy drinking at this particular time. An arresting fact soon became obvious to the town's barflies; no speakeasy that Warren Lincoln patronized was ever raided while he was on the premises. Of course not. Lincoln knew, from overhearing conversations between his wife and brother-in-law at home, what retreats had the Indian sign on them.

Lincoln chewed cloves and coffee beans and otherwise took precautions to kill a whiskey breath at home, and got away with it for a long time. He began to tip off speakeasy proprietors of impending raids. Then one night he made the mistake of going from a speakeasy, where he had spent the afternoon, and the dinner hour, direct to prayer meeting. His wife and brother-in-law saw the awful light. Not only was Lincoln a secret drinker, but he was a traitor —a betrayer who had tipped off liquor sellers to hide their inventory just before a white-ribbon descent.

A mortified wife and an enraged brother-in-law propelled Warren Lincoln through the night to the privacy of the cottage on the outskirts. Lincoln was not seen for two weeks. When he did appear, he looked like a model for an accident-insurance advertisement. He told fellow railbirds in a Joe-sent-me haven that he had met with a household mishap, which, in a way was true.

In the summer of 1922, Lincoln decided to put his love of sweet peas on a paying basis. He constructed a small greenhouse in the rear of the cottage. He was a handy man with tools; he put the place up himself.

The greenhouse was an immediate success. Lincoln had to make it larger as he branched out to raising other kinds of flowers to meet commercial demands. He hired an assistant—an easygoing big fellow named Frank—to do the heavy work, such as moving barrels of lime around. Frank liked his job so much that he frequently puttered around in the greenhouse until late at night.

In January of 1923—about two years after he had ambled over the Aurora horizon—Lincoln took to brooding at the mahogany, and addressing unintelligible remarks to his image in the mirror behind the bar. Once in a while he would pull a letter from his pocket and ponder it. Somebody looked over Lincoln's shoulder when he was reading the letter one day. The communication was short, being confined to one page. It read:

Lina Dearest,
Meet me the same place and the same time Chicago Tuesday. Don't worry about the little runt. He won't suspect anything.
A big hug for you.

George

Lincoln caught the snooper in the act. Since the cat was out of the bag, he wasn't reluctant to discuss what was causing his mental anguish. In spite of everything, he loved his wife. Yes, they quarrelled occasionally, but who didn't? Now that he had learned that there was somebody else in Lina's life, his heart was broken. He began to carry around with him a photograph of a young brunette beauty—the Lina Shoup of a bygone day.

Women are seldom heroines in saloon conversation. The battle line of the war between the sexes was clearly drawn when it developed that Lincoln's wife had a lover. Every man in the joint chipped in with advice to the wronged husband. Totalled up, the advice was that Lincoln should go home and put an ultimatum up to his wife. She would either give up her lover and also tell her brother to get to hell back to Nebraska, or she and her brother could pack up and get out.

Lincoln demurred. He said he was afraid to carry out the advice. He was afraid of what Shoup might do to him.

The let's-you-and-him-fight characters were not to be denied. They poured amber-colored courage into Lincoln and sent him on his way.

Next day the little man appeared in the speakeasy shortly before noon. It was a different Warren Lincoln whom the bartender and the early patrons beheld. The old Warren Lincoln had been a quiet, beaten little man. The new Lincoln was louder and openly belligerent. He downed a double rye. "There was nothing to it," he said, in answer to a question. "I was surprised myself. I just laid the law down and they went packing. No argument whatsoever."

"But you loved your wife, Mr. Lincoln," said the bartender. "What you goin' to do without her?"

"Absence makes the heart grow fonder," said Lincoln. "She'll come back to me of her own accord. See what the boys in the back room are drinking."

Frank, Lincoln's helper, ambled in for a quick one. "I was just telling the boys about last night, Frank," said Lincoln.

Frank grinned. "I didn't think the boss had it in him," he said. "There was hardly a peep out of either Mrs. Lincoln or Mr. Shoup. They just said, 'All right, we'll go if that's how you feel.' "

A couple of weeks later, one night while Lincoln had

gone to bed early to read, Frank, working late in the green-house, became conscious of someone peering at him through one of the panes. He ran outside to see what was up. He was too late to catch up with the person who had been doing the peering, but he saw him running off into some fields that separated the Lincoln cottage from the home of the nearest neighbor—a few hundred feet distant.

Frank didn't say anything to Lincoln about the matter. A few nights later, Lincoln himself appeared at the back door of the cottage, in an old-fashioned nightshirt and sleeping cap, and shouted for Frank in a voice heavy with alarm. He told Frank that he had caught sight of a man peering into his bedroom window.

The mysterious figure put in a third appearance about ten nights later, when Lincoln had gone downtown to the movies. This time Frank almost caught up with him as he chased him through the fields.

In the morning, Lincoln reported the matter to Chief of Police Michels. "Gee whiz," said the chief, "I'll bet some-body's spying on you, Mr. Lincoln."

The chief went out to Lincoln's place. The weather had been unseasonably warm and the earth had been soft enough clearly to record the footprints of the mystery figure.

The chief, Lincoln, and Frank followed the trail of the prints. The impressions had been made by a man with a fairly large foot. Judging from the depth of the prints, and the wide separations between them, the fleeing one had travelled at top speed.

Lincoln began to act like a man with something unpleas-ant on his mind. Even the not-too-observant Frank noticed that. Lincoln wasn't sleeping very well, or very much. He was often at work in the greenhouse before Frank arrived in the morning. Sometimes he puttered around the green-house, alone, until the small hours of the night.

Late one afternoon, when Frank was almost through for the day, Lincoln called him into the house. "Frank," he said, "I don't want to alarm you, but there's something I've got to tell you. I've been a lawyer, and I know how things work. I know who that man is who has been loitering around here lately."

"Who, Mr. Lincoln?"

"A private detective. There's no doubt about it."

"How do you figure that, Mr. Lincoln?"

"My wife has been unfaithful to me. After I ordered her and her brother out of this house, I found a stack of love letters written to her by a man named George. The letters are now in a safety deposit box in my bank in Chicago. That private detective is hanging around, trying to get those letters. My wife knows that they would be evidence in a divorce suit against her."

Frank, a moral man, was flabbergasted. Then he asked, "Why are you tellin' me all this, Mr. Lincoln?"

"Something could happen to me. There's no telling what a man or a woman will do when they're desperate. I'm telling you all this because if something does happen to me I want you to go to Chief of Police Michels and tell him what I have just told you."

Toward the end of April, Lincoln began to act a little more normal. He had gotten hold of a new kind of fertilizer, and he was anxious to see what effect it had on his sweet peas.

The little cottage seemed ominously still when Frank reported for work on the morning of April 30. Suspicious, Frank was unable to get any response to repeated knocks on the back door. He forced an entrance. The inside of the cottage was a shambles. There was blood all over the place, and things had been literally turned inside out. Lincoln was gone.

Frank phoned Chief of Police Michels and told him everything—about what he had just discovered, about the mysterious loiterer and about what Lincoln had told him to tell the chief in case anything, such as this, ever happened to him. "Gee whiz," said the chief, "I bet Mr. Lincoln's been murdered."

Three sets of footprints led from a point under Lincoln's open bedroom window through some fields. One set was an exact duplicate of those left in the wake of the loitering mystery man. The others had been made by a man who wore a size 12 shoe and by a woman who wore a size 8 shoe.

Chief Michels, who was now caught up in a chain of circumstances that was to lead to his shining hour, quickly established, from local shoe stores, that Byron Shoup had worn a 12 E shoe and that Mrs. Lincoln had worn an 8-C. There could be little doubt—in fact, no doubt whatsoever—that the shoes of Byron Shoup and Lina Lincoln had made two of the three sets of footprints that were of such vital concern to Chief Michels.

A minute search of the fields containing the footprints yielded two finds—one fascinating, the other alarming. The alarming find was Warren Lincoln's nightcap, literally soaked with blood. The fascinating find was a name card bearing the legend:

MILO DURAND
Private Detective
Chicago

Chief Michels did not consider himself a master of deduction. He didn't have to be to deduce that Warren Lincoln had been abducted, by his wife, her brother, and a private detective working for them. Judging from the amount of blood on the nightcap, and in the bedroom, it didn't seem possible that the ex-barrister was still alive.

For six weeks a futile hunt was instituted throughout the Middle West for Warren Lincoln's body. Byron Shoup and Lina Lincoln might as well have gone up in smoke, so far as Chief Michels and other officials who tried to locate them were concerned. As for Milo Durand, he might as well never have existed. There was no trace of him in the Chicago phone book or city directory. The Chicago police, who were more than passingly interested in the case because Warren Lincoln had pulled several fast ones on them, told the Aurora police chief that they had never heard of Milo Durand.

And then, one wonderful morning in June, a neighbor of Lincoln's, who had, the previous night, looked upon the grape when it was red, groped his way to a bedroom window to look out at the day and forthwith decided never to touch another drop. This man had seen many things as a result of alcohol. But on this particular morning, he was seeing a ghost. For there, puttering around outside of the greenhouse, as big as life and twice as natural, was little Warren Lincoln.

It was Lincoln, all right, in the flesh. Word of the man's reappearance, as if he were someone risen from the dead, reached Chief Michels within the hour. The chief went over to hear what Lincoln had to say.

Lincoln's story fitted certain known facts. He had been abducted by his wife, his brother-in-law, and a second man whose name he did not know. "That," interrupted Chief Michels, "was a private detective named Milo Durand. We can't get any trace of him. Supposed to come from Chicago."

The abductors had taken Lincoln to an automobile, taped his eyes, and driven him a great distance. He found himself a prisoner of hired gangsters in a windowless room stripped of everything that would serve later to identify it. The abduction motive had been to get a batch of love letters that a man named George had written to Mrs. Lincoln and which the woman had neglected to take with her when Lincoln had ordered her and her brother out of the house in January.

"Where are the letters?" asked Chief Michels.

"In a safety deposit box in my bank in Chicago."

Lincoln had been beaten and tortured by his captors in an effort to wring from him the hiding place of the love letters. He had not been able to convince his captors that the letters were in a safety deposit box, and, therefore, unobtainable without him. He had finally escaped, learned that he had been in Cleveland, and made his way back to Aurora.

"Why didn't you come over to my office and tell me you were back?" asked the chief. "You must of known we'd be goin' to a lot of trouble after findin' things as we did the last day of April."

"I didn't want to cause a lot of fuss," said Lincoln.

The chief wanted to know how the captors had tortured Lincoln.

"Come into the house," said Lincoln. The ex-lawyer stripped. His body was a mass of bruises and welts. Among other things, he had been lashed across the back by a whip.

The chief, hot on the biggest case of his career, began to ask Lincoln for details about the appearance of the captors hired by the plotters, the name of the street in Cleveland where he had been held, and so on. Lincoln put his hands to his head. "Tomorrow, or some other time, Chief," he said. "I've been through so much I don't want to think about it for a couple of days."

That sounded reasonable enough to the chief, so he left.

A couple of days later, he went out to see Lincoln again. Lincoln was sitting on the front porch of the cottage, his feet up on a box filled with sweet peas. "Chief," he said, more his usual self now, "take a look at those sweet peas in the box there. Tell me, did you ever see anything as beautiful?"

The chief wasn't what you would call a sweet-pea fancier, and anyway he was anxious to get on with the questioning. He said the sweet peas were certainly beautiful.

"New kind of fertilizer," said Lincoln. "Never been used before."

Lincoln described his Cleveland captors. There had been three of them, working in eight-hour shifts, around the clock. He also named the street on which the kidnap house had been located, but did not know the exact number. That was because, he explained, he had not stopped running after his escape until he was several blocks from the house.

The chief went away, and passed the information on to the Cleveland Police by long-distance phone. He was back again in a few days. Lincoln was watering the sweet peas in the box on the porch. "I thought," said Chief Michels, "that maybe if we went into Chicago and got those letters that this George wrote to your wife that maybe we could get a clue from them about where your wife is now. That is, maybe we could get some trace of this man George, and if Mrs. Lincoln is still going around with him, then we'd have her."

Lincoln said he'd rather forget about the whole thing. Chief Michels began to suspect that he was still in love with his wife, in spite of everything. But the chief wasn't going to let the one big mystery he had ever been connected with peter out. He insisted that he and Lincoln go to the safety deposit box and get the letters. He was so insistent that Lincoln finally consented.

The letters certainly should have been written on asbestos. They went into steam-heated boudoir details.

"You can see now," said Lincoln as the chief read them, "why I was reluctant to let anybody else see them. It's very embarrassing, Chief."

The letters had been addressed to Mrs. Lincoln to a post office box at the general post office in Chicago. They had borne no return address. That omission seemed to be explained by references in several of the letters to the fact that George was married. The chief could well imagine a married man taking the precaution of not putting his name and address on a letter to a mistress.

Michels did a sleight-of-hand act. He slipped one of the letters into his pocket before he returned the pack to Lincoln, who put them back in the safety box. The chief figured that the letter might somehow come in useful eventually, though he had no idea just how.

The first week in July, three weeks after the return of Warren Lincoln, the chief made a call at the little cottage on the outskirts. He had discouraging news to report. The Cleveland police were getting nowhere. The flower box on the porch was missing. The chief asked where it was. Lincoln said he had covered it with cement and used it to buttress one end of his front porch, which had begun to sag. The box was about the size of a Belgian block, and was ideal for the purpose to which it had now been put.

The next day, Warren Lincoln was gone again. This time there were no signs of violence in his wake. But there were signs that he had packed enough belongings for a very extended trip—somewhere.

The chief began to brood over why Lincoln had gone a second time. This second disappearance just didn't make sense.

The chief sought out Frank, Lincoln's one-time helper, whom Lincoln had not rehired upon his return. Michels figured that if he talked to Frank long enough some clue might develop. The chief was a great reader of detective stories, and he had read story after story wherein eternal questioning had paid handsome rewards.

Michels got to talking to Frank about the night Lincoln laid the law down to his wife and Shoup. Frank talked about the episode as if he had been an eyewitness. The chief discovered, however, upon closely questioning the man, that he had not actually *seen* anything, but had only *heard* Lincoln talking to Shoup and Mrs. Lincoln, and the latter two answering.

Now Michels began to really go into the story about the man, presumably Milo Durand, the private detective, who had appeared three times before Lincoln's abduction. He learned that Frank had seen the man on two occasions, once when Lincoln was presumably in the cottage asleep and another time when Lincoln was supposed to be downtown at the movies. In each instance, the chief now realized, it would have been possible for Lincoln himself to have assumed the role of the loiterer. The first time, he could have slipped out of the darkened cottage, played his part, and returned to the cottage. The second time, he could have sneaked home early from the movies, and then, after appearing as the mystery man, kept out of sight until the hour of his normal return from the movies. When Lincoln himself had told Frank that he had seen a man peering into his bedroom window—a totally uncorroborated statement —Frank, because of his own previous experience, had naturally believed him.

The chief went into Chicago and enlisted the aid of the Police Department in canvassing all establishments in the city that printed name cards. It was a long job, and a long shot, but it paid off. In September, two months after the canvass started, the establishment that had printed the Milo Durand card was located.

The Durand card, and the man it had been made for, were clearly recalled, although the job had been done the previous December—a month before Mrs. Lincoln and Byron Shoup had disappeared from the Aurora scene. The job was clearly recalled because only one card had been ordered. Just a single, solitary card, not fifty, or a hundred or five hundred. The little man who had ordered it had appeared very furtive, as if he had been up to something. He had had a bald head and large, blue eyes. He had not given any name. He hadn't had to. Chief Michels knew he was Warren Lincoln.

The fact that the Durand card had been ordered a month before Mrs. Lincoln and big Shoup had last been seen added a slightly sinister note to the composition of mystery. Lincoln must have been very sure they were going to disappear in January when he ordered the card in December.

Now Michels consulted the rental records of boxes in the main Chicago post office. The records showed that the box to which the George letters had been sent had been rented not by Mrs. Lincoln, but by Warren Lincoln. It was, then, a foregone conclusion that handwriting experts would pronounce the George letters as the penmanship of Warren Lincoln. The chief still had Lincoln's bloodstained sleeping cap. The blood proved to be the life fluid of a chicken, not a human.

The various scenes of the whole horrible scenario now began to fall into proper juxtaposition in the mind of Chief Michels. Lincoln, his life made miserable by the presence in his household of his bullying, sadistic brother-in-law, had finally been goaded to murder. Possessing a legal mind, he had planned the perfect murder. He had created the fiction that his wife had a lover, and established a motive for his ordering them out of the house. He had even maneuvered things so that several speakeasy patrons had urged him on to kick out his wife and Shoup.

The chief had read in a detective story somewhere that there is no such thing as the perfect crime. What spoils the average well-planned murder is that it is either underdone or overdone. This one had been overdone. It had been perfect, up to the point where Lincoln, not quite sure that everybody would believe his story that he had kicked his wife and Shoup out, set out to *prove* that he had done so. His proof took the form of staging his own abduction, with the clear implication that the abduction had been plotted by Lina Lincoln and her brother.

Lincoln had had all night long to simulate the three sets of footprints, and he had made a good job of it. He had a small foot. He had worn first a pair of his wife's shoes, then a pair of Shoup's, and then a third pair to simulate the prints of Durand, the private detective.

But if murder had been done—if Nina Lincoln and Byron Shoup had been done to death in the cottage the night Lincoln supposedly ordered them out—where were the bodies? The Lincoln cottage was turned inside out, and so was the greenhouse. The sweet-pea beds were plowed up. There was no trace of the missing pair.

Lincoln was secretly hunted throughout the country. He couldn't be found. Then, in January of 1924, he came back again.

Chief Michels charged Lincoln with the murder of his wife and brother-in-law. Lincoln made one of the most memorable answers in the history of criminology. "Sure I killed them," he said. "But go to hell and prove it."

The chief wanted details. Lincoln, the lawyer, supplied them. "Chief," he said, "you've got to have a body, or enough of it to establish identity, to prove murder. Well, nothing remains of either my wife or that————brother-in-law of mine."

And now a singular killer spilled a singular story. Despising both his wife and her brother, he had begun to work on the details of their murders months before the crime. He had hired the post office box and begun to write the George letters and had the Durand card made up. Then he had seen to it that a barfly looked over his shoulder as he read one of the letters.

He had shot his wife and Shoup with a silenced gun the night he had supposedly ordered them out of the house. After the murder, he had staged a loud argument, simulating Shoup's voice and his wife's voice, for the benefit of Frank, whom he knew would be listening. Both victims were big, and he had a major disposal problem on his hands. He cut each body in pieces. Late of a night, he would burn the pieces of the human jigsaws in a roaring furnace in the greenhouse. Early of a morning, he would retrieve the bones from the furnace. The bones he ground into a fertilizer. He used the fertilizer on his sweet peas, including the ones in the box on the porch.

The night he had staged his own abduction, he had, as suspected, worn shoes of his wife and Shoup, which he had retained in case he would need them for the purpose. He had actually gone to Cleveland. He had hired a man there to lash his back with a whip and to otherwise mark him up.

"The fellow thought I was crazy," Lincoln said to Chief Michels, and the chief could see what he meant.

"What did you do with the heads?" asked the chief, who had once read somewhere that it is hard to thoroughly dispose of a human head without leaving some trace.

"That's where I put the crowning touch to my crime, Chief," said Lincoln. "Remember that box on the porch that I pointed out to you—the ones with the sweet peas in it?"

The chief nodded, and shuddered.

"The heads were in there. I put the heads in that box and covered them with quicklime. I then put some earth over the quicklime and planted some sweet peas in the earth. They grew very nicely, especially with the fertilizer I made out of Lina and Byron."

The chief knew that quicklime would, in time, reduce the heads, even the dental work, to a state where positive identification would be out of the question. Lincoln divined what the chief was pondering. "Yes," he said, "the heads will be reduced to nothing now. That's why I went away for a while. I wanted to give the quicklime a real chance to do its work."

The box containing the heads was taken from its place as a support under the front porch and opened—just as a matter of curiosity. The heads of Lina Lincoln and Byron Shoup—victims of the most singular torso crime of all— were far from unrecognizable. On the contrary, they were in a remarkable state of preservation. Something had gone far awry.

The torsos may have long since been reduced to smoke and fertilizer, but these heads remained to accuse the super-plotter. They sent him away to prison for life.

Before he died in prison in 1941, Warren Lincoln had ample time to ponder the caprices of fate. The heads had been preserved because of an error. There had been two barrels of lime at the entrance of the greenhouse—one deadly quicklime, and the other harmless, slaked lime. Lincoln had always warned Frank, his dull-witted assistant, to be careful not to get the barrels mixed up. Which was, quite obviously, precisely what Frank had done. Lincoln had dipped liberally into the barrel that was supposed to contain the quicklime the night he had packed the heads into the flower box. And, instead of quicklime, the barrel had contained the harmless slaked lime. Lincoln had often said that he thought he had made a mistake in hiring such a blundering fellow as Frank. Now he was sure of it.